IMAGES
of America

AFRICAN-AMERICAN LIFE IN PRESTON COUNTY

IMAGES
of America

AFRICAN-AMERICAN LIFE IN PRESTON COUNTY

Nancy Jane Copney

ARCADIA
PUBLISHING

ISBN 978-0-7385-0133-8

Published by Arcadia Publishing
Charleston SC, Chicago IL, Portsmouth NH, San Francisco CA

Printed in the United States of America

Library of Congress Catalog Card Number: 99-63803

For all general information contact Arcadia Publishing at:
Telephone 843-853-2070
Fax 843-853-0044
E-Mail sales@arcadiapublishing.com
For customer service and orders:
Toll-Free 1-888-313-2665

Visit us on the Internet at www.arcadiapublishing.com

In memory of Mildred Grace McDonald,
who was the Sunday school superintendent for 50 years
and was a shining inspiration for many people.

CONTENTS

ACKNOWLEDGMENTS

One cloudy Sunday afternoon while walking up the railroad tracks to my grandparents' house, when I came to the trestle, I stopped, looked into that water, and crying, I told God all about an incident with a traveling salesman who wanted to take away my mother's silverware because she couldn't make the payments. I told God if he would allow me to grow up and get a job, that my parents would never want for anything again. When I finished praying, the sun began to shine, and I knew my request had been granted. I was eight years old. This incident is my mountaintop experience, for God has kept his bargain, and I have done all I can to keep my end of it today.

I would like to thank that local Kingwood businessman who loaned me the money to go to Washington, D.C., to work. When I was younger, every summer, I would ask my parents to send me to visit my girlfriends in Morgantown. After only two days away, I would cry to come home, and they would have to pick me up. Later in life, I knew better than to ask them for $150 to get to Washington, D.C., so I asked a local businessman to loan me the money. I took my grades and my job offer with me, and he loaned me the money. To him I am eternally grateful.

I want to dedicate this book to my immediate family. First, to my mother, Margaret, who stood by me during the school integration process and cleaned houses in Kingwood and Morgantown so that I might have the necessities to complete high school. "No weapon that is formed against thee shall prosper . . ." (*Isaiah* 55:17) was the Bible verse she instilled within me.

Second, I would like to dedicate this book to my father, Henry, who walked ten miles from our home to Miller Mines to dig coal and then walked those same miles back home, in all conditions of weather.

Third, I would like to acknowledge my brothers, Charles and Melvin, who helped me whenever I wanted to relocate or needed assistance with my church projects.

When I relocated to Kingwood in 1990, I was not working, and my aunt Mabel suggested that I go to the courthouse to do research on the Younger family. I am so glad that I followed her advice, for when this book project came along, I had already gathered a lot of the necessary information. To Aunt Mabel, I say, "Thank you."

I would like to honor the "Ladies of the Gospel," Mrs. Marietta Goines, Mrs. Beulah Hall, Mrs. Louise McDonald, and Ms. Ruth Barnett, for their singing truly blesses my soul.

Finally, I want to thank the entire Kingwood community for all acts of kindness toward me and my church families.

Author's Note

Raised with my three brothers, the late Ray Franklin, Charles Cramer, and Melvin Eugene, I grew up in a segregated community. Before 1954, all black children went to a one-room school, Beverly Hill Elementary School, which was established on July 22, 1924, when the Preston County Board of Education purchased property from Mrs. Israel Schaffer. In this school, we had one teacher who taught all the subjects to all the students, from grades one through eight. In the history of black teachers at Beverly Hill, only one was a male, Mr. Charles Cranford. All of the teachers roomed with black families, and many of these teachers over the years roomed with Rheta Ann Walker and Leanna Strothers.

Like most one-room schoolhouses, Beverly Hill had no indoor plumbing. On one side of the school building was a two-seater toilet for the girls, and on the other side, there was a two-seater toilet for the boys. A hand pump stood in the yard until about two years ago. I remember a stone jar would be filled with water and placed in the classroom, and each student had his or her own drinking cup. I still have mine.

The school's room was heated with a pot-bellied Burnside #2. My brothers, Charles and Melvin, and I made the fire in the stove and swept the wooden floor before school time for several years. At first, children brought their lunches to school. The winters were very cold, and it snowed often. On occasion, I remember being treated to hot chocolate (cooked Hershey's cocoa and milk), which was served by Mrs. Evelyn Paige and my mother, Margaret. My mother and Mrs. Paige would also bring soup or chili. When this happened, all of the children thought we had "died and went to Heaven," so to speak. Later on, the Welfare Department distributed dry soup, beans, butter, bread, and cartons of milk to the school. Mrs. Ruth Smith would prepare the soup beans at home and deliver them to us at lunch time. It was decided at the PTA that each school "mom" should take turns cooking at the school. They purchased a two-burner oil stove, placed it right in the front of the classroom, cooked, and served the beans.

This all took place before computers. Hide and seek, leap frog, marbles, checkers, softball, and fishing were some of the games we played. Our fun consisted of dunking for apples in a tin tub filled with water, pinning the tail on the donkey (blind folded), and potato sack races. When we graduated from the eighth grade, the Preston County Board of Education issued letters to students telling them they could ride for free the Osgood bus from Kingwood to Morgantown, West Virginia, to attend another black school—Monongalia High, located in Westover. The Osgood bus line was a commercial bus providing transportation for workers and shoppers. The first bus left from Schwabs Drug Store at 6 a.m. and departed from the Greyhound Bus Station in Morgantown at 5:30 p.m.—I left in the dark and came back home in the dark. After arriving in Morgantown there was a two-hour wait for school to open. After school was out, there was another two-hour wait to return home.

Having been notified that the schools were going to be integrated and our school was going to be sold, the black community decided to purchase the building. Sarah McDonald Goines, along with myself, canvassed the neighborhood both by car and on foot, soliciting donations to purchase the school property. Dinners and bake sales sponsored by several families were also held. Transported by Mr. Herbert McDonald Sr. and Mr. Jesse McDonald Jr., the choir made guest appearances in various churches throughout West Virginia and Maryland to receive donations. Sporting blue robes with golden ties, this choir had around 20 members at one time. For several years, I traveled with this choir, singing and playing the piano.

Schools were integrated in Preston County in 1954. A public sale of the school and land was held at the front door of the courthouse on July 17, 1954. The trustees were John Henry Younger, Jesse McDonald Jr., and Henry Copney. The purchase was for $450. While attending Kingwood High School (KHS), I enrolled in Typing I, II, III, and Greg shorthand. I earned several typing and shorthand certificates. When the recruiters from several government agencies came to KHS, I along with my classmates were tested. We also filled out job applications. Test scores were sent from Washington, D.C., directly to students along with job placement offers. On May 23, 1957, along with Joseph Douglas Paige and the late James Garrett Paige (twins), we were the first black students to graduate from Kingwood High School. Armed with my new "White, Pearl-Covered Bible," given to me by Mrs. Margaret McIntire, I accepted the job offer with the Central Intelligence Agency. I remained at this agency for six and half years when I transferred to the Department of Health, Education, and Welfare, now known as Health and Human Services, from which I was given an "Early Retirement" in 1989 when my elderly mother suffered a stroke.

While public education was a big part of my life, religious schooling was very important to my parents, and they believed that my brothers and me should attend Sunday school every Sunday. Upon our return home from Sunday school, my parents discussed our lessons with us. If one us had a "sick" Sunday, he or she had to stay in the house all day—needless to say, there were very few "sick" Sundays. Furthermore, our beloved superintendent, Grace McDonald, would place a "Gold Star" by your name each Sunday you were there.

I have many fond memories of growing up. We heard the news broadcast from a battery-operated radio and listened to Lowell Thomas end each 7 p.m. broadcast with "And that's all from Washington at this time." In our household, we all had our favorite shows; my brothers enjoyed the Shadow and the Lone Ranger, while my favorite was Junior Miss. My mother followed the stories of the Romance of Helen Trent and the Guiding Light. I remember how the battery would "run out" right in the middle of one of our shows, and we would have to wait until our father was able to purchase another battery. In the early 1950s, my aunt and uncle purchased a combination record player with a 5-inch television screen. Every Saturday morning, the neighborhood kids were invited to watch TV from 8 a.m. until noon. They were the only black family to have a television.

After living away for so many years, I finally returned to Kingwood in 1990. Upon my return, word soon got around that I was back, and a dinner was held at a restaurant with 12 of my former classmates. On June 11, 1991, I was hired as a payroll clerk at the Preston Memorial Hospital, and this challenging position has allowed me to meet and serve some of the most wonderful people in the world. Also, I have been able to do some nice things for my family, friends, and my church. I am very grateful to the Preston Memorial Hospital Administrative Board and Staff for allowing me to serve in this capacity.

One

PEOPLE

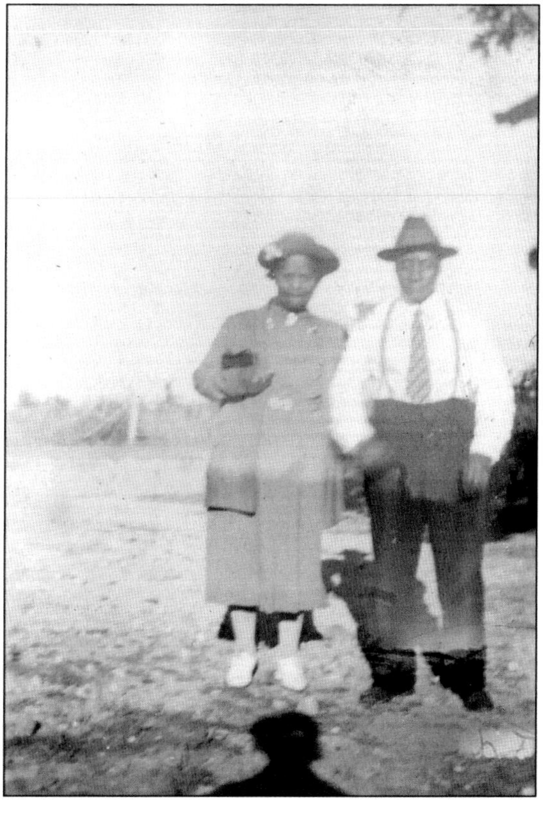

Mary Frances Price Younger and Henry Younger were married on September 1, 1897, at Beverly Hill Methodist Episcopal (M.E.) Church in Kingwood. Mary was born in Danville, Virginia, on December 3, 1876. She came to Kingwood to work as a domestic for the Crogan family, and, in the 1930s and 1940s, she served as a midwife to several area families. They are pictured here *c.* 1940s.

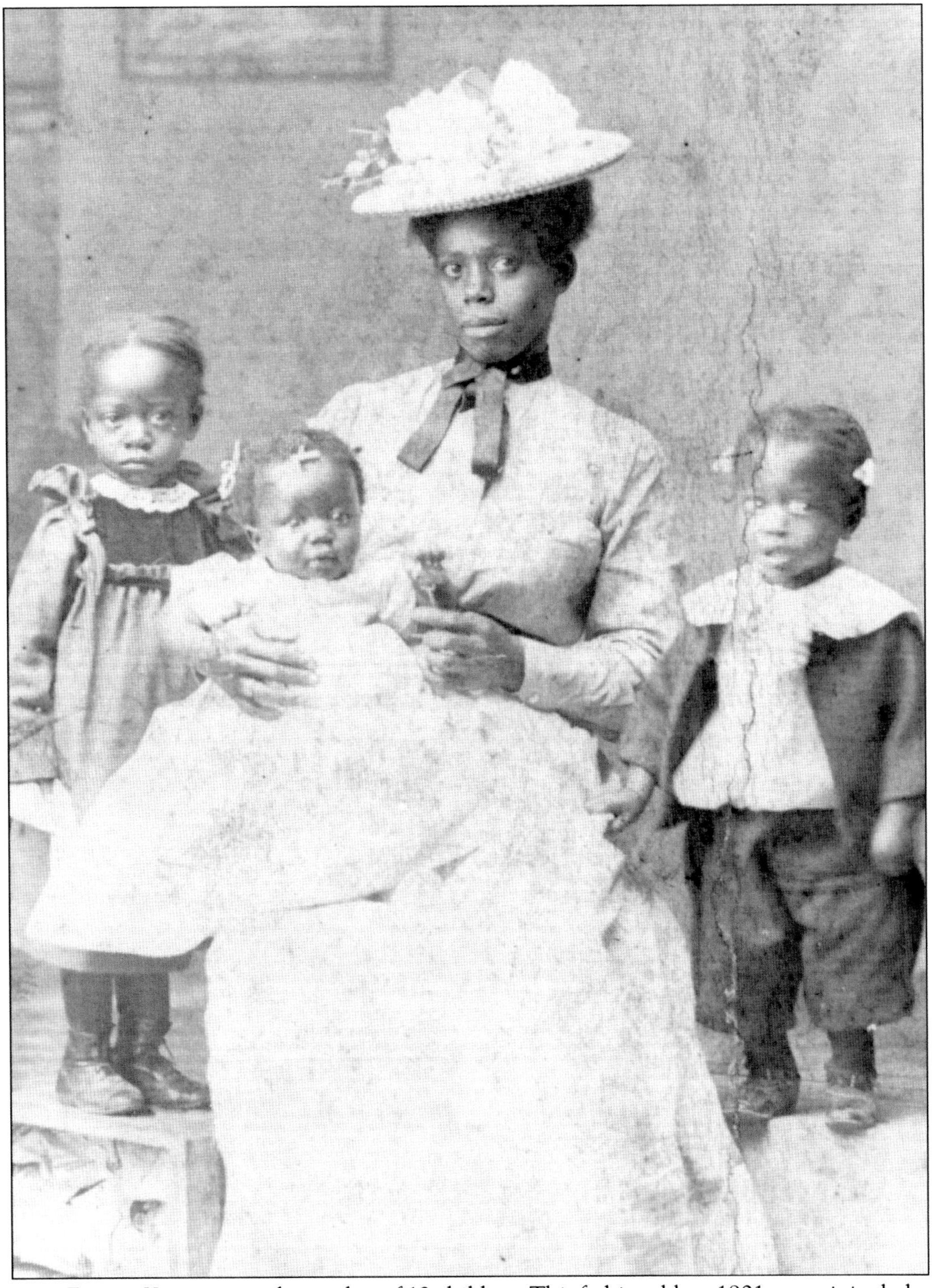

Mary Frances Younger was the mother of 12 children. This fashionable c. 1901 portrait includes three of those children, from left to right: Cora Lee, born on May 14, 1900; Laylor Jane, born on October 9, 1901; and Walter, born on November 12, 1898.

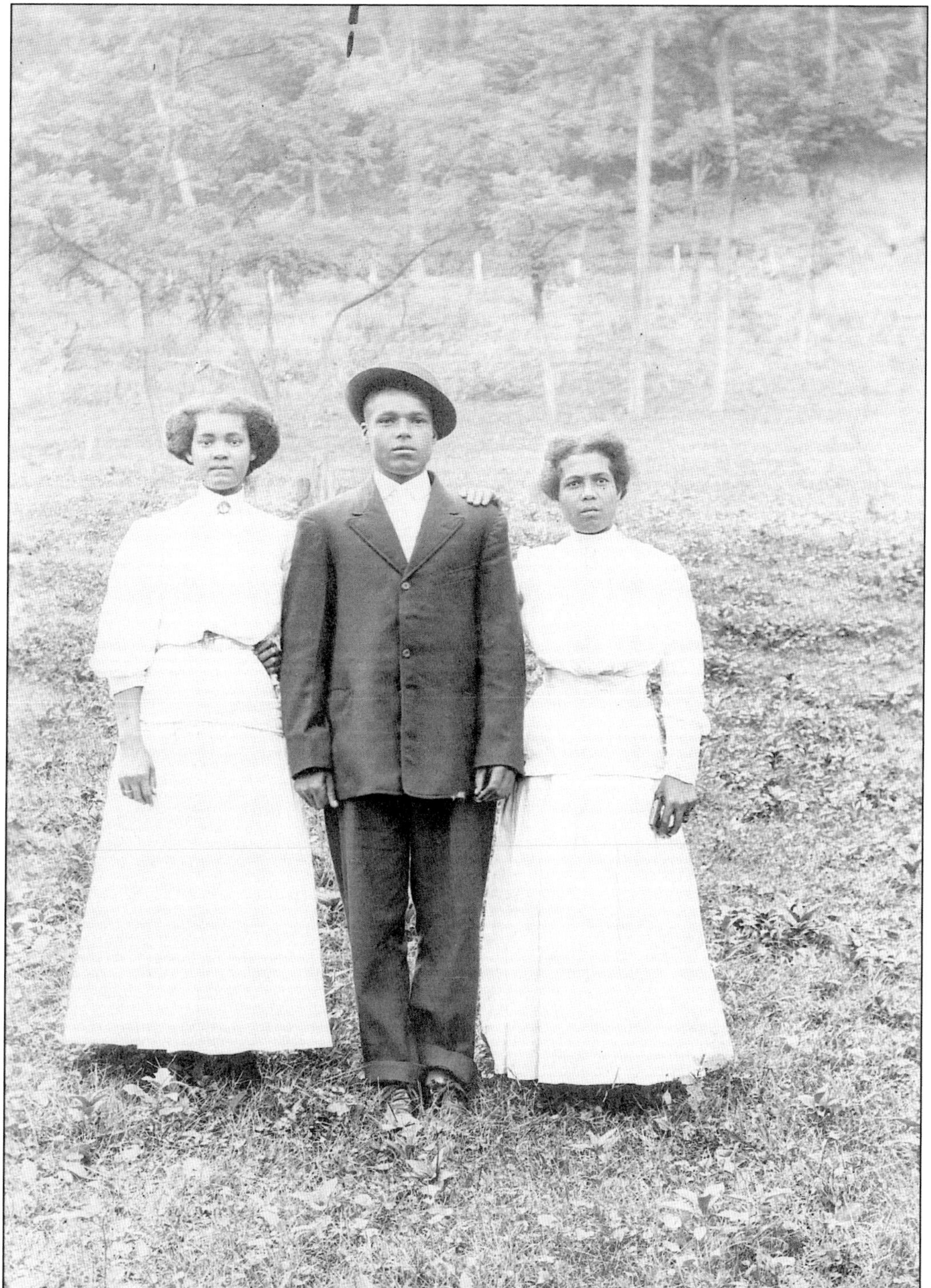

This picture of, from left to right, Jean Younger, George Ashby, and Mary Ashby Younger was taken in the 1920s.

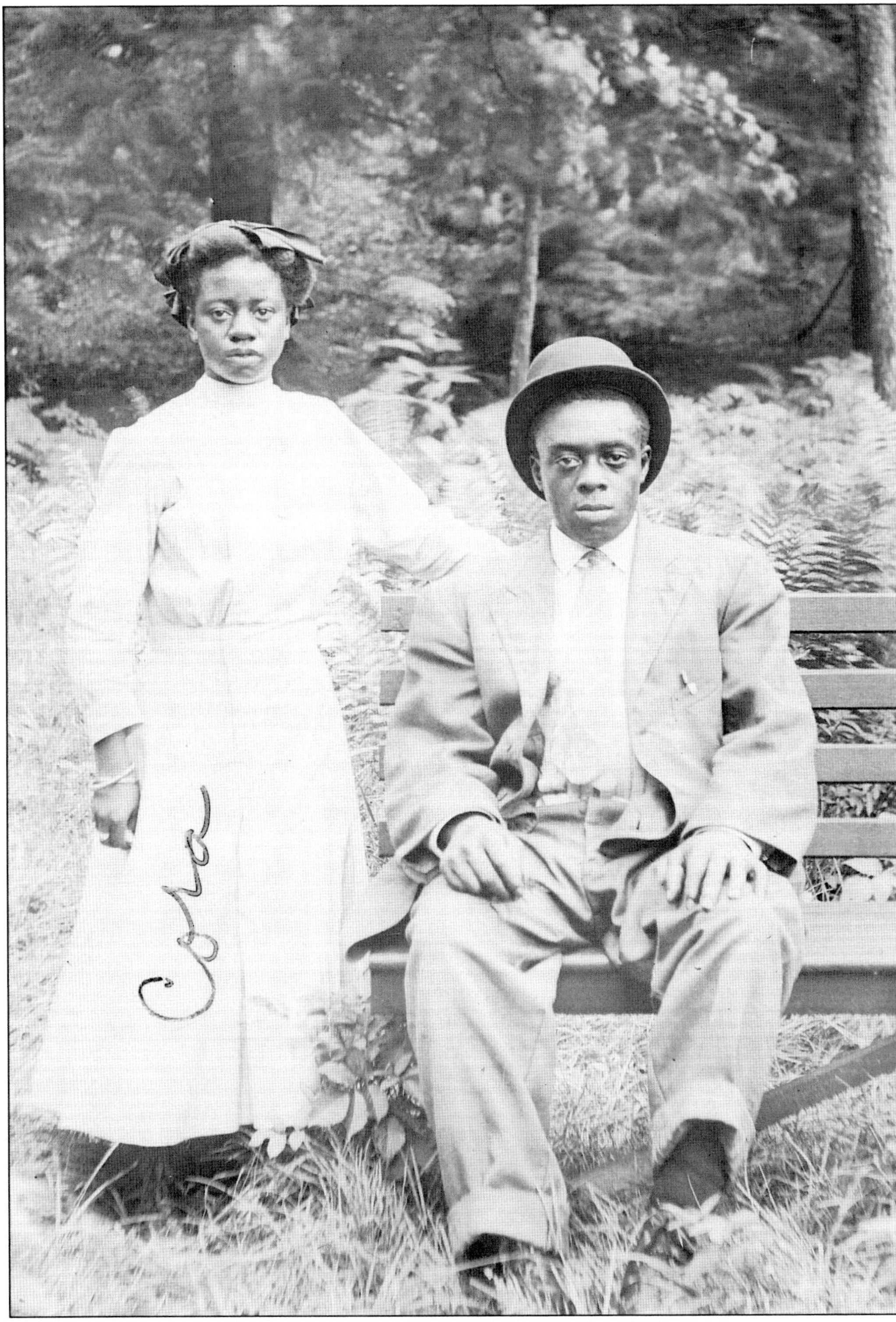

Cora Lee Smith and John Younger posed for this portrait in the 1920s.

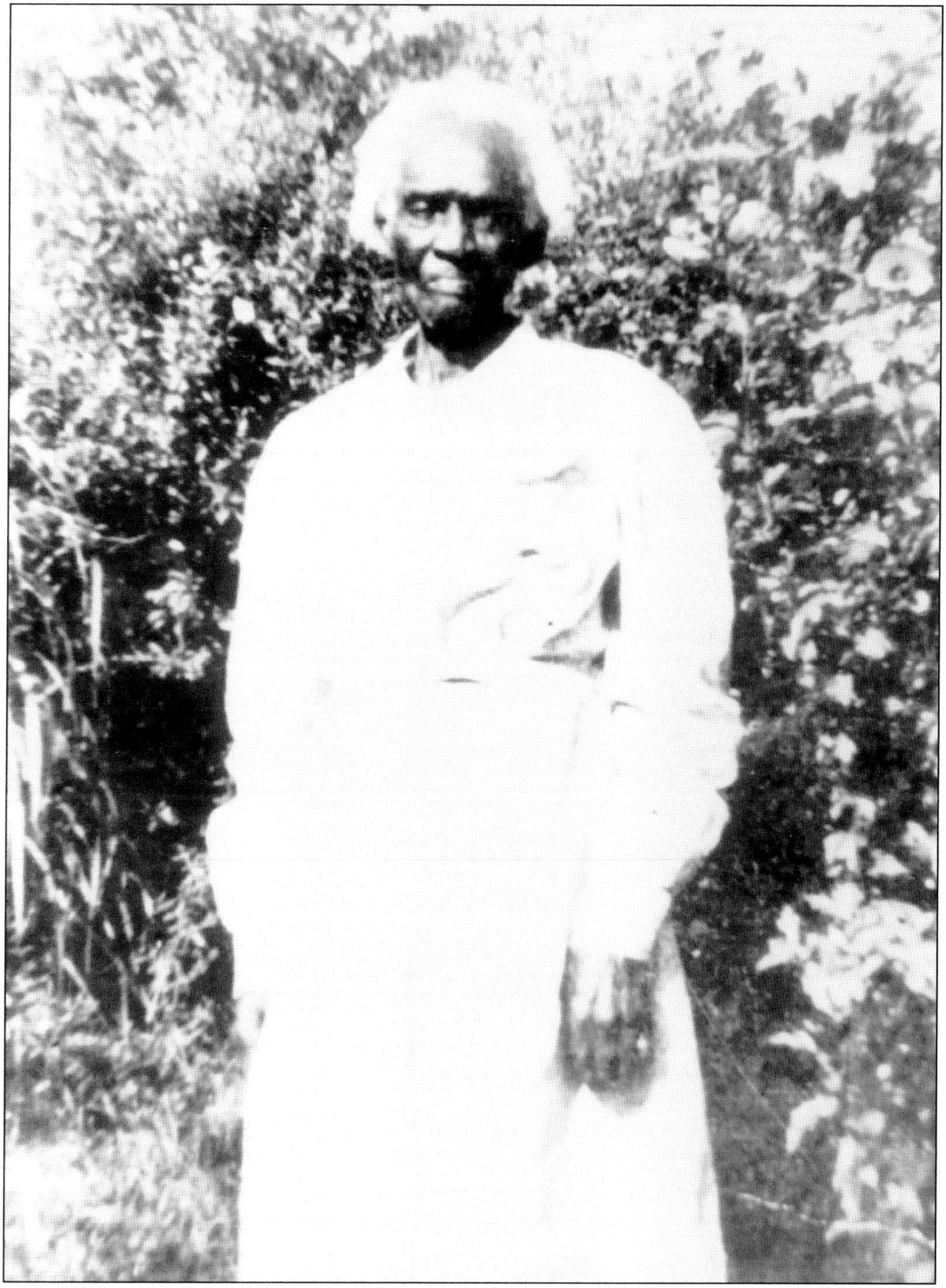

Mary Price Younger was one of the daughters of the strong, old woman pictured here. Jane Flippin was born a slave in Danville, Virginia.

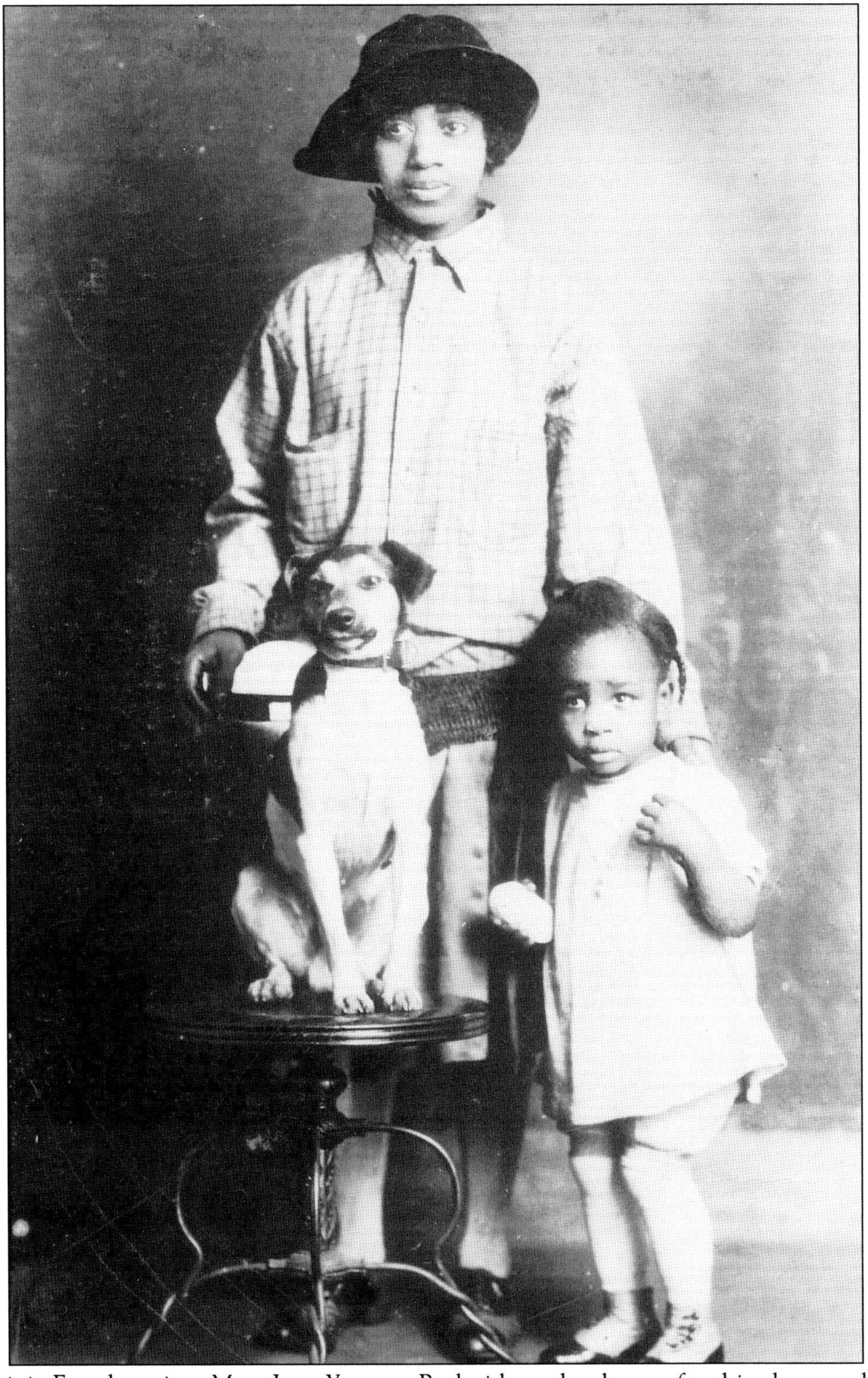

Virginia Fort, her niece Mary Jane Younger Beckwith, and a dog sat for this photograph, c. 1922. Notice the spats and stockings on the little girl.

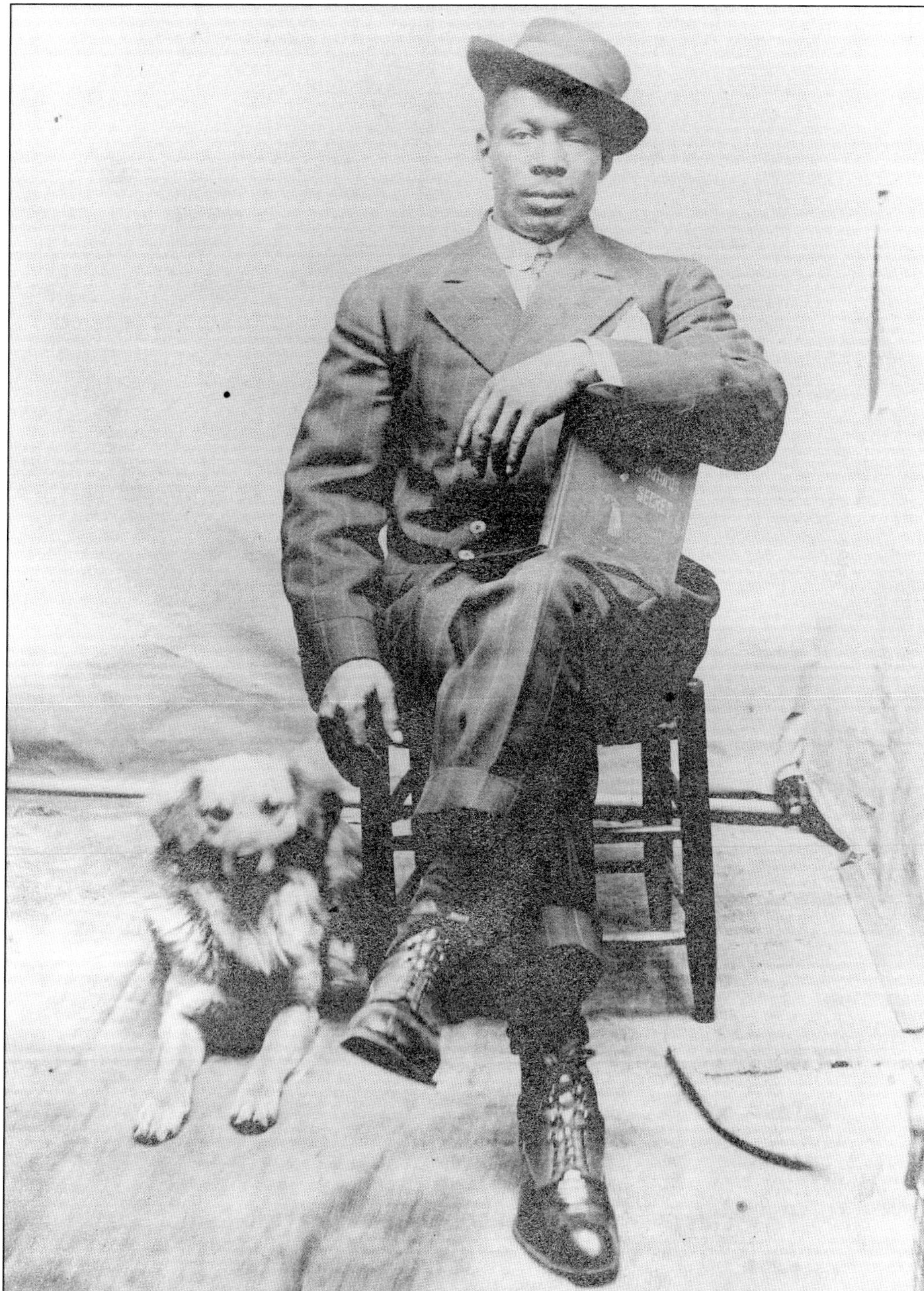

This stunning portrait of a man and his dog was taken in the early 1900s. The subject, Joseph Whitley Jr., was the husband of Lula Flippin. He worked as a barber for the African-American people in the surrounding area.

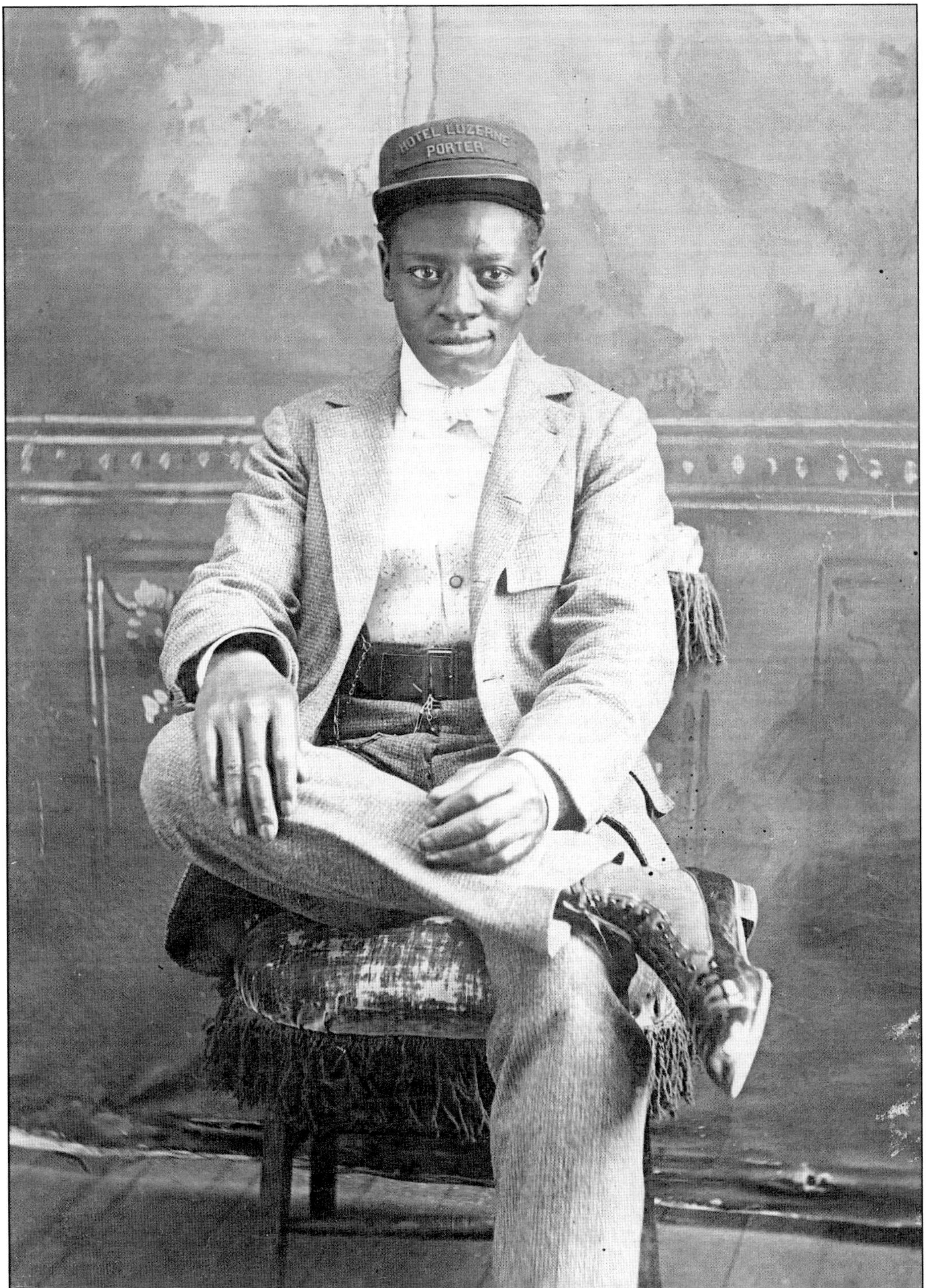

Thomas James Younger was born on June 8, 1879, and eventually married a young woman named Lucy. Dressed in his smart uniform for this portrait, Younger worked as a janitor at the Hotel Luzerne in Belington, West Virginia.

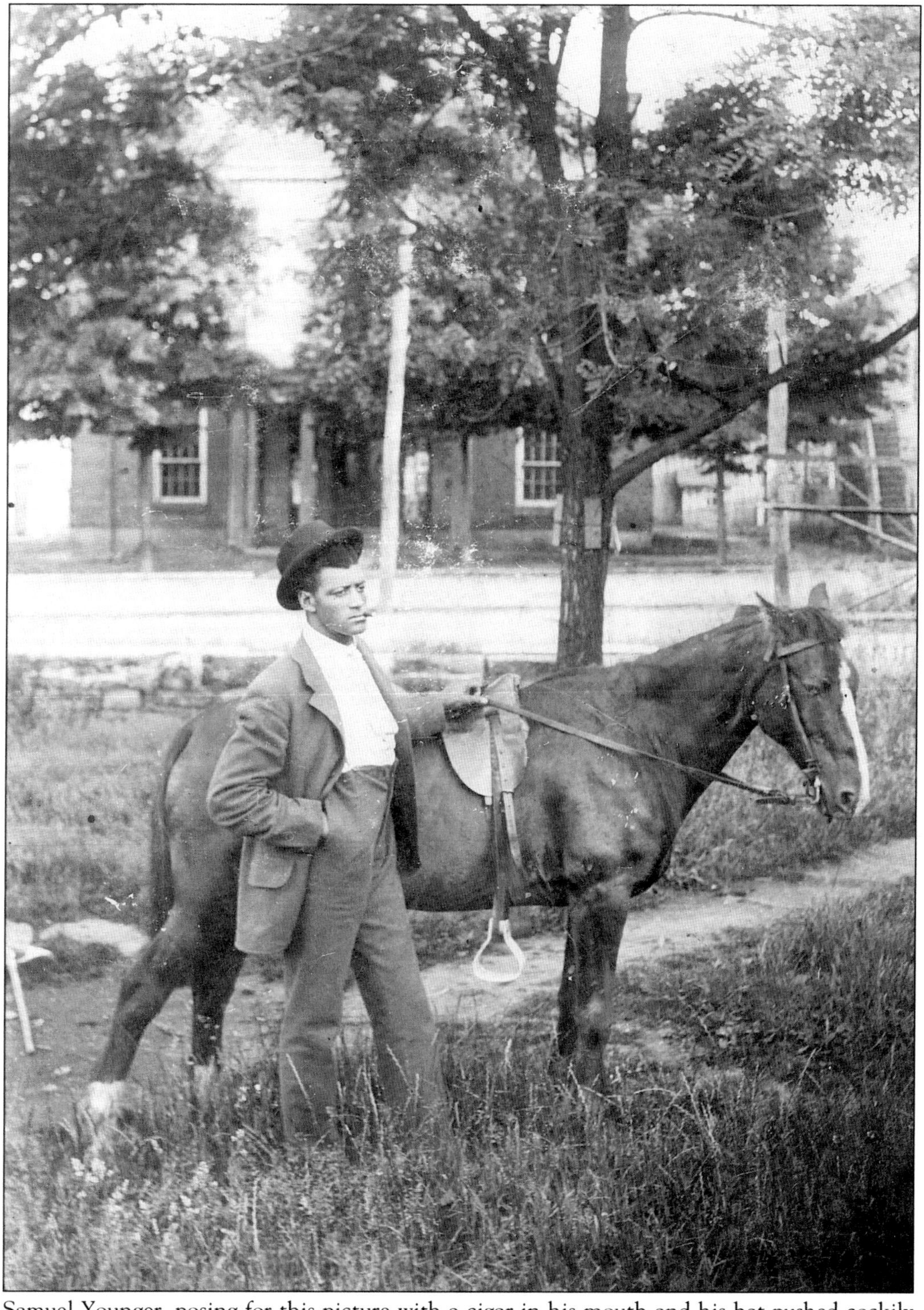

Samuel Younger, posing for this picture with a cigar in his mouth and his hat pushed cockily back on his head, was born on February 11, 1873. Known to friends and family as a great Republican, Younger was a sanitation worker for the city of Kingwood.

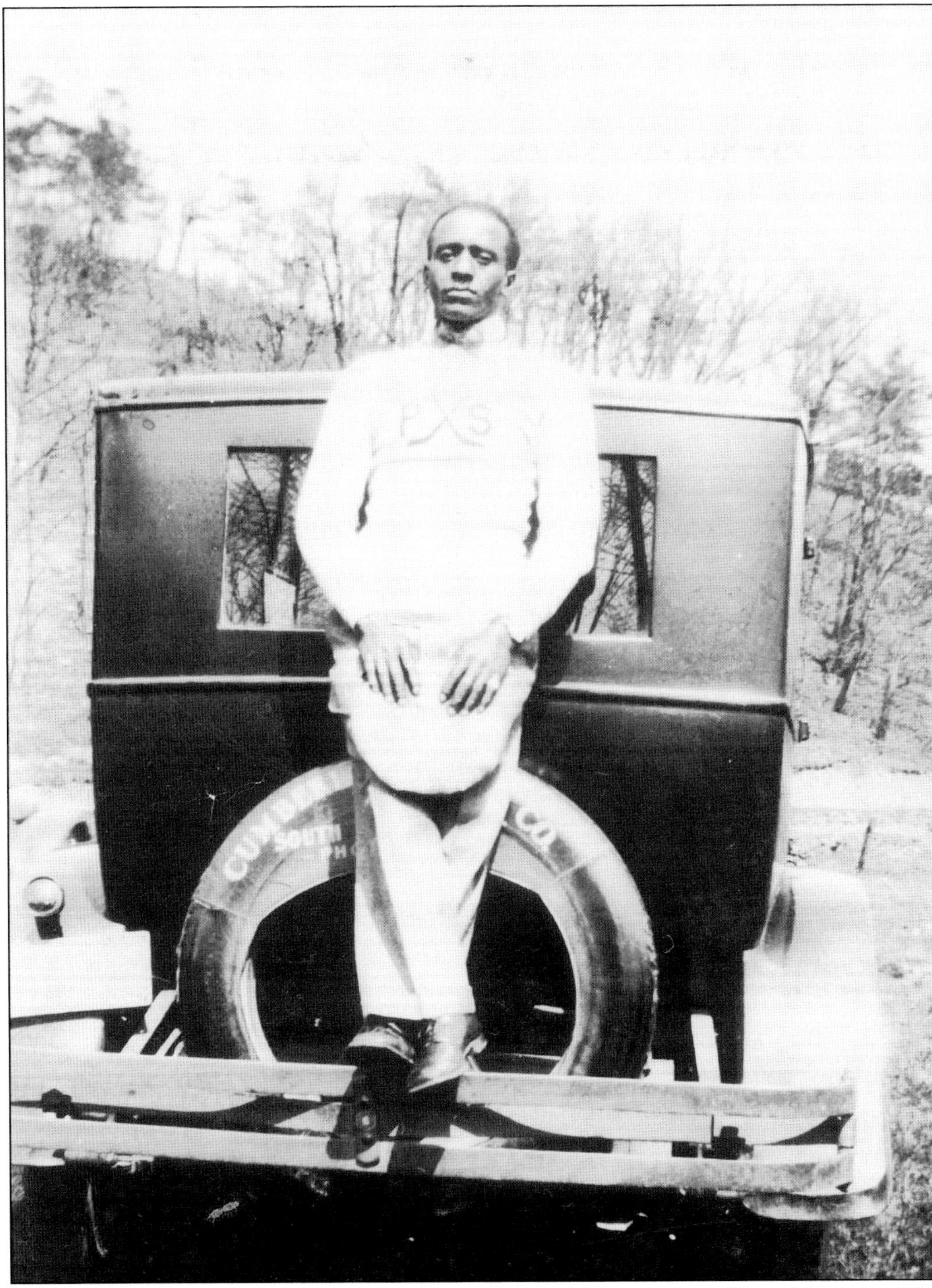

Walter Younger is pictured here standing on the wooden bumper of an old automobile. Younger was the son of John Henry and Mary P. Younger and was born on November 19, 1898. He married Henrietta Johnson and had one daughter, Mary Jane. He eventually moved to Cumberland, Maryland.

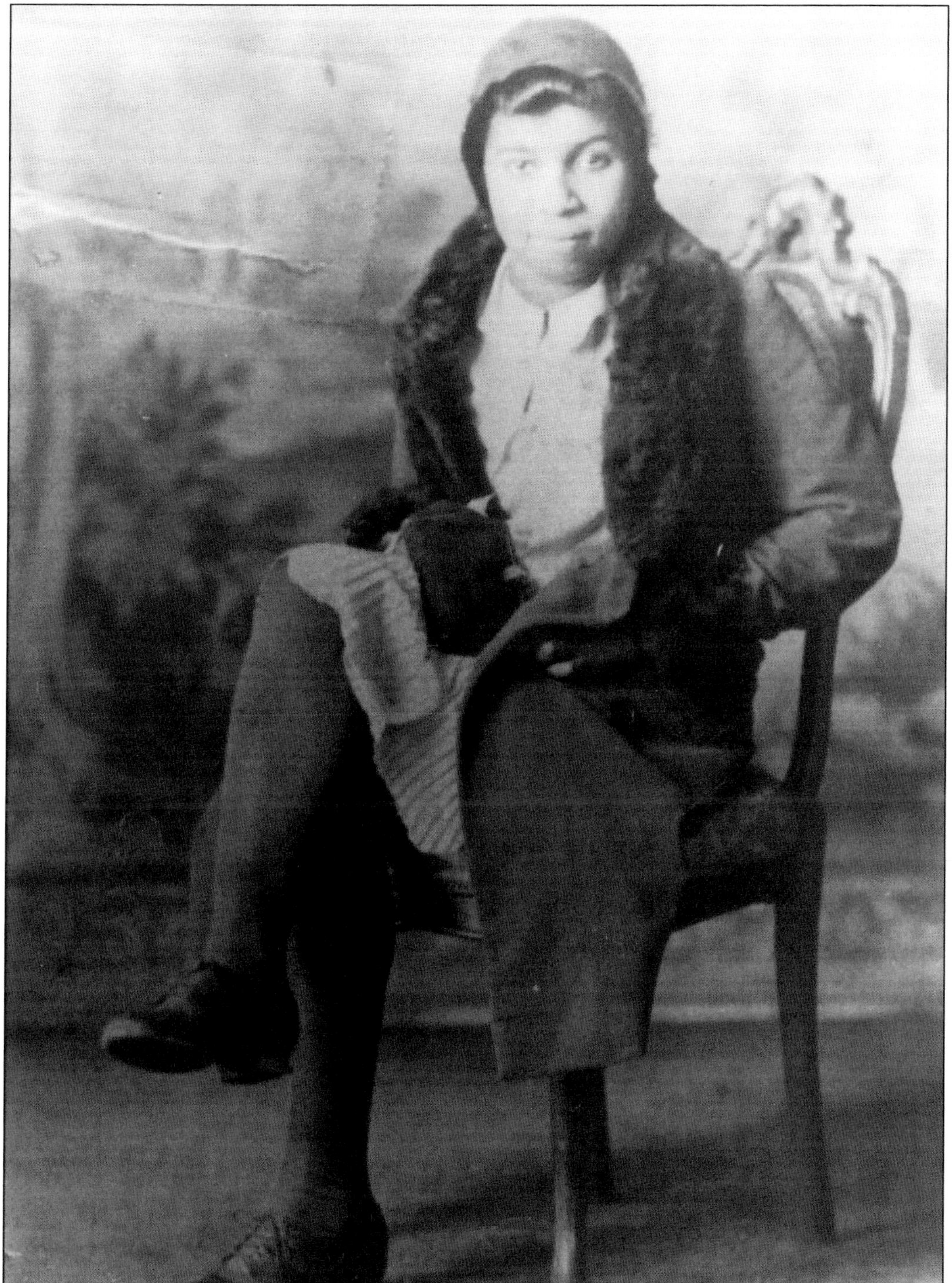

Elizabeth Selene Smith Younger is pictured here in a hat and fur-collared overcoat when she was just 18 years old in 1931. Born on October 6, 1913, she became the mother of 16 children, including two sets of twins.

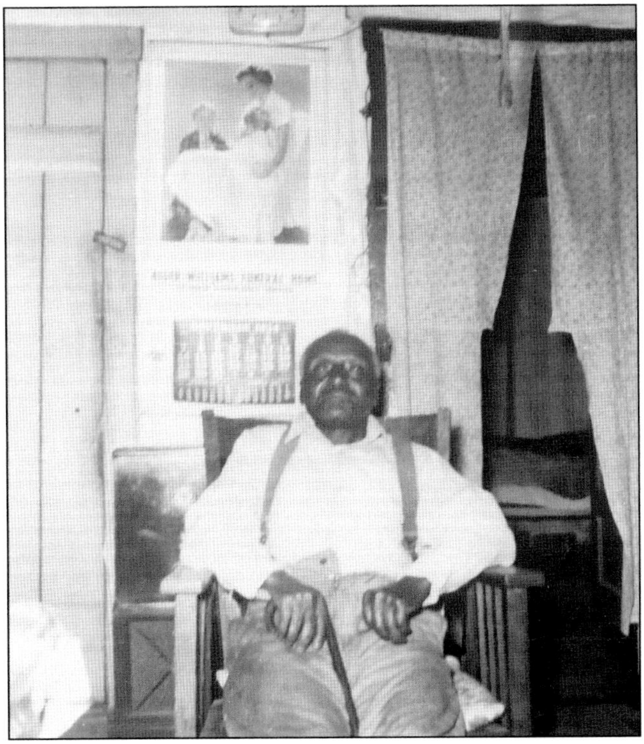

This September 1954 photograph shows John Henry Younger relaxing in a chair. Even though he never learned to read or write, Younger was in charge of a Work Projects Administration (WPA) program that distributed lumber and other supplies to qualifying local residents.

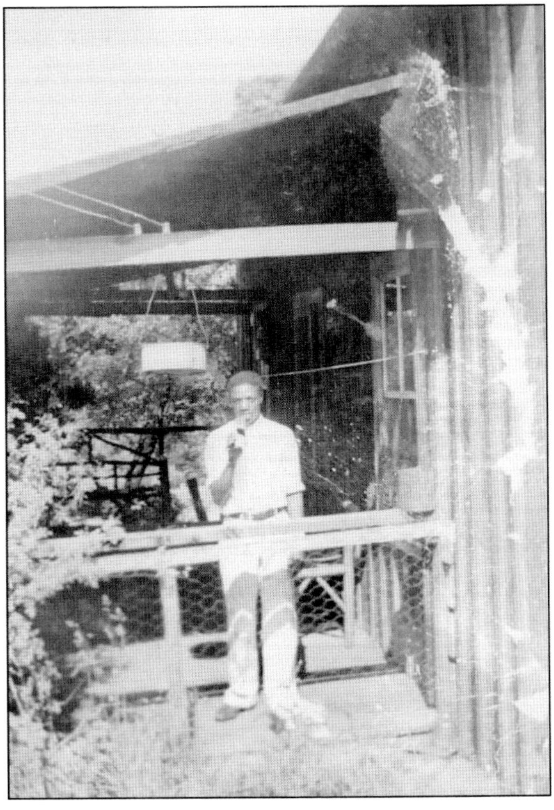

The Reverend George Staley is pictured here.

Thomas Staley poses for this outdoor portrait in a cap and knickers.

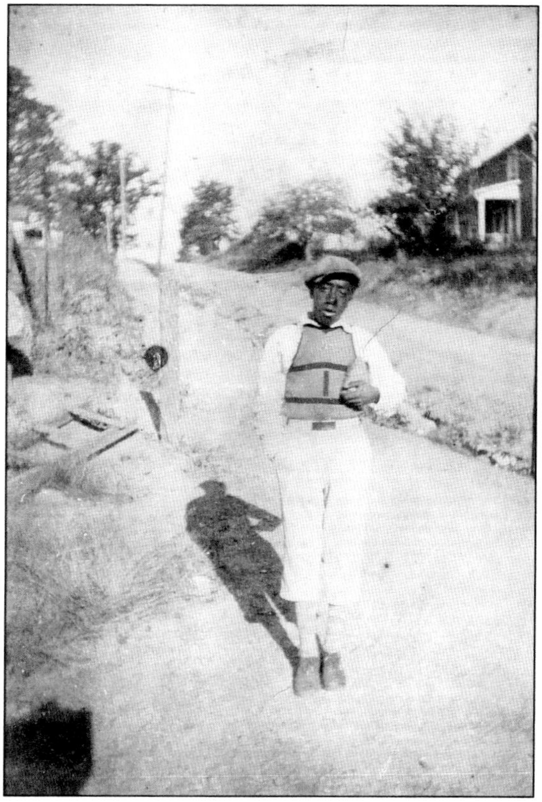

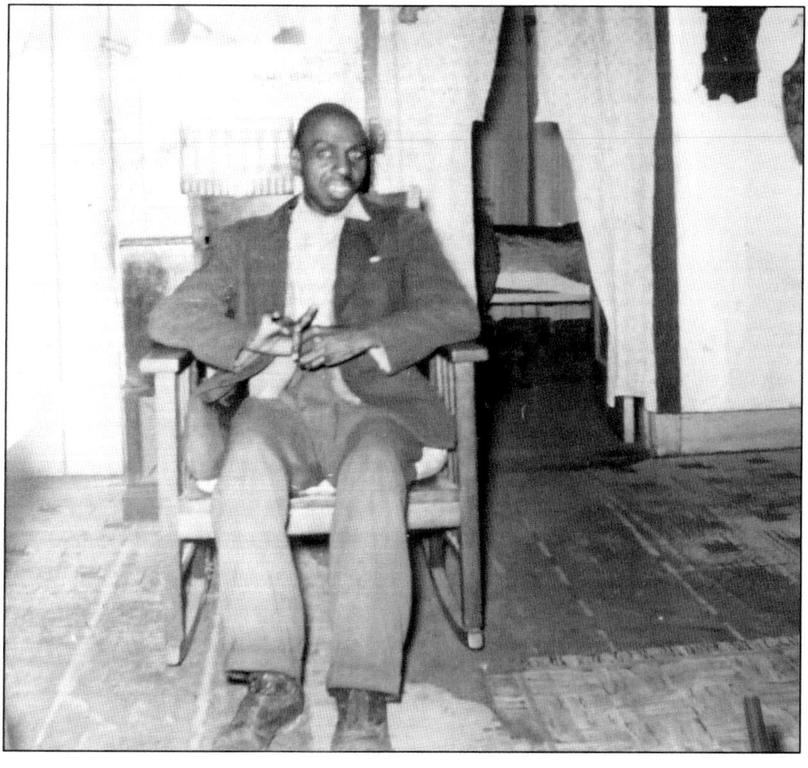

Albert Younger smiles for his portrait. George Staley, Thomas Staley (both pictured previously), and Albert Younger were the three sons of Cora Lee Younger Staley Smith.

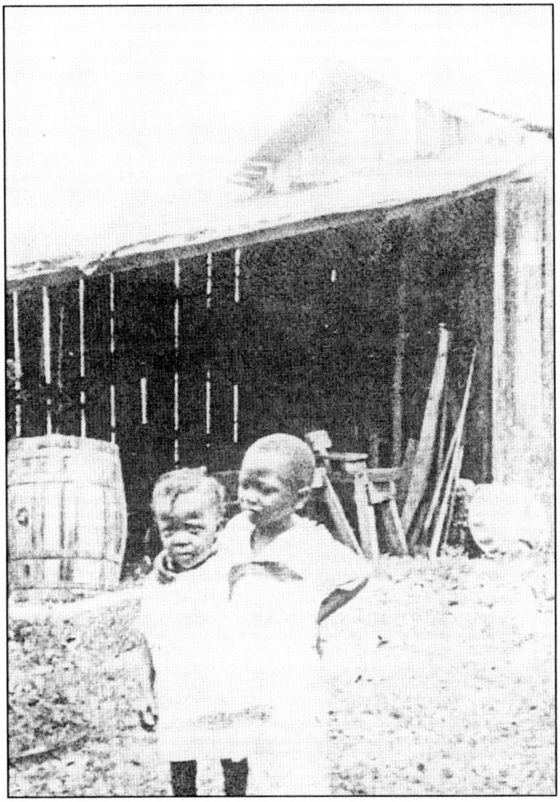

Wilma Jean Younger and Ray F. Copney play together in front of Henry Younger's tool shed in this c. 1935 image.

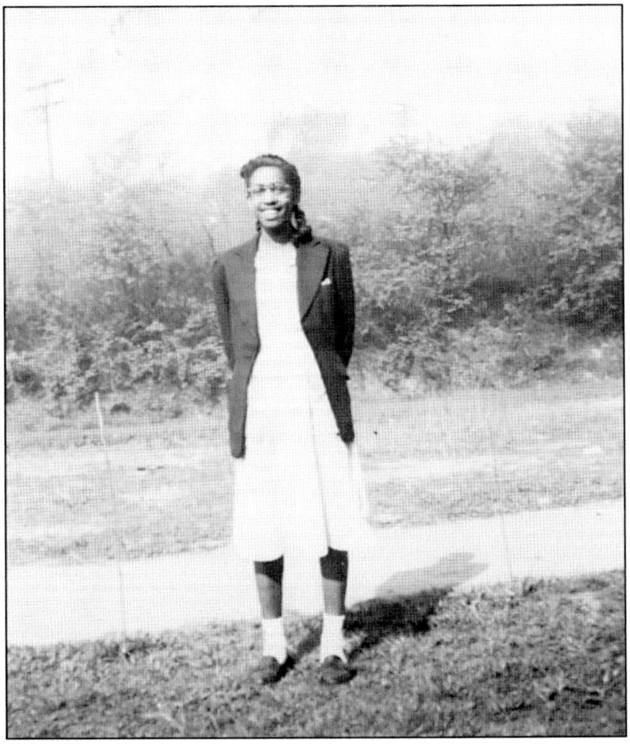

A teenaged and bespectacled Peggy Young stands outside to have her picture taken. She worked as a "clothes hanger" at Hills Department Store in Clarksburg, West Virginia, upon graduation from Monongalia High School in 1949, and she has just recently retired.

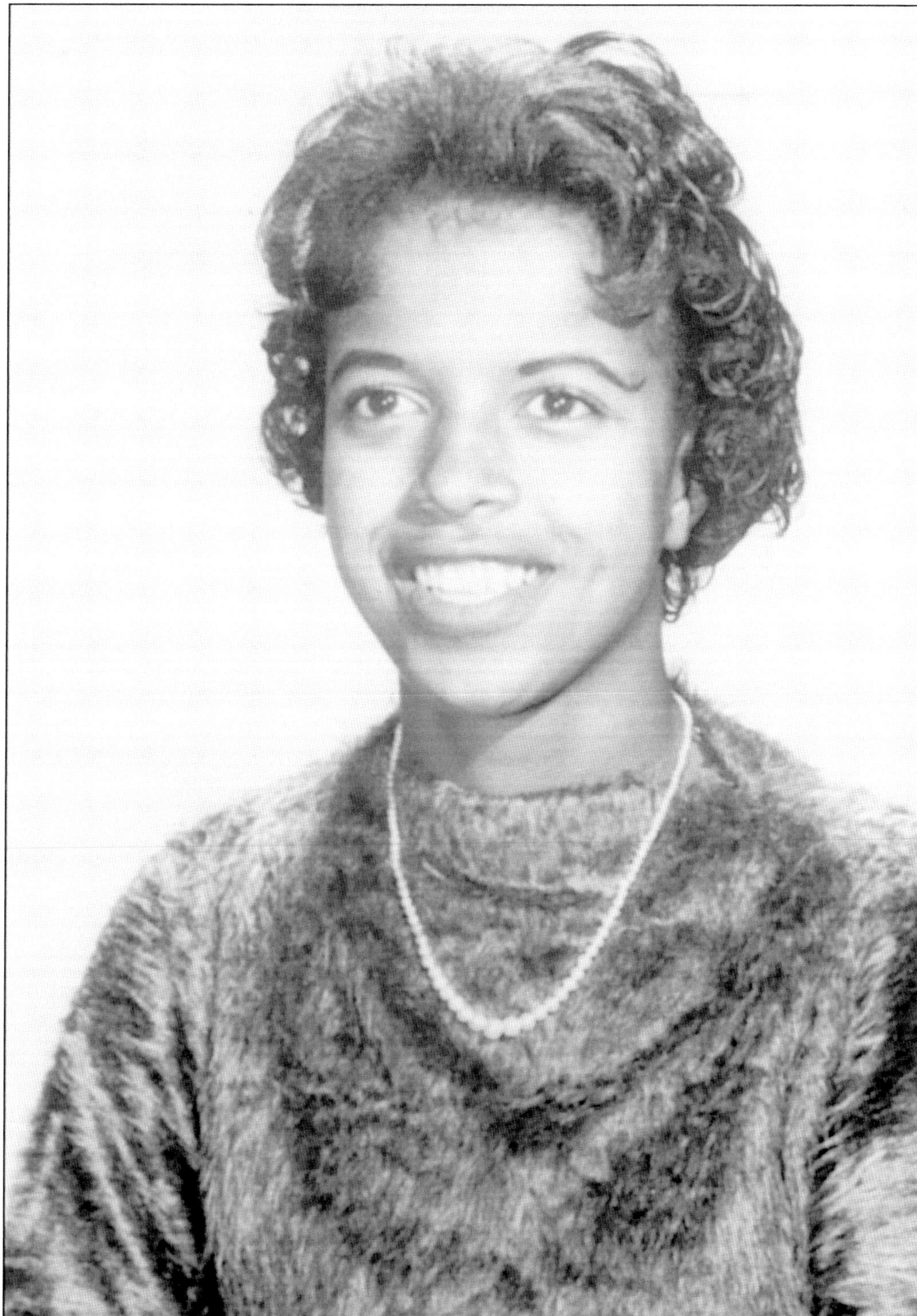

Phyllis Young smiles brilliantly for this posed photograph.

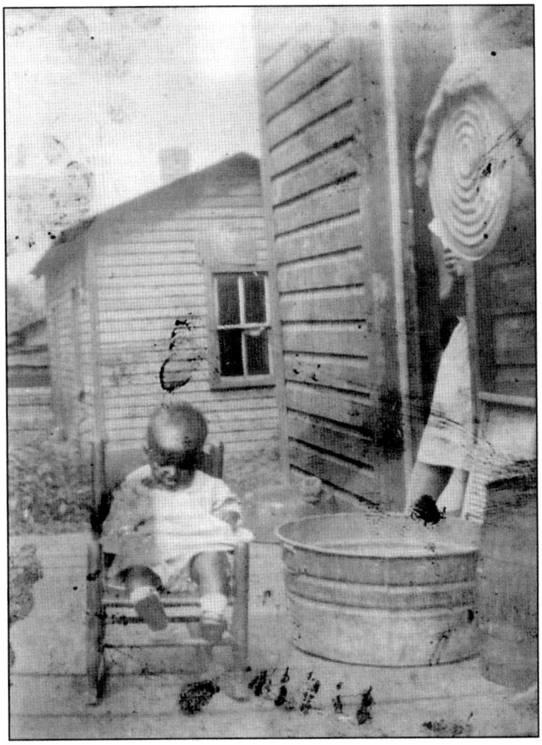

This childhood picture of Ray F. Copney sitting in a small rocking chair was taken in the early 1930s. The tin wash tub seen next to Copney was used not only for washing clothing, but also for washing children.

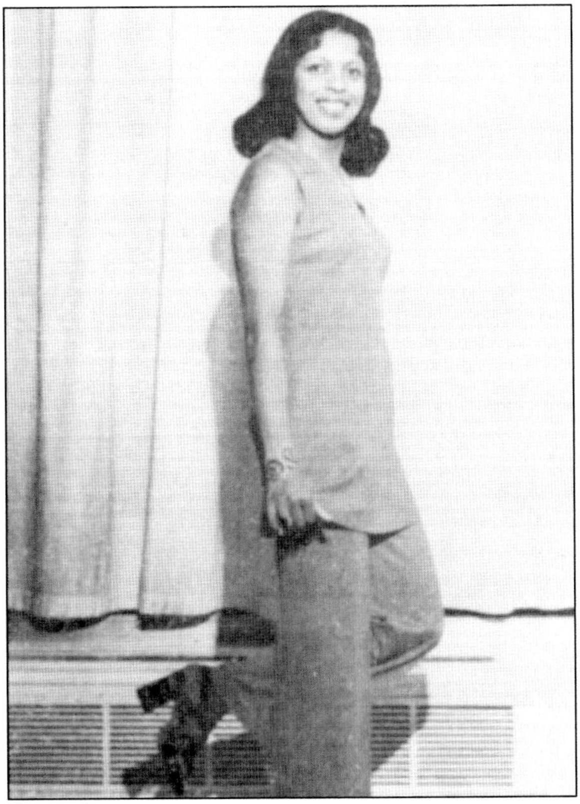

This picture of Phyllis Young was taken on August 28, 1995.

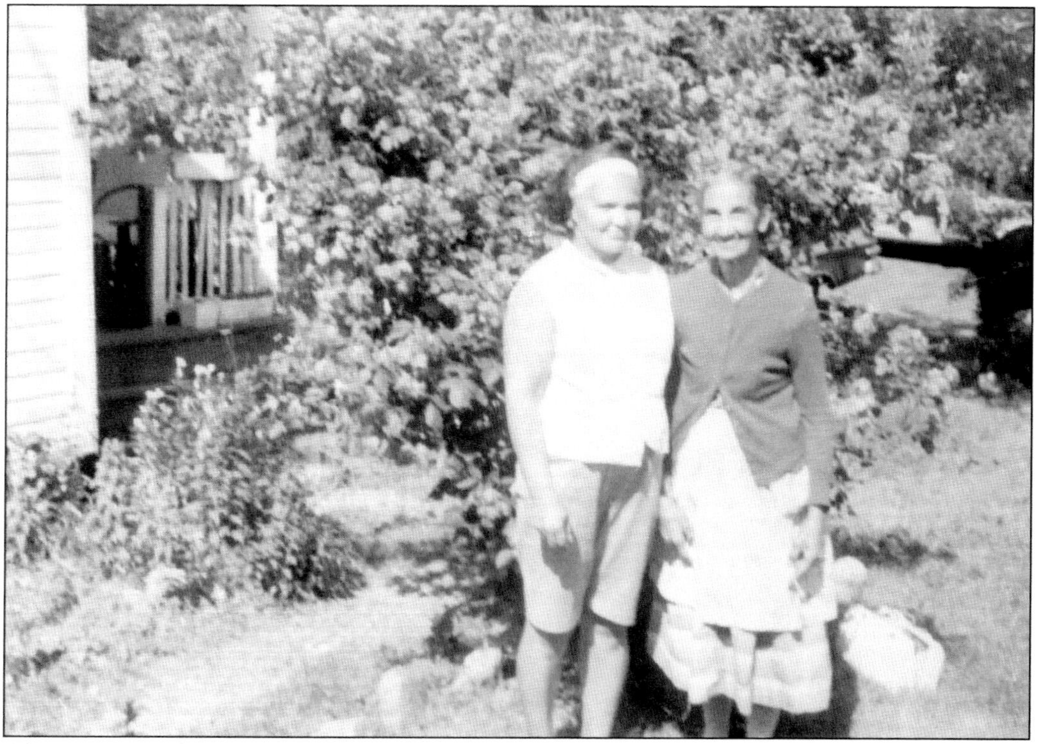

Alice Young and Icie Young are pictured here in a garden. Alice (in shorts) married Herbert Young, the son of Icie Young.

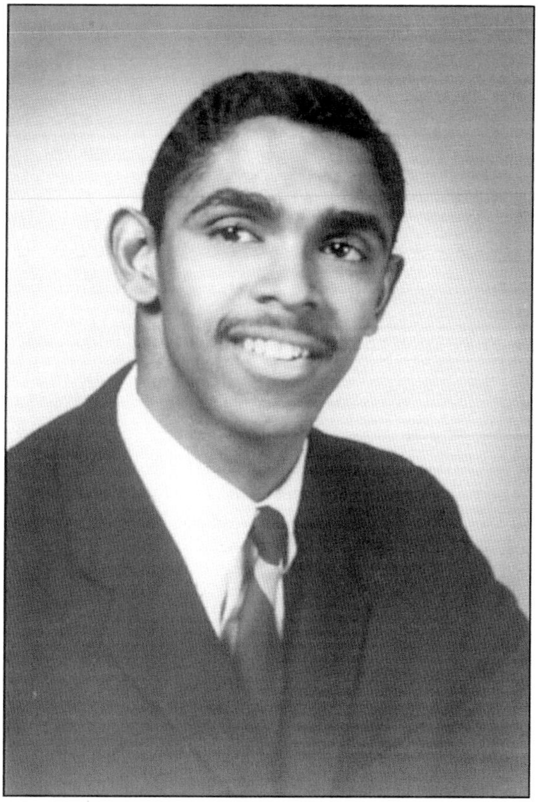

Calvin Young poses in a suit and tie for this portrait.

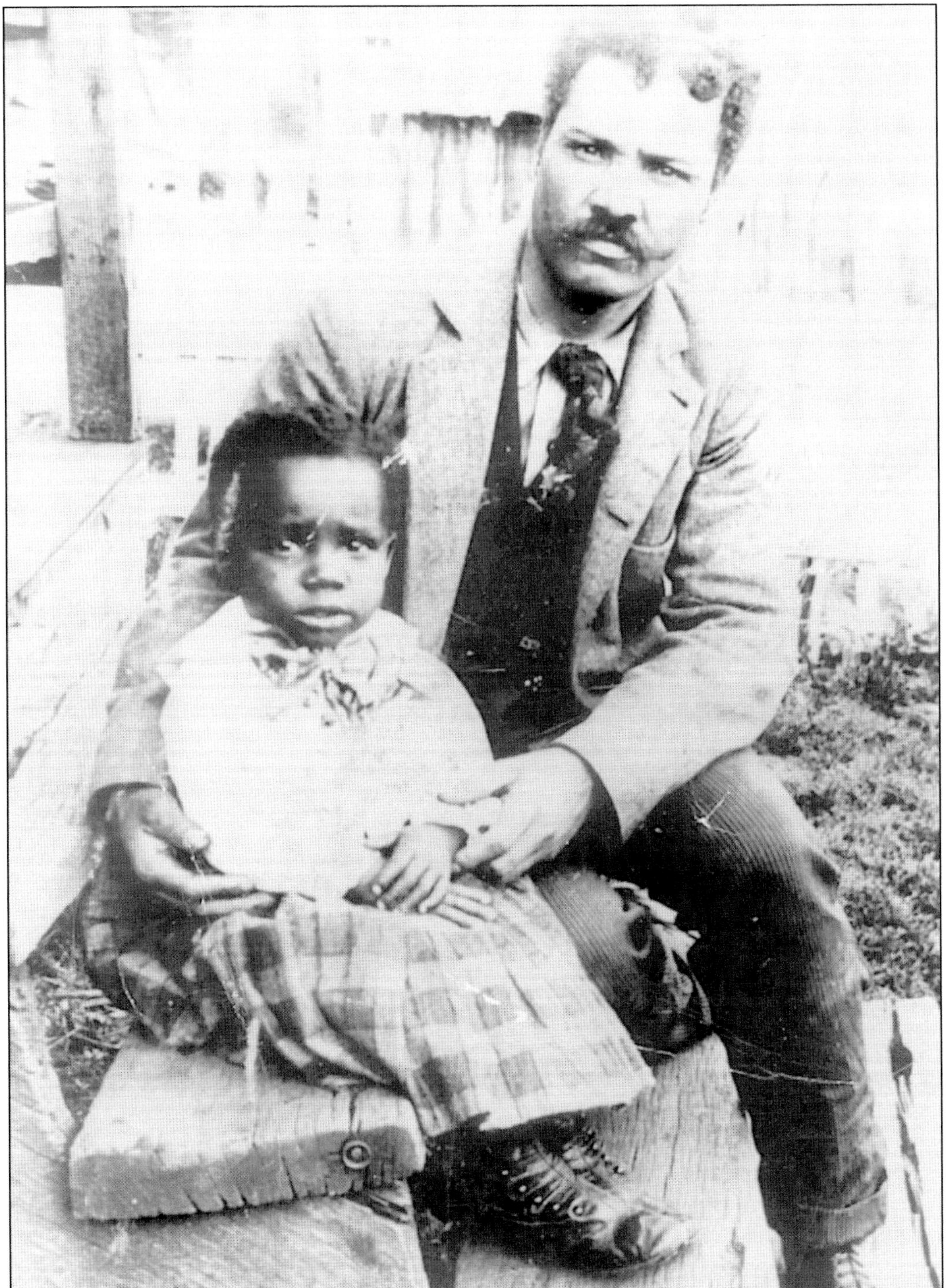

John McDonald is pictured here with his son, Jesse McDonald, in the late nineteenth century. Jesse was later raised by Lula Whitley and eventually married Laylor Jane Younger. Notice the child's interesting outfit and shoes.

Joseph Younger looks lovingly at his wife, Grace, and provides her with a seat in this picture. Grace Younger, "the Song Bird of the South," worked for the Anderson family, who owned the Alpine Theatre. W.G. "Bill" Williams Jr. tells the following story about Joseph Younger. When Bill was only a child in the 1920s, he attended a circus that was set up in a tent located on North Price Street. The circus ringmaster offered $20 to any man who could stay in the ring with his champion boxer, and upon hearing this, some of the local white men went looking for Joseph Younger. Joseph Younger took up the ringmaster's challenge and, with the first blow, knocked out his opponent. The ringmaster didn't want to give Joseph the $20 and claimed the fight hadn't been fair, but when someone mentioned that the tent might be burned down, Joseph got his prize.

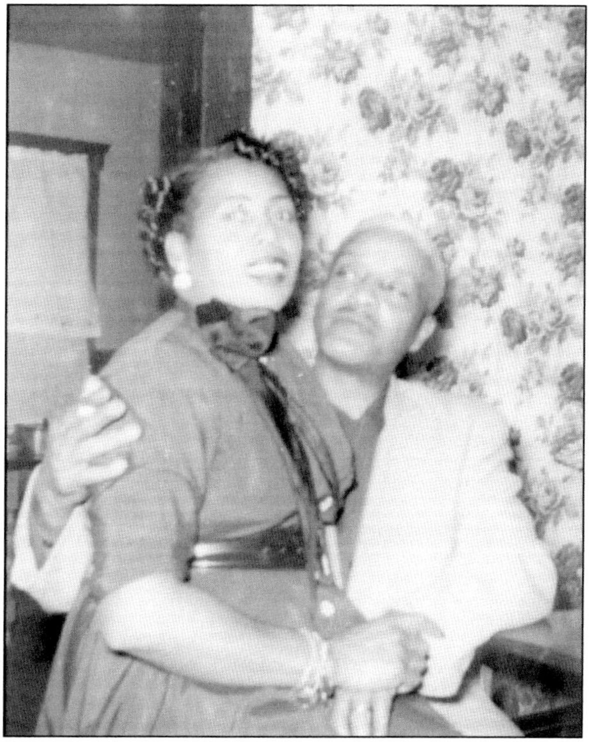

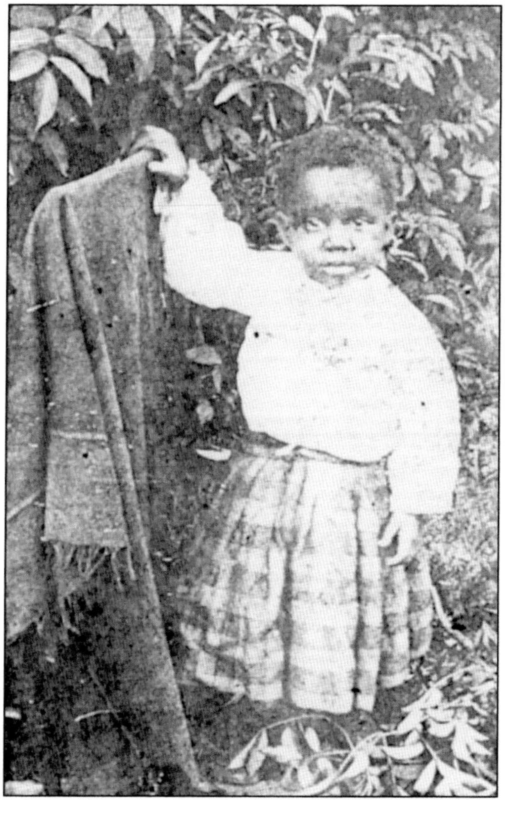

Jesse McDonald, once again pictured in the traditional clothing of the period, was born in Newsburg on January 4, 1898.

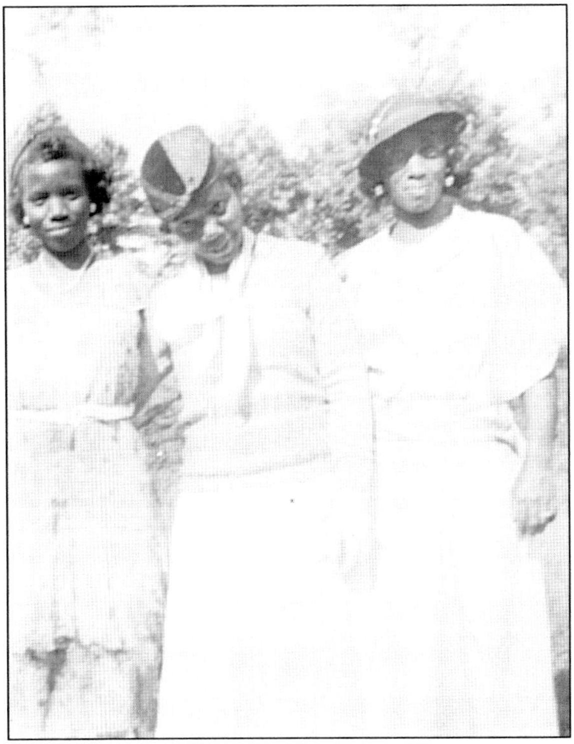

The Younger sisters, Margaret, Mable, and Virginia, pose together for this snapshot.

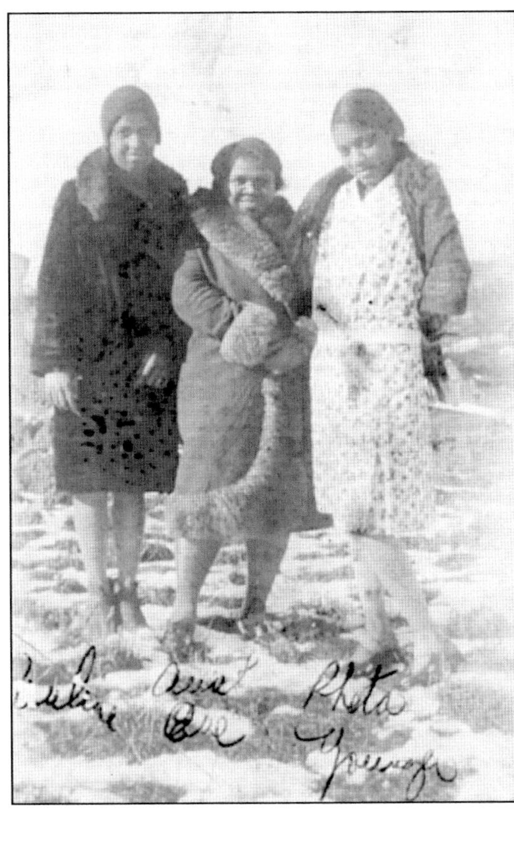

On what appears to be a cold day judging by the girls' warm coats and hats, Pauline Gray, Ava Younger, and Rheta Younger still managed to smile for this portrait.

This simple, yet elegant photo portrait is of Helen Younger.

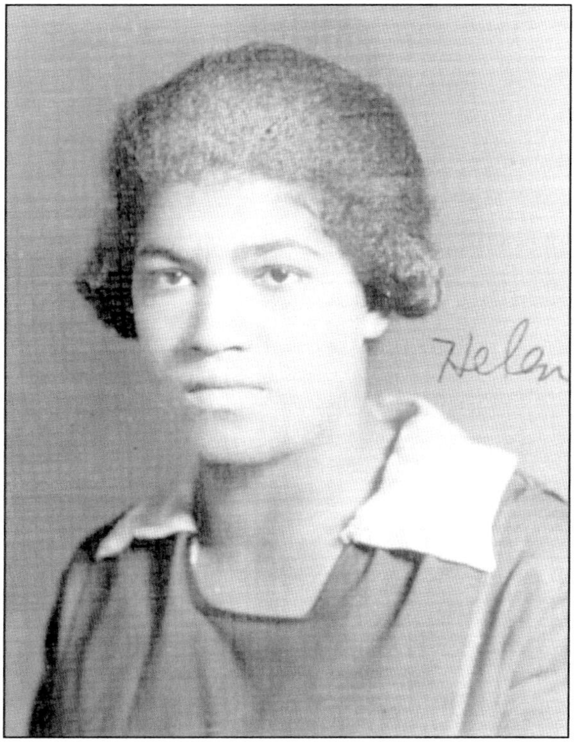

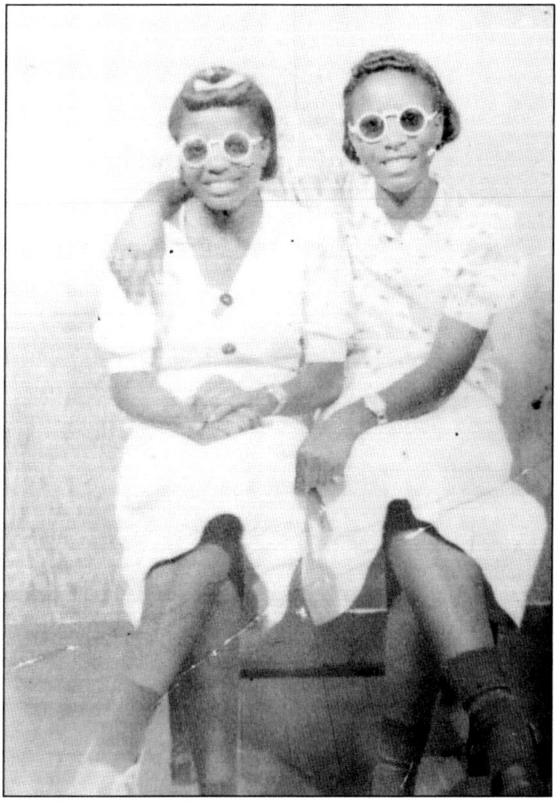

Wearing outrageous sunglasses, first cousins Eva Smith Jones and Mary Jane Beckwith shared a chair for this silly picture.

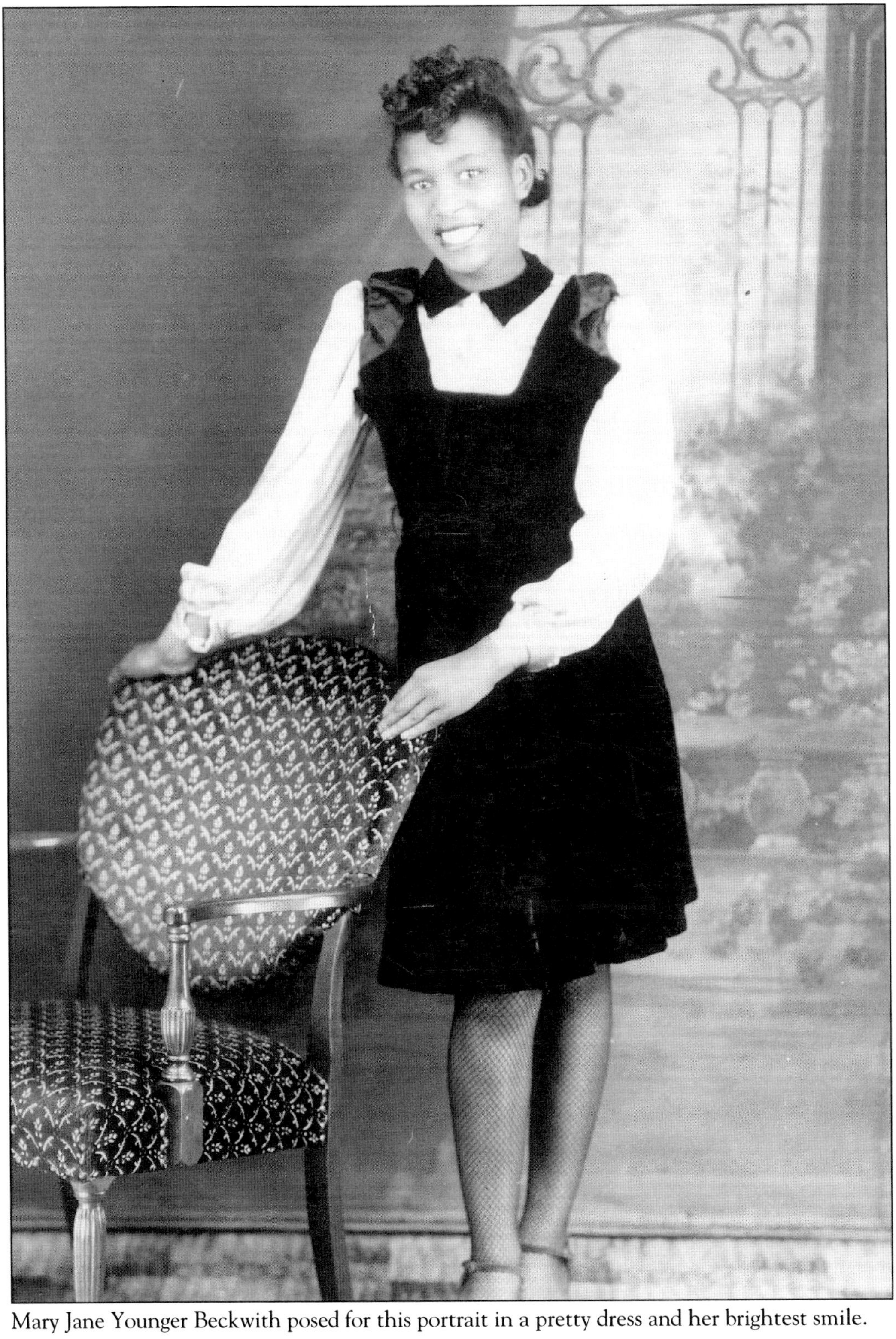

Mary Jane Younger Beckwith posed for this portrait in a pretty dress and her brightest smile.

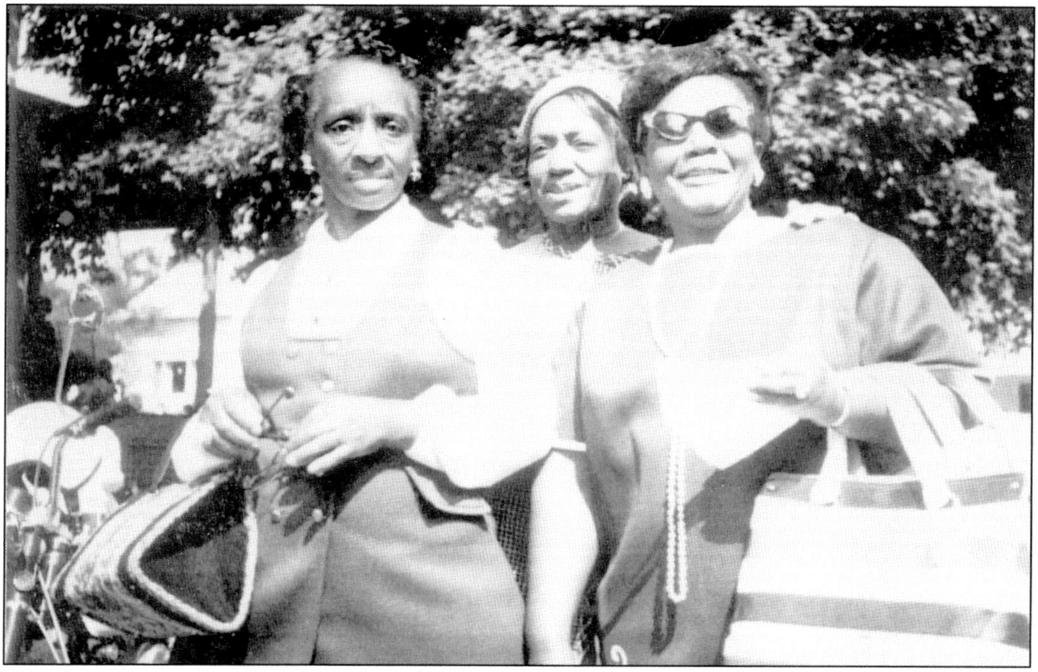

The three sisters seen here are, from left to right, LuLa Spencer, Virginia Fort, and Margaret Copney.

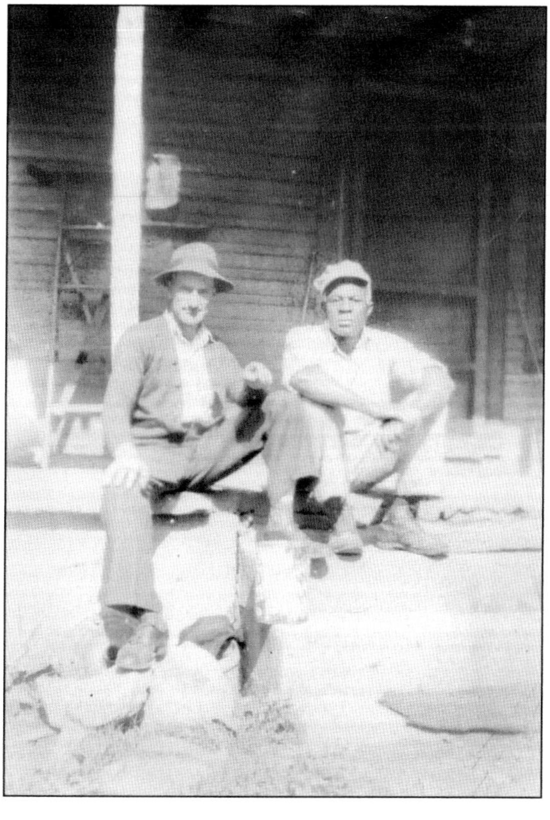

Benjamin Rivers, at right, is pictured here with his neighbor, a man by the name of Moore. Unfortunately, Rivers was murdered in the 1940s.

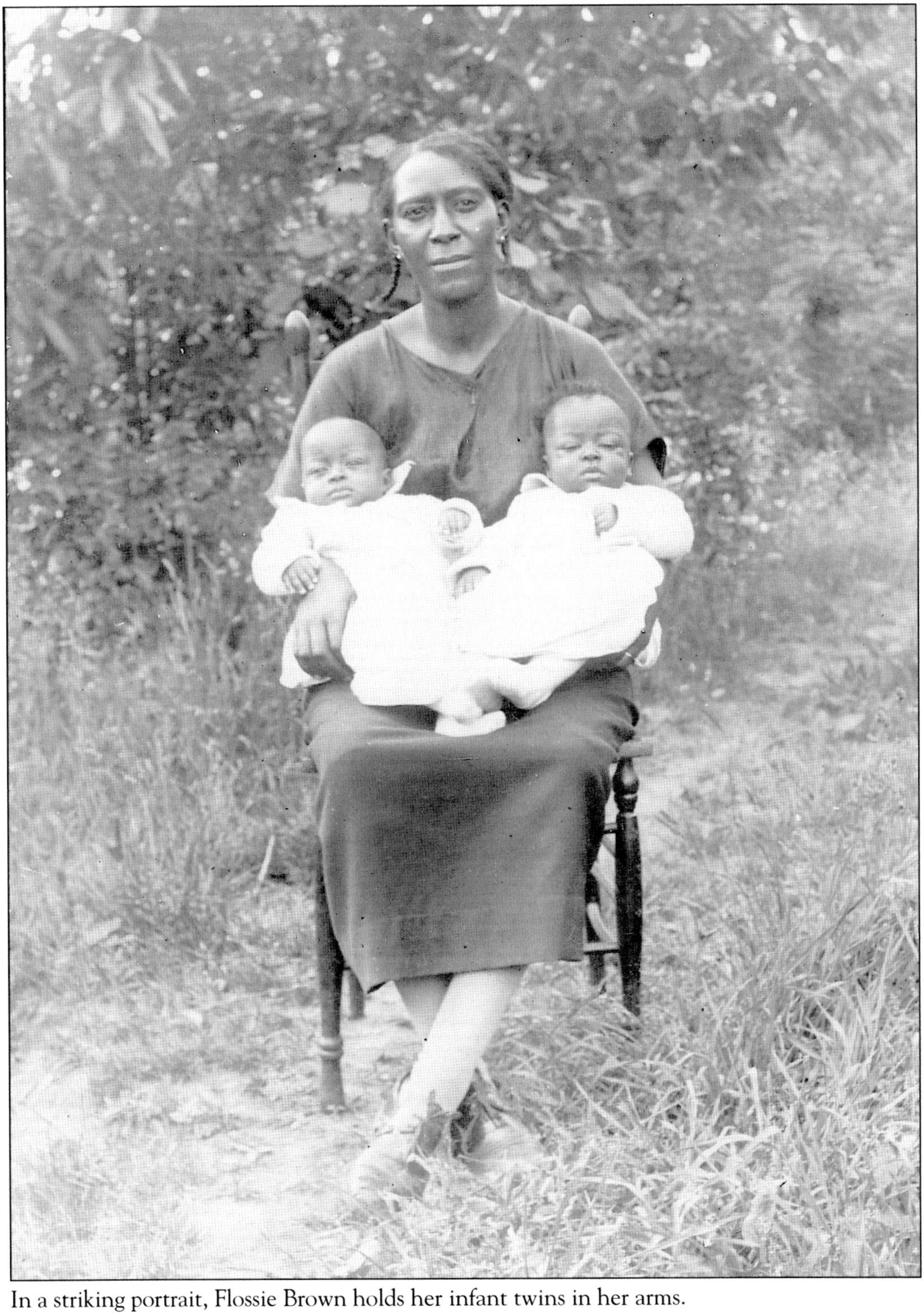

In a striking portrait, Flossie Brown holds her infant twins in her arms.

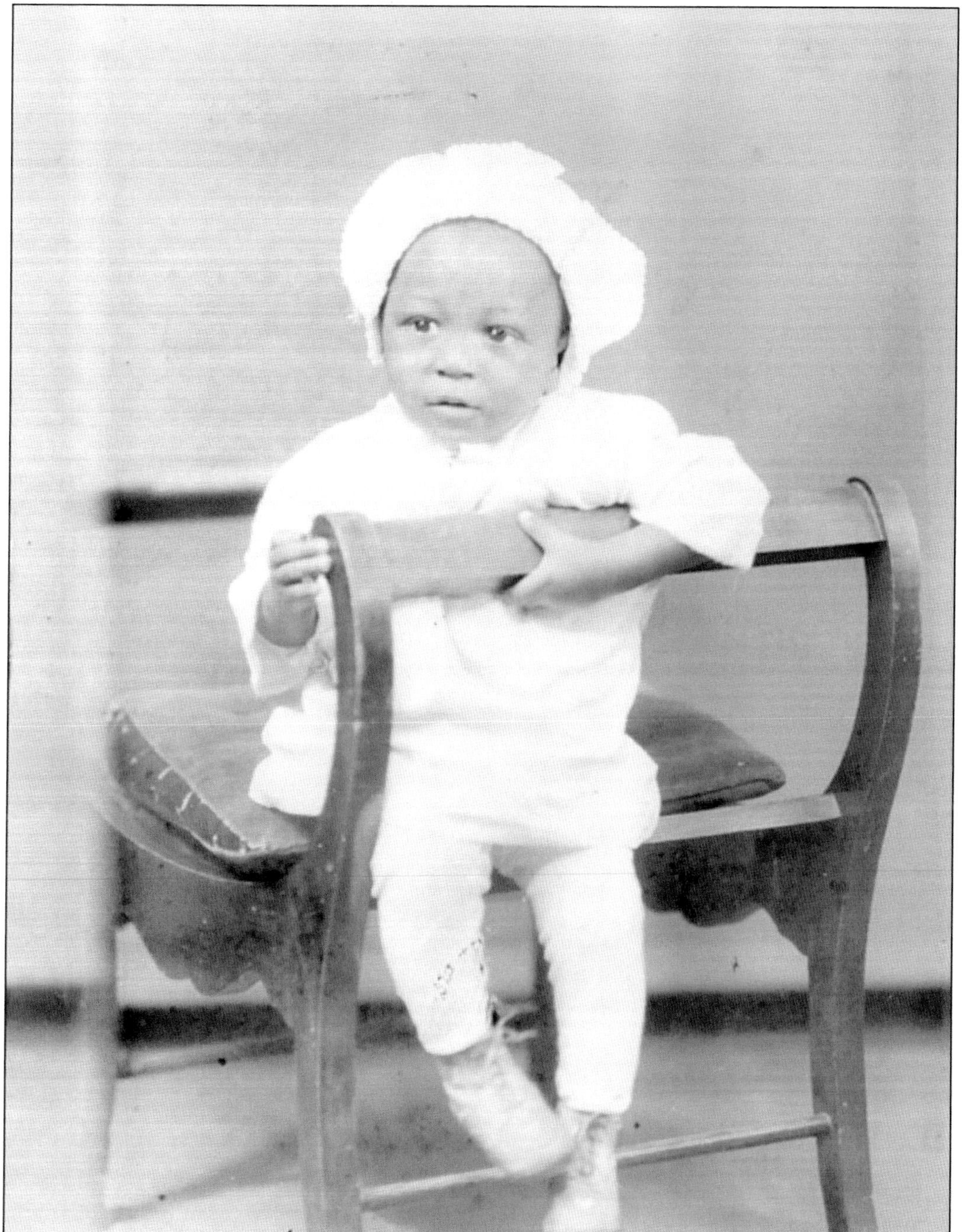

Ray Franklin Copney was born on January 9, 1933, to Henry and Margaret Copney. Notice his adorable white clothes and shoes.

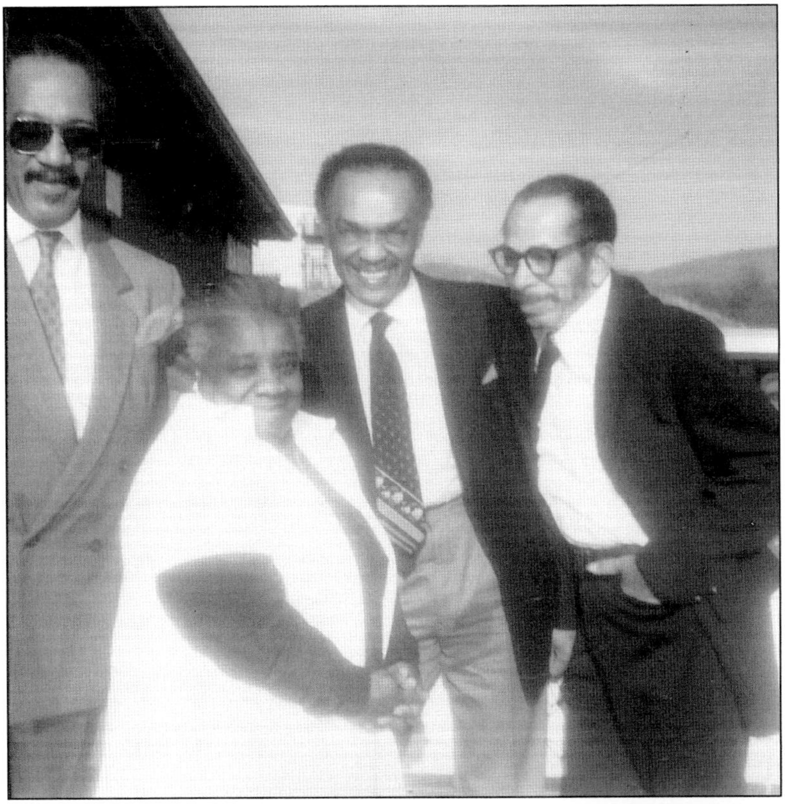

Pictured, from left to right, are James Paige, Marietta Goines, Joseph Paige, and Eddie Barnett.

Marietta was a dedicated teacher and worked with the Head Start program for children.

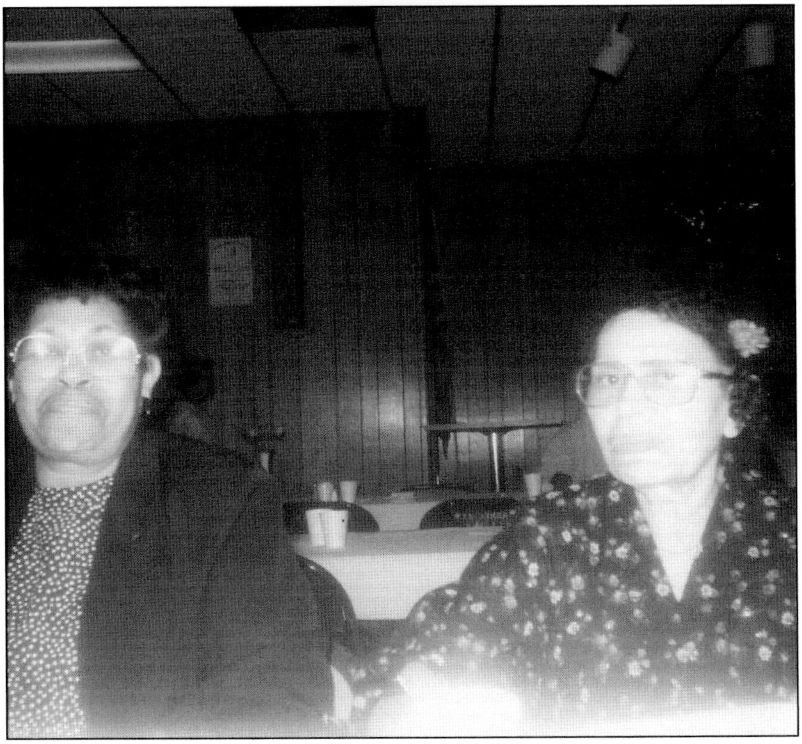

Ruth Barnett and Viola Barnett pose for this quick snapshot.

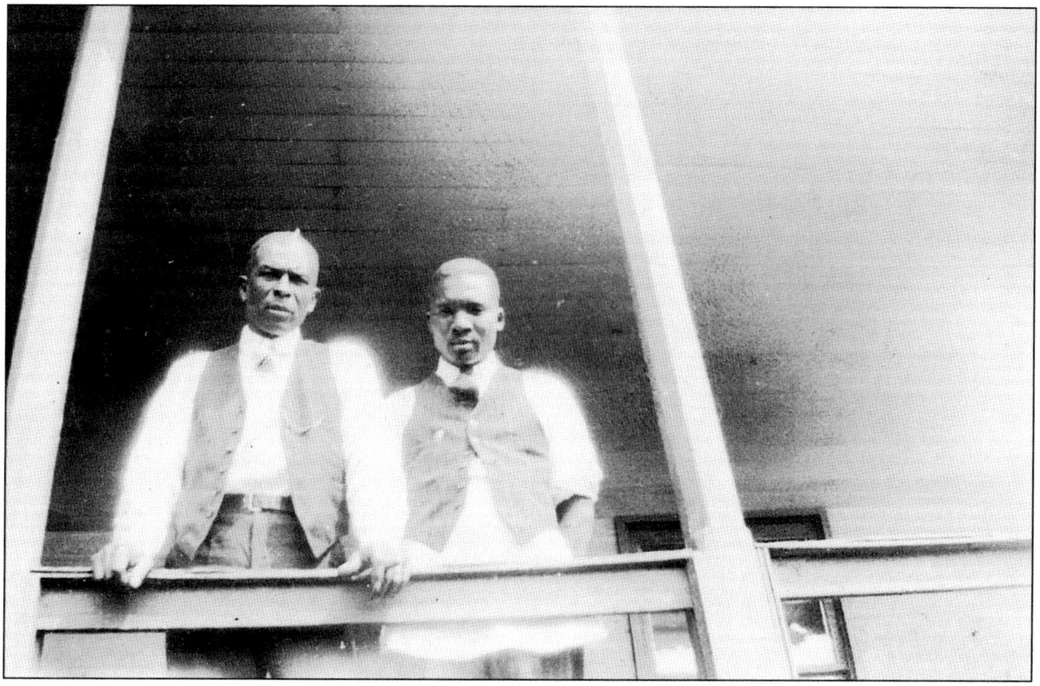

Wearing smart vests, D.C. Spencer and Richard Fort are captured in this photograph taken from below.

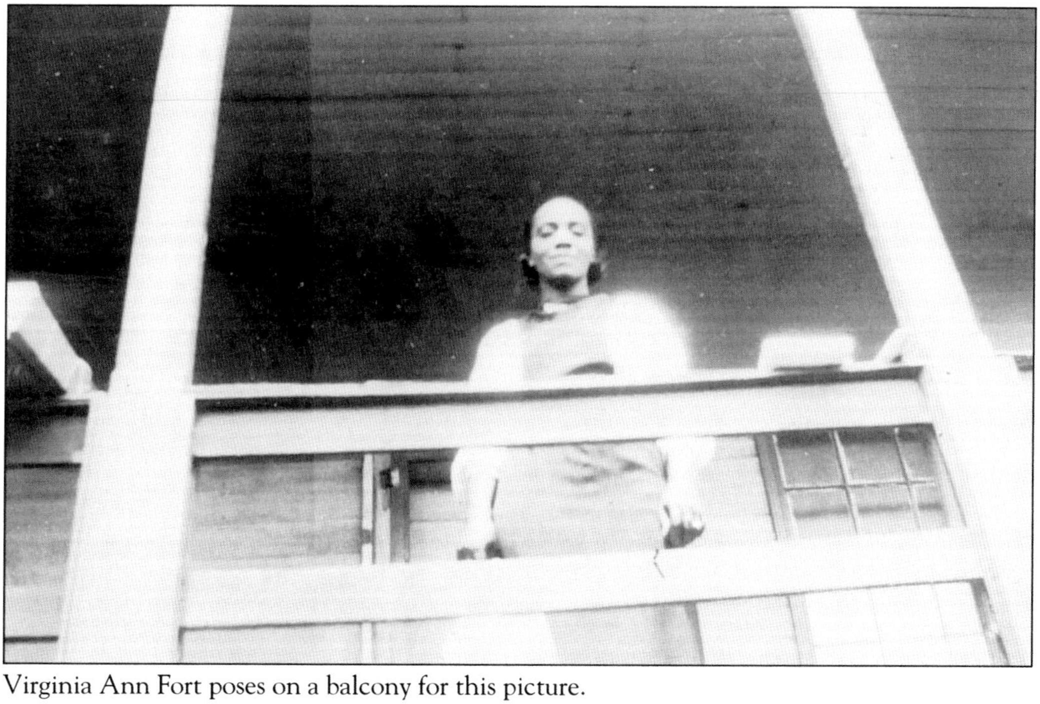

Virginia Ann Fort poses on a balcony for this picture.

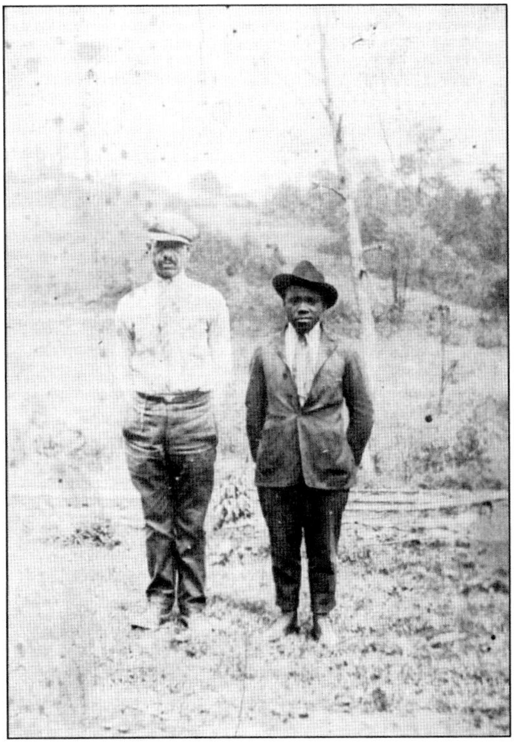

George Staley Sr. and Jesse McDonald Sr. stand rigidly with their hands behind their backs for this outdoor portrait. Mr. McDonald helped organize and marched in a "Colored" band in the late 1920s. His ceremonial sword, engraved with his name on it, has been passed down to his grandson, Marcus McDonald.

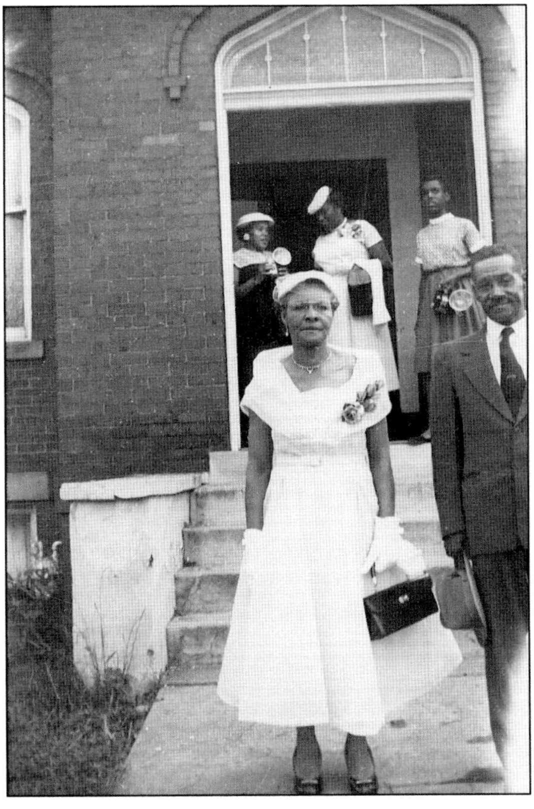

This July 1957 image shows Mr. and Mrs. James (Zella Holland) McDonald at Mt. Hermon Baptist Church on their daughter Claudette's wedding day. Also identified is Frances McDonald Dobbs in the background at far left.

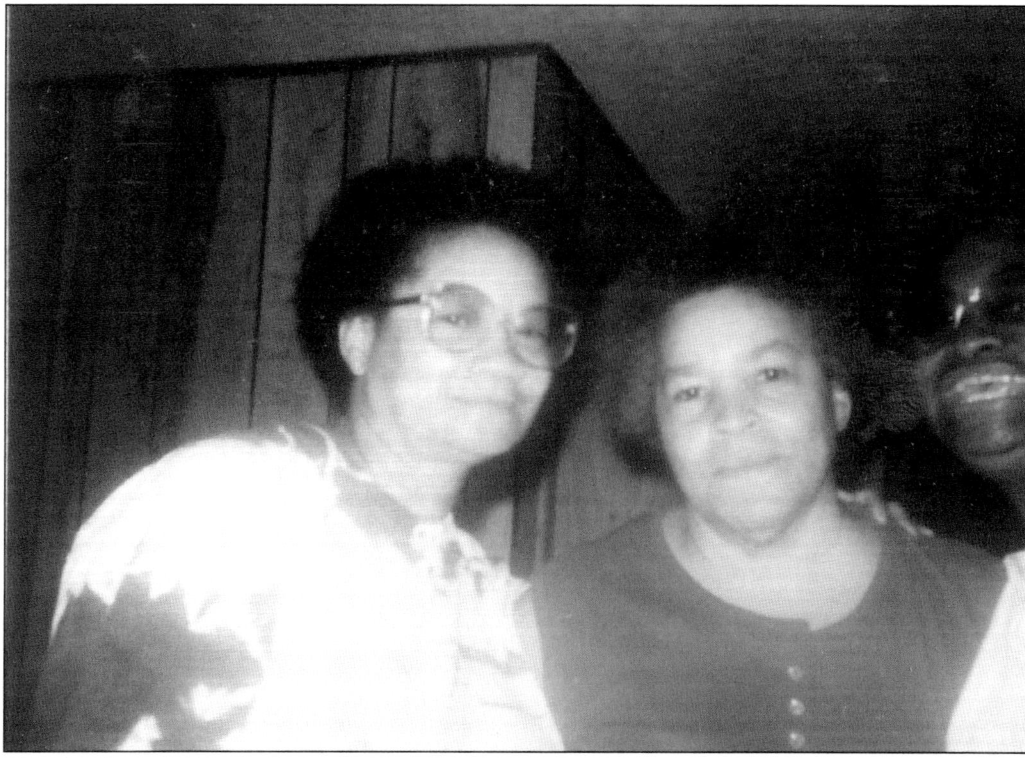

The daughters of Mr. and Mrs. James McDonald are pictured together here. They are, from left to right, Carolyn, Frances, and Claudette.

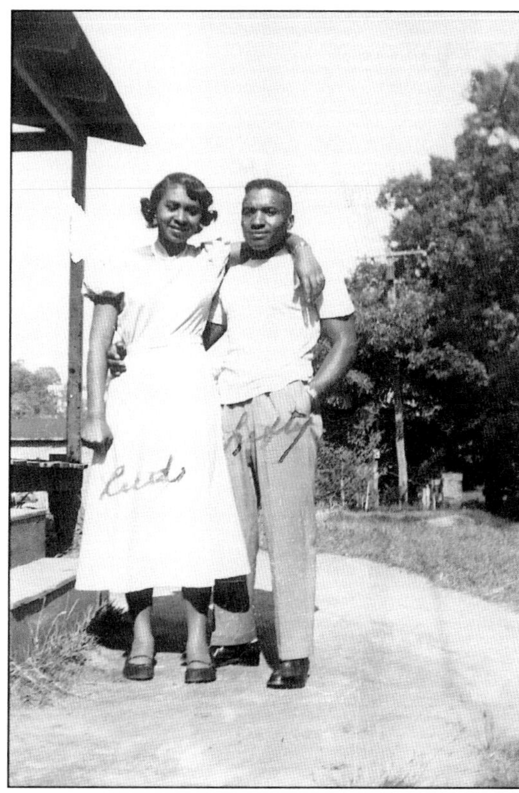

Ruth and Cornelius "Lefty" Smith, with arms around one another, posed for this photo in 1953.

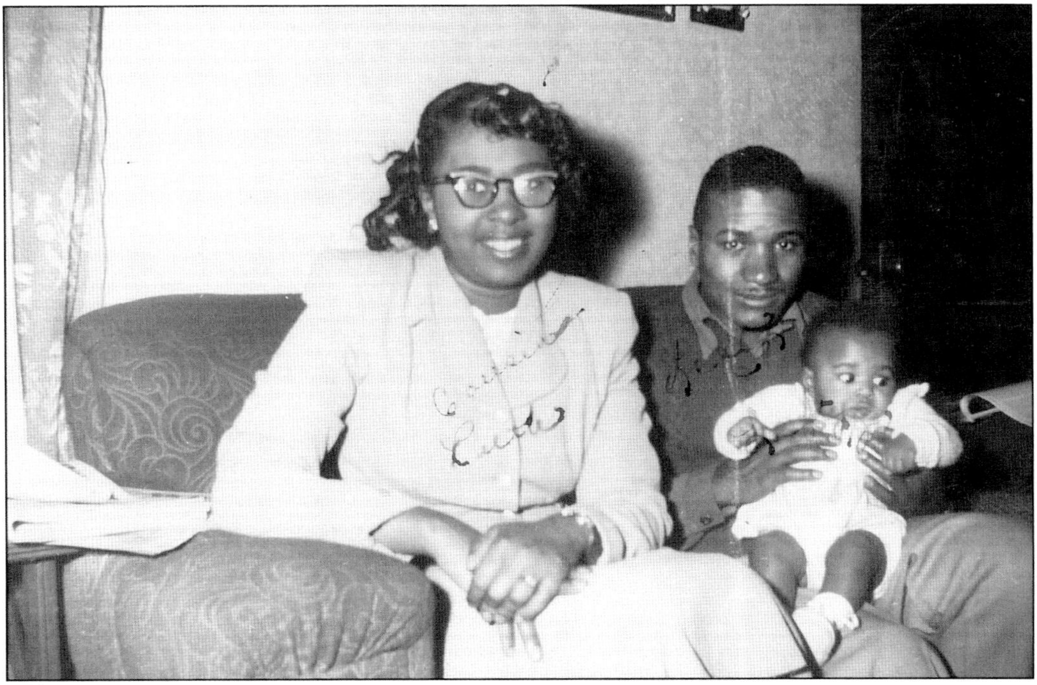

The following year, Ruth and Cornelius Smith are joined by their son Cornelius Jr. in this January 31, 1954 image.

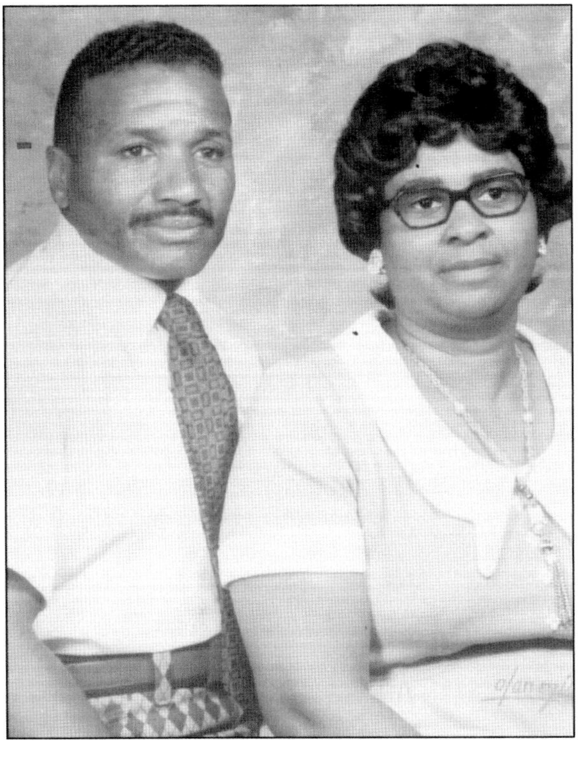

Cornelius Smith and Ruth Smith are seen in this portrait many years later.

Eva Smith Jones and Dorothy Lee Smith share an affectionate moment around the table in this simple snapshot.

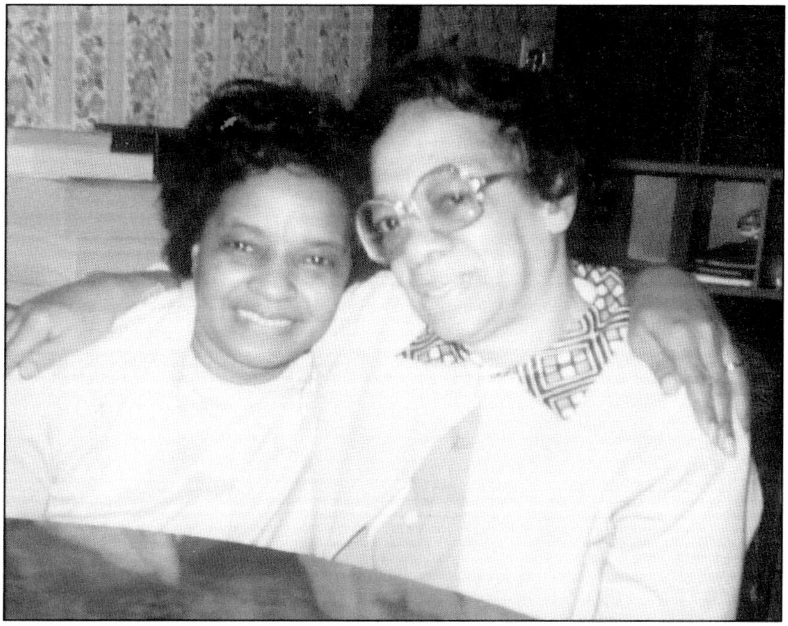

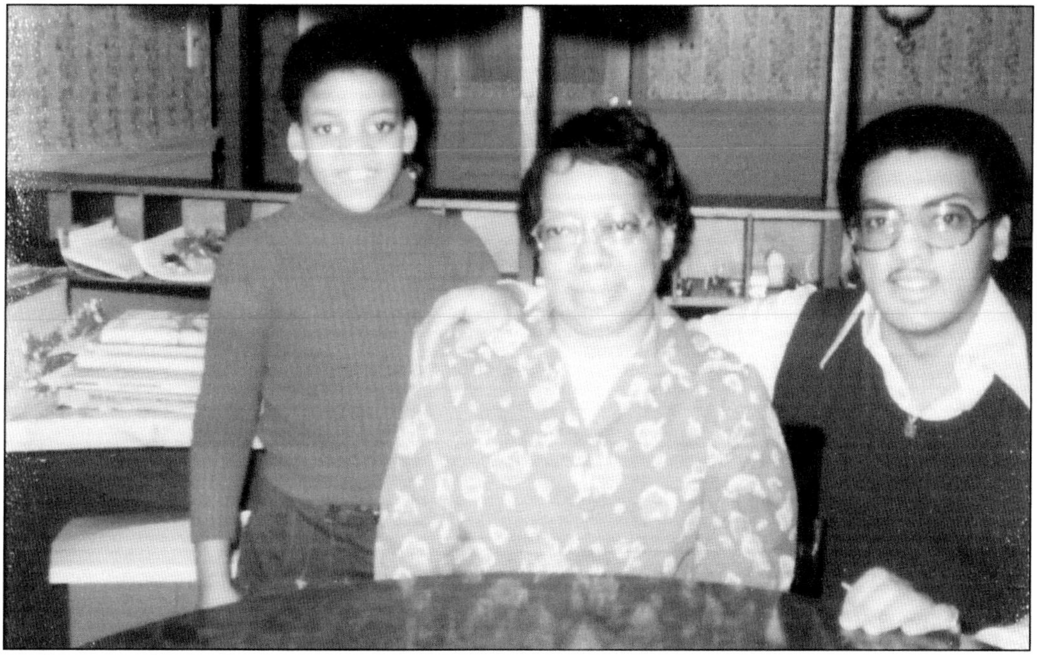

Andre, Dorothy, and Leonard Smith take a family picture together. Leonard Smith was born in Kingwood, West Virginia, on April 10, 1946, to a single mother, Dorothy Smith. Leonard had the distinction of starting school at the age of five at the one-room school his mother and those before her attended. He spent his childhood going to school and learning the fundamentals of baseball from his Uncles Ed and Lefty.

His mother was a domestic worker and supplemented her small income by taking in laundry. Leonard was always amazed how white and starched those shirts turned out. She often took on more work so that she could keep him in necessities and see that he wanted for nothing. She instilled in him a solid work ethic and a deep appreciation of family and church.

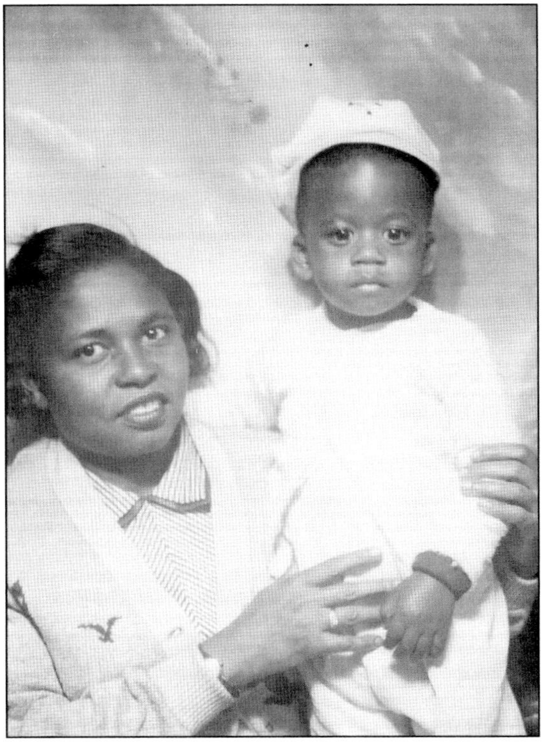

Elizabeth Dobbs Smith brought her son "Peewee" along for this cute portrait.

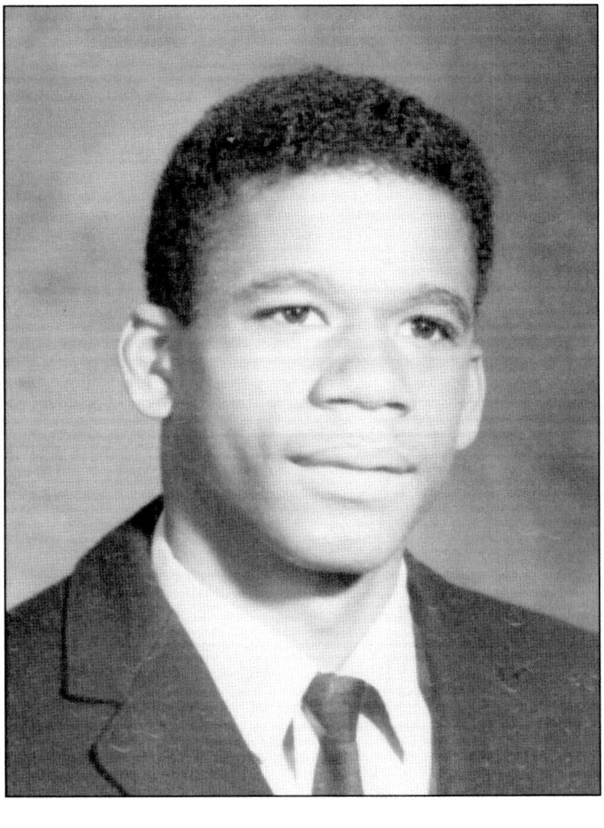

This is a picture of Elizabeth's son Richard Smith. Richard graduated from KHS in 1969. He joined the Navy in 1972 and was Honorably discharged on January 5, 1975. He then joined the Army Reserves in 1978 and was employed at Fibair for 14 years. Richard married Lisa Johnson on July 7, 1984. They had a son, D.J., born June 12, 1991, and a daughter, Jackie, born July 16, 1995.

Margaret and Henry Copney have both retired from the Sheidow Bronze Corporation.

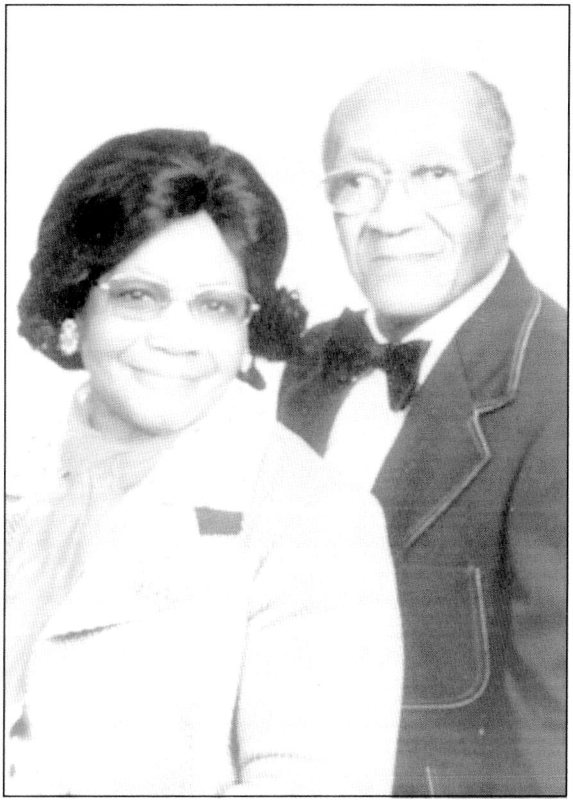

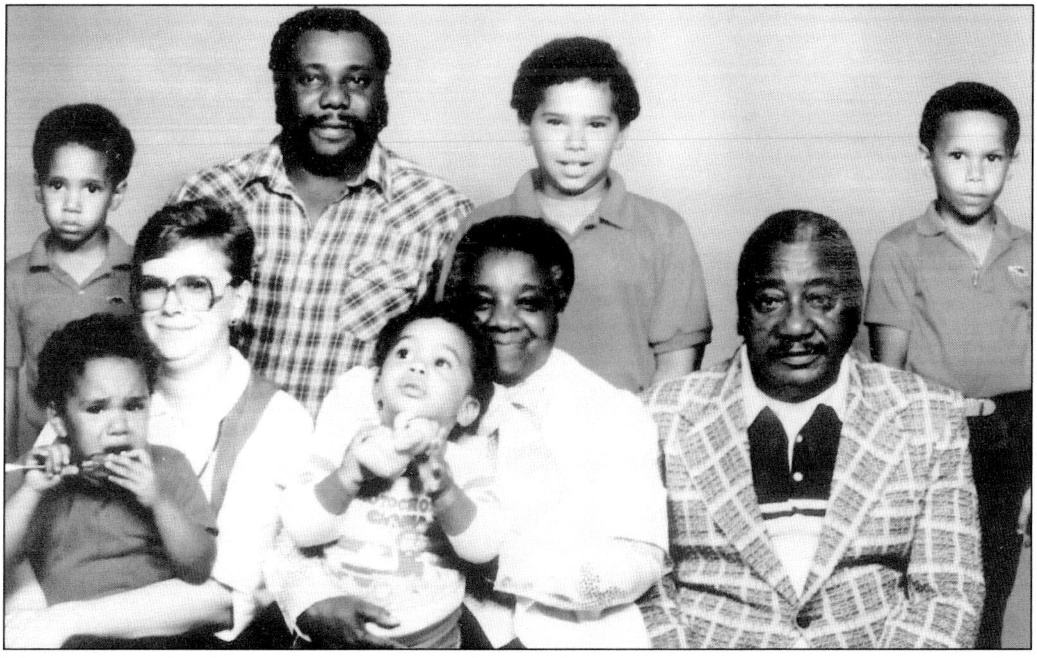

This Goines family portrait includes, from left to right, (front row) Paula (holding John), Marietta (holding Frank II), and Russell Goines Sr.; (back row) Jason, Russell Jr., Jeremy, and Jesse.

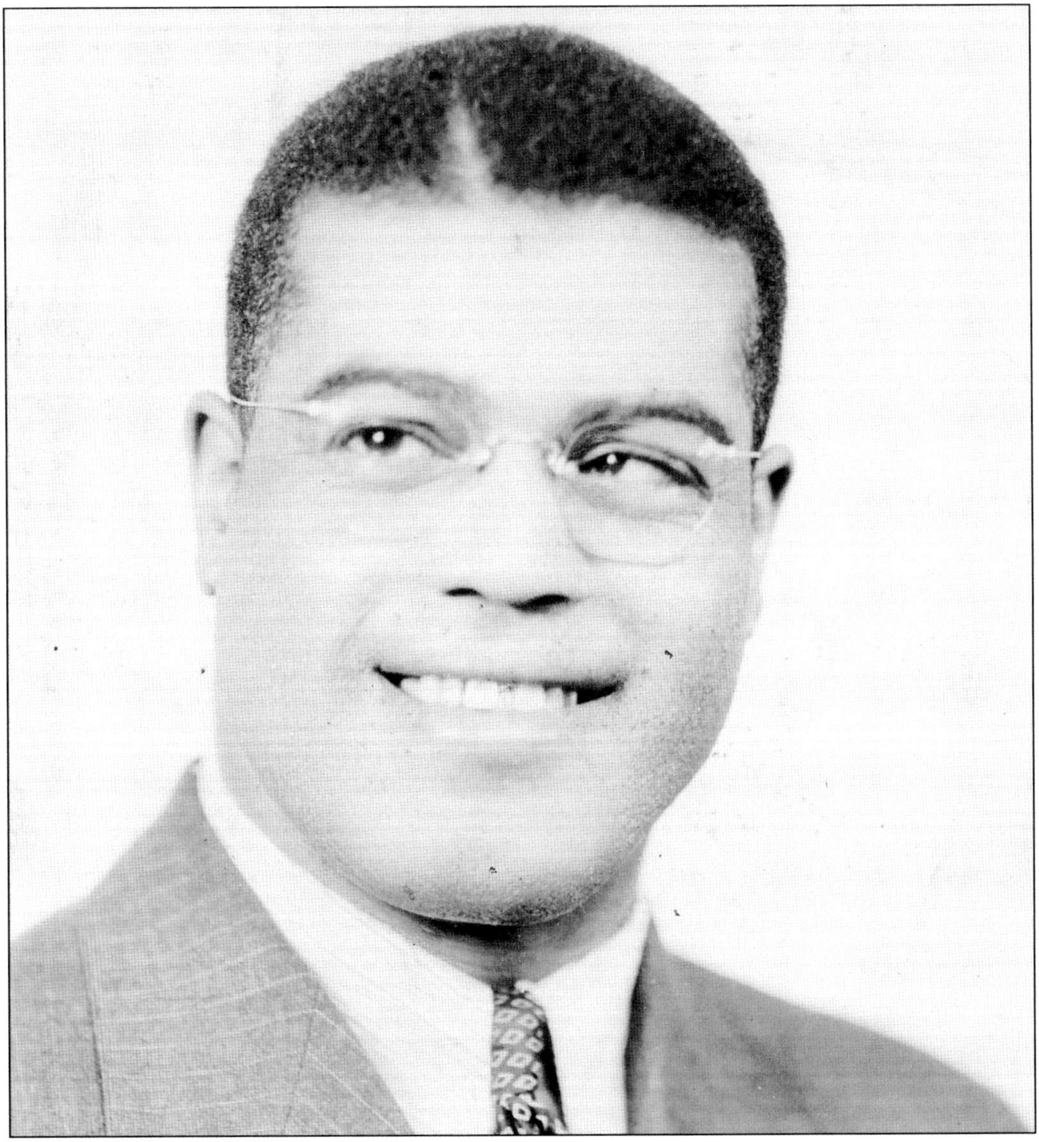

When Charles "Charlie" Younger was a boy, in Kingwood, schools were segregated and there was no high school for African Americans. So when African-American children completed eight grades, the boys would get jobs in the coal mines and the girls would get housework. When Younger was 26 years old, he would sometimes peek through the windows of the high school's auditorium when the white students held a dance. Some of the boys inside knew that Younger was a good singer, and they invited him in to sing for them. Word of his musical talent spread throughout the community, and Besse Hardesty, the president of the Loyal Workers Sunday School Class at Wesley Methodist Church, called Younger's mother and asked her to have her son sing for them. After Younger sang, Hardesty addressed the group, telling them that she thought it a shame that this man had talent and couldn't do anything about it. She said, "I move that we get this man in a school," and they agreed. They sent him to Piney Woods School in Piney Woods, Mississippi, a trade school. From there, Younger won a scholarship to Elseworth Conservatory of Music and College, and he was able to major in English, voice, and plumbing.

Herbert Sr. and Louise McDonald are the proud parents of five children. Herbert retired from the coal mines and now regularly visits the sick in the community and is a loyal volunteer at Love Chapel Church. Louise sings in the choir and is a lay leader at Love Chapel. When the church was organized on December 5, 1954, it was at her suggestion that the church was named after the presiding Bishop Edgar Love.

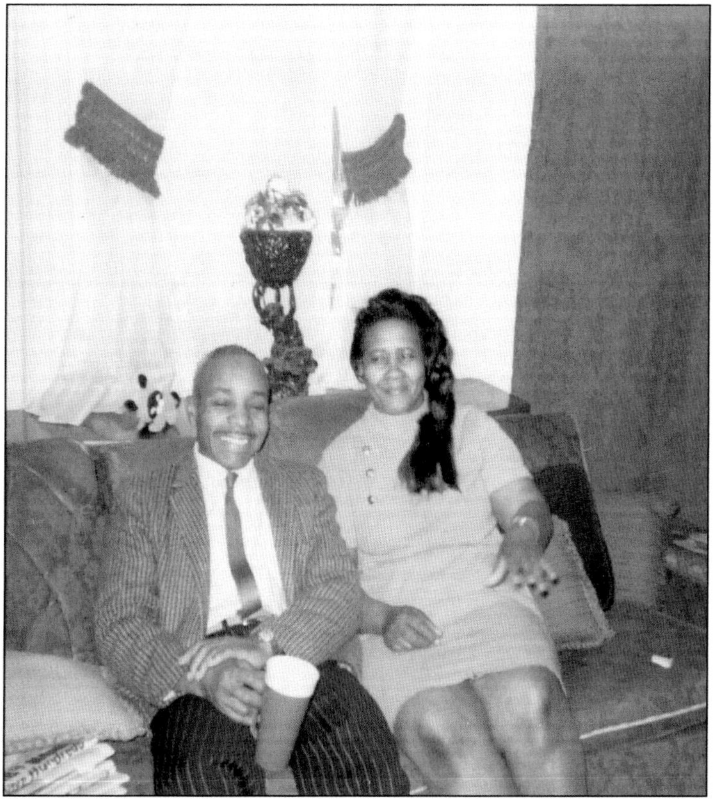

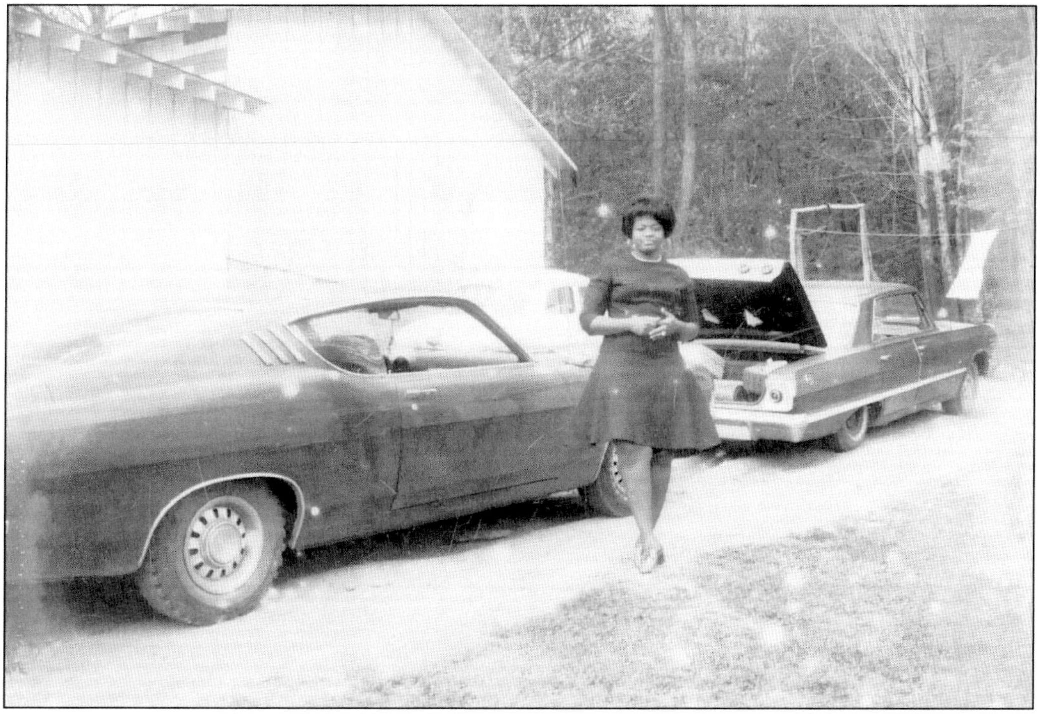

Sandra Jefferson Spencer is all dressed up for this outdoor portrait.

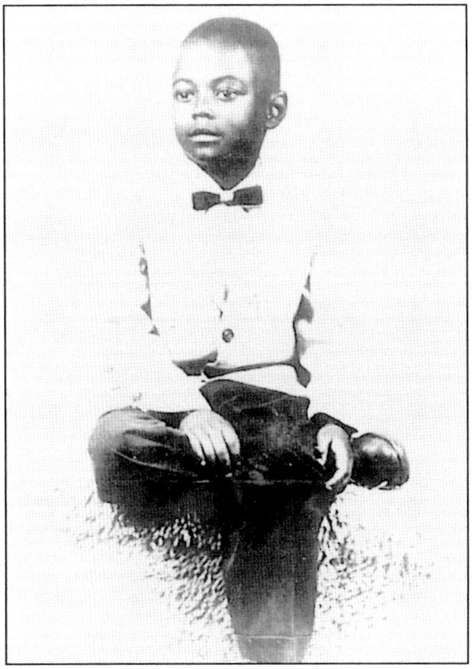

William "Billy" Miller, pictured here in suit and bow tie, is the stepson of Jesse McDonald Jr.

Annie Copney Dove, a visitor from White Plains, New York, in the bottom left corner, and Robert Spencer had this picture snapped in 1975.

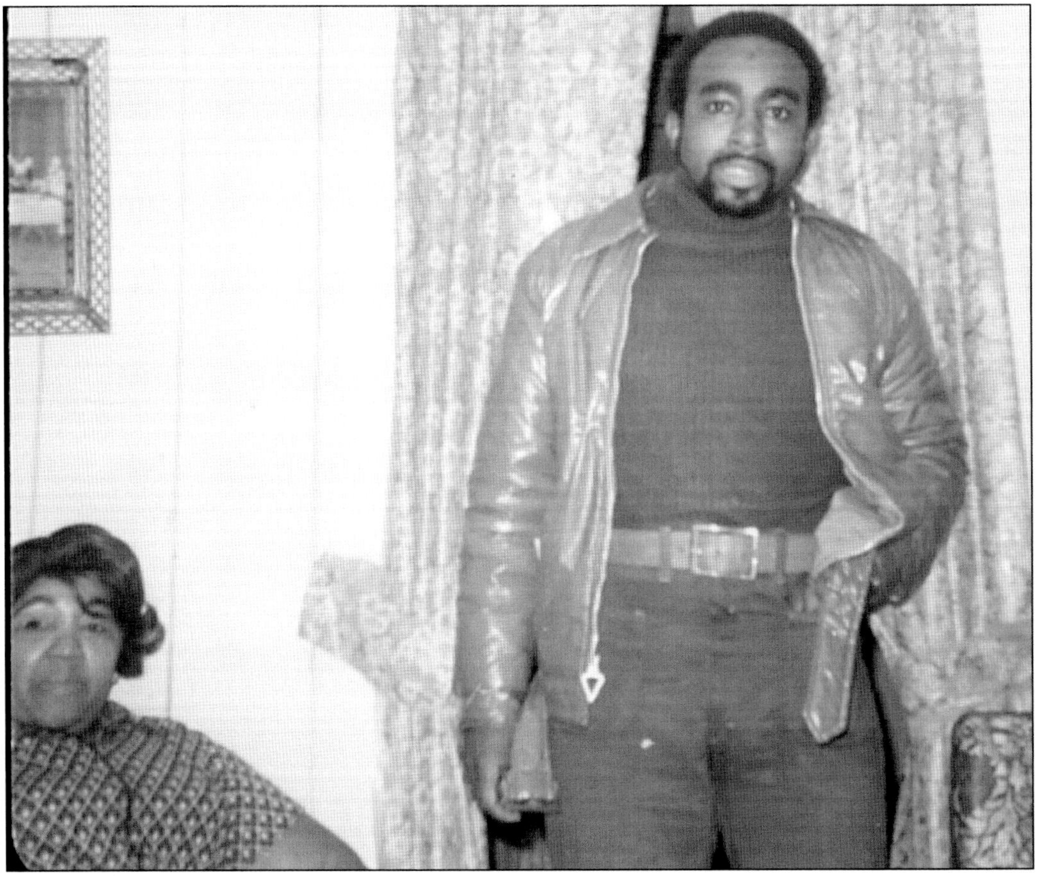

Little Benjamin McGee looks as if this picture took him by surprise.

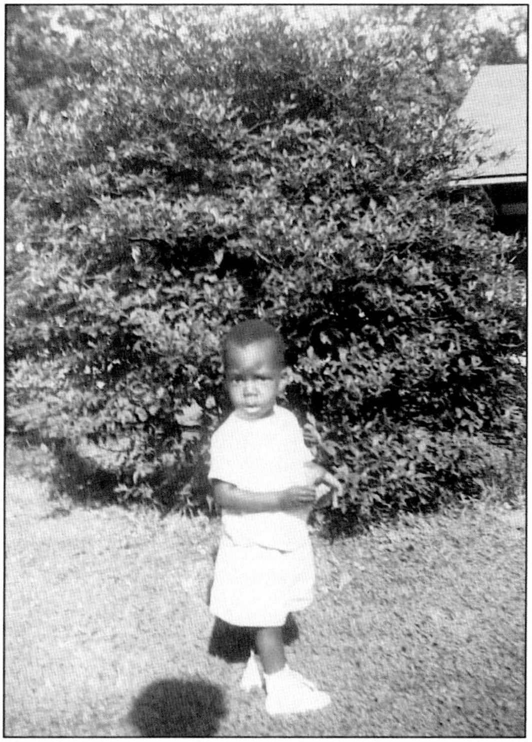

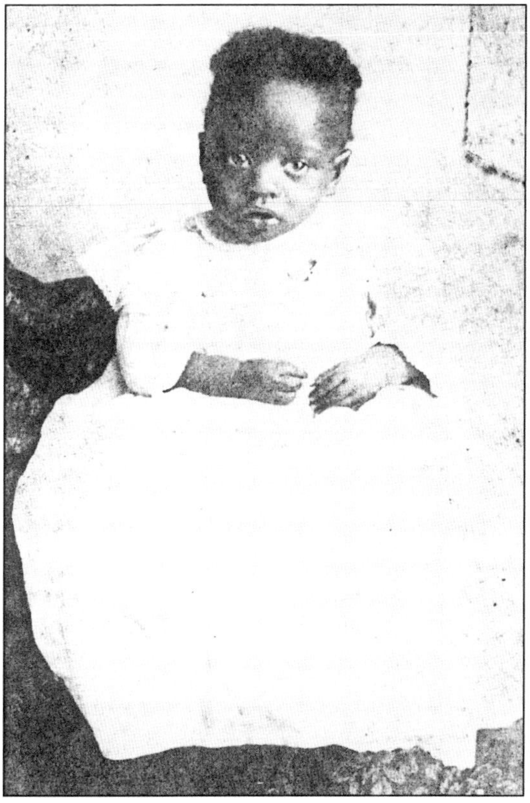

Cora Lee Younger Smith, seen in this formal portrait, was born on May 14, 1900.

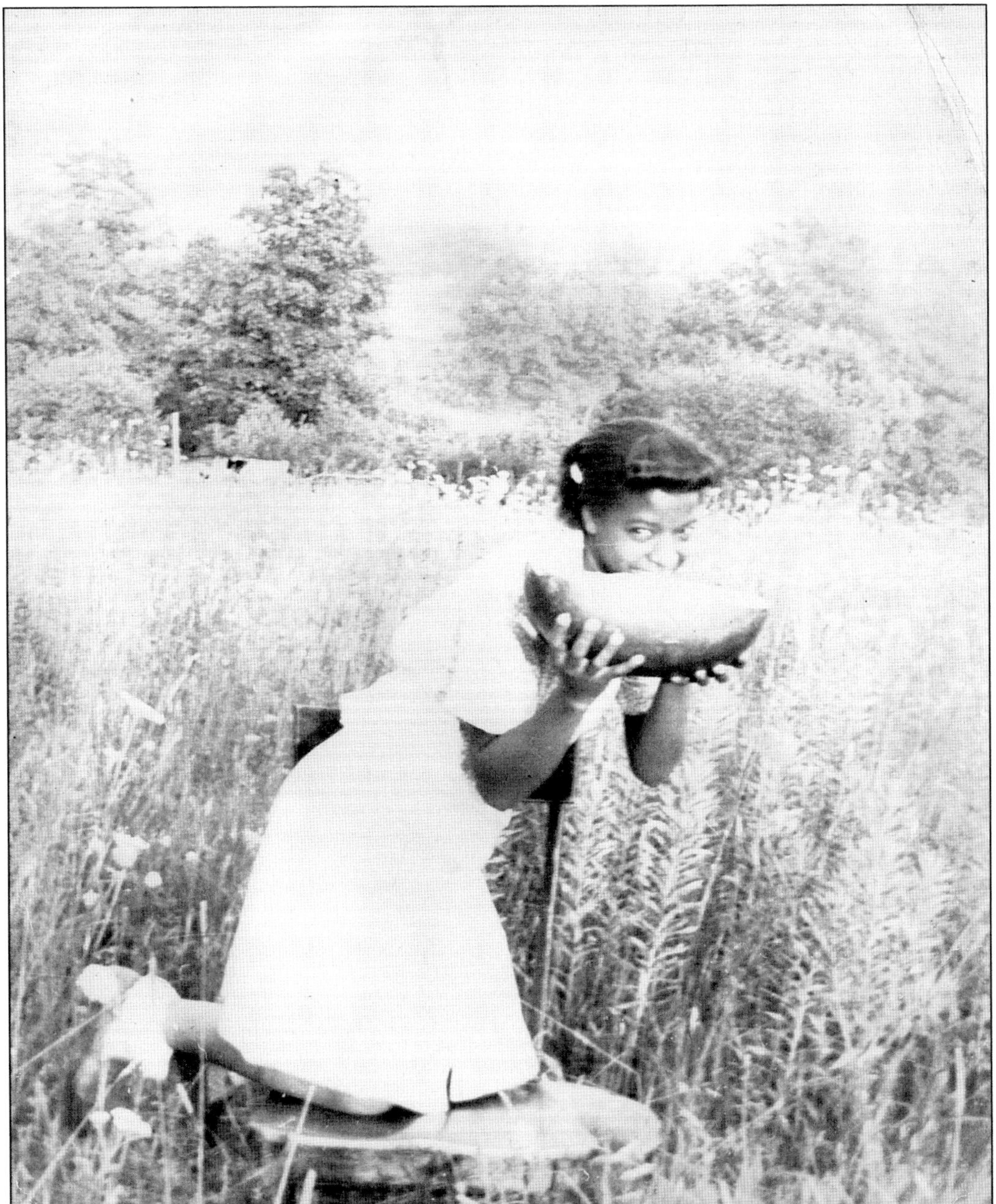

Eva Smith Jones was testing a watermelon when this photograph was taken early in the 1930s in Mr. Charlie Harner's field.

William Younger Sr., holding his granddaughter Esther at left, his wife, Eva, and John Hall all smile broadly for this 1940s photograph.

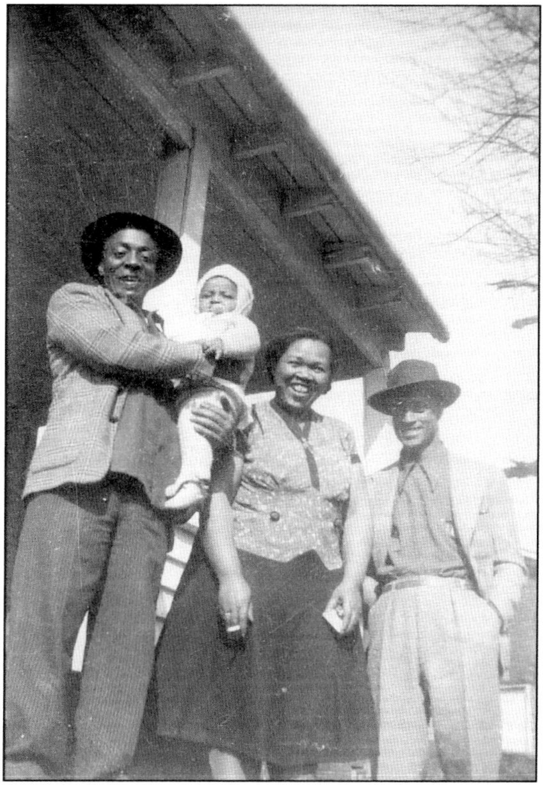

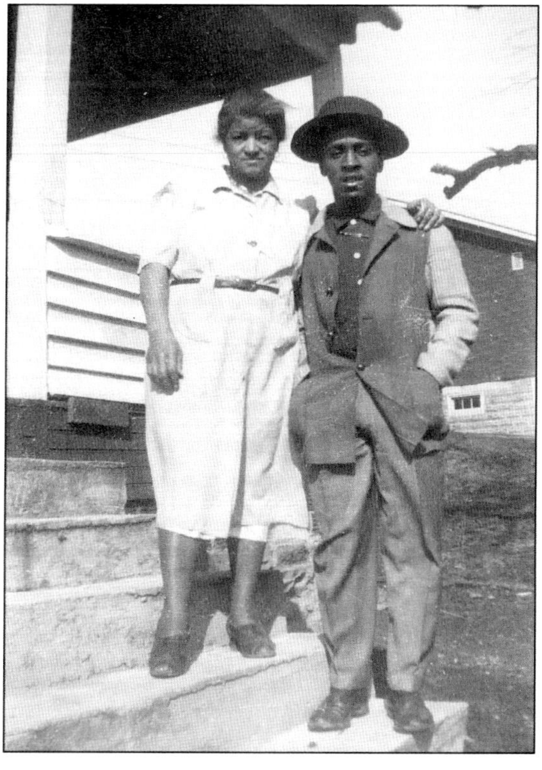

Helen Rivers and William Younger Jr. take a moment to pose on the steps for this picture.

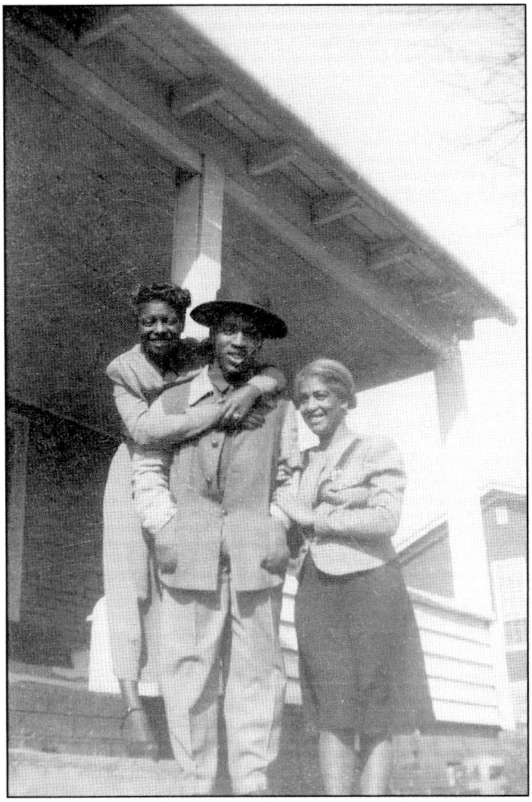

Esther Holland, with her arms draped around William Younger Jr., and Pauline Gray were the subject of this early 1940s picture.

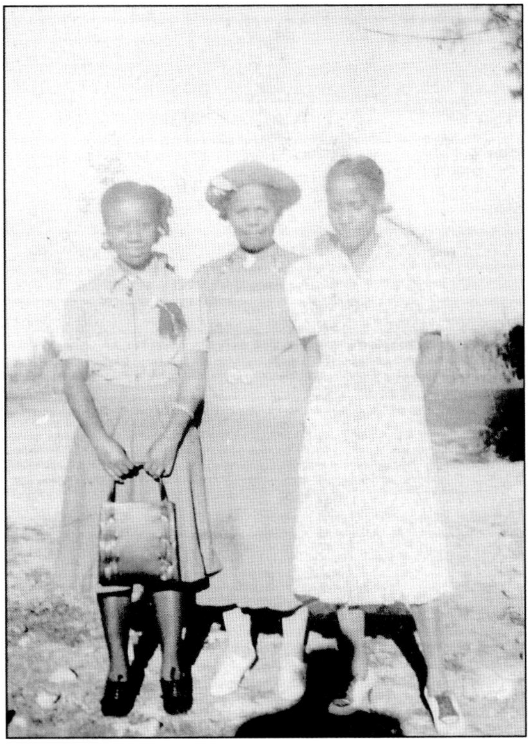

Pictured from left to right, Mable Younger, her mother, Mary, and sister Virginia had this group shot taken in the 1930s.

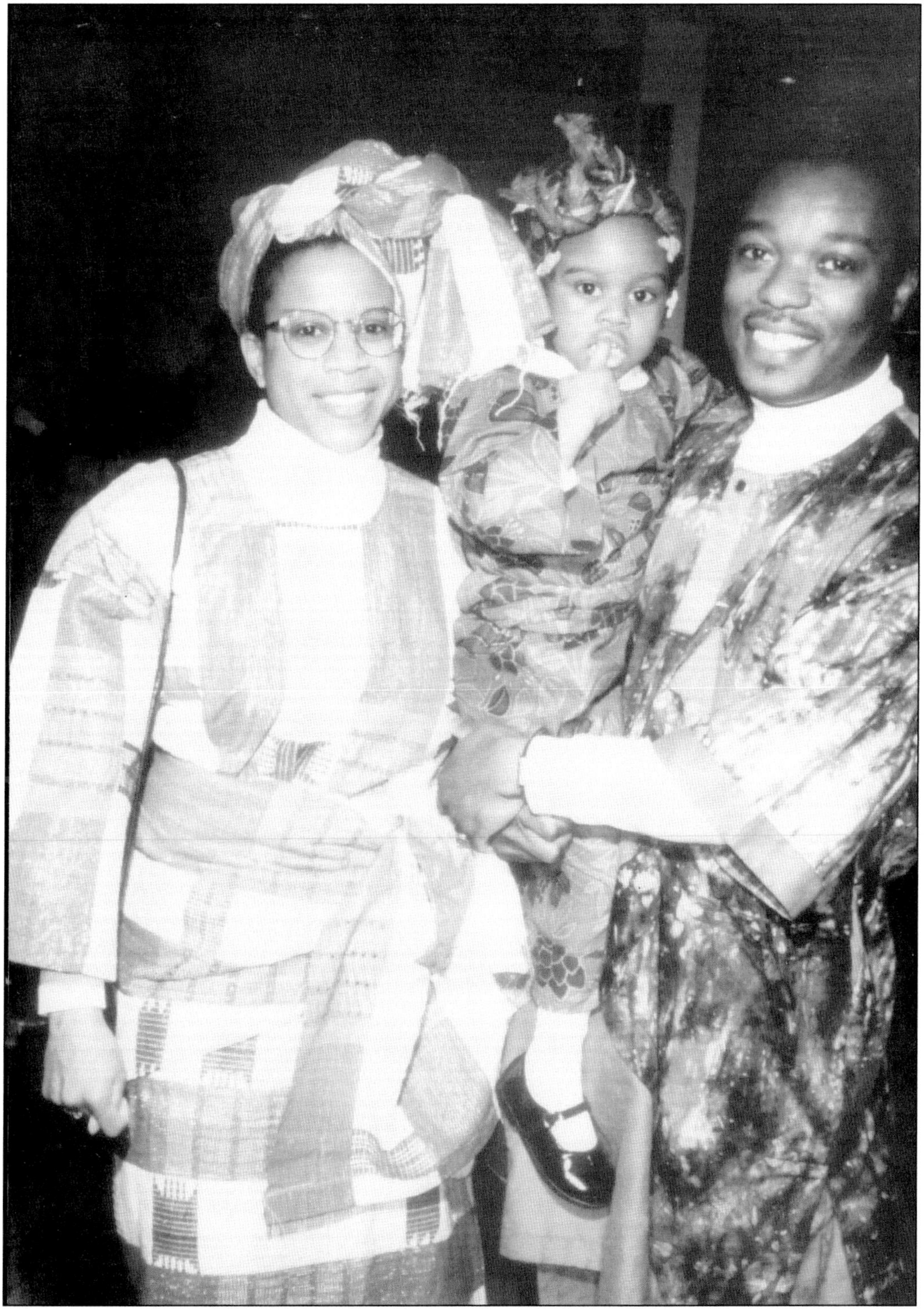

Carolyn McDonald Ayodeji and her husband, Wale, are pictured here with their daughter. Mrs. Ayodeji is a federal government employee in accounting, and her husband is a civil engineer.

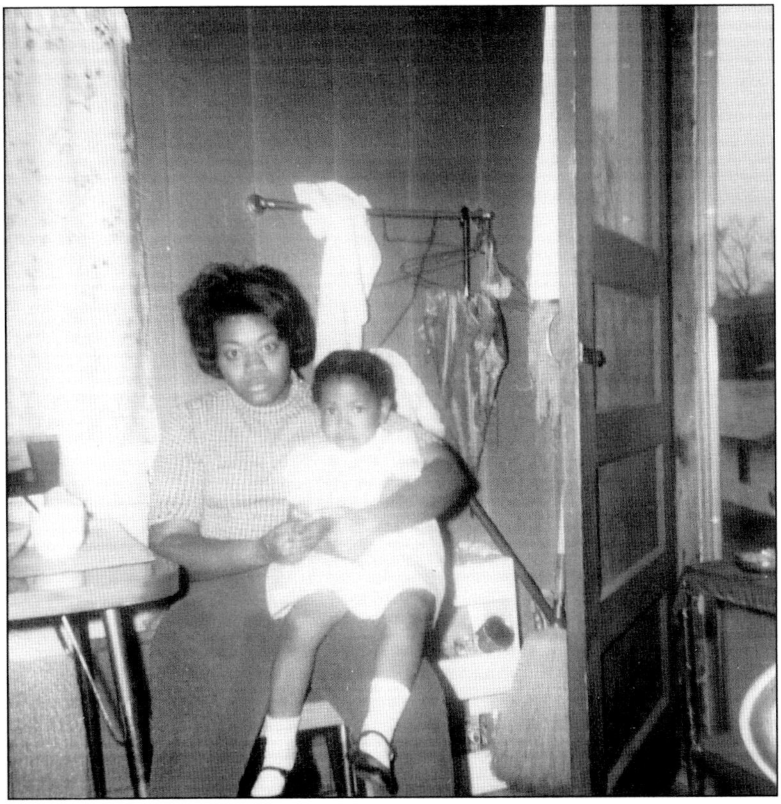

Sandra Jefferson Spencer holds Amy Jones on her lap in this 1966 picture.

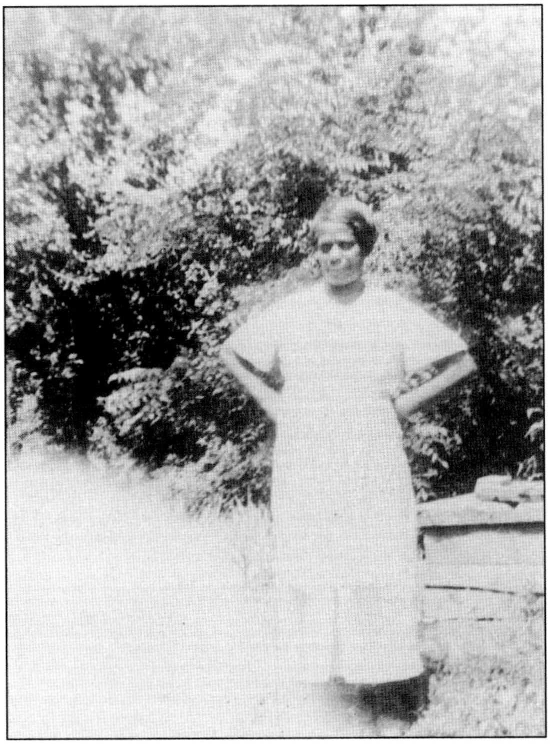

Mary Frances Younger stands, with hands on hips, for this old portrait.

Mildred Grace McDonald was very active in church work and was a Sunday school superintendent and teacher for nearly 50 years. This picture was taken in the early 1960s.

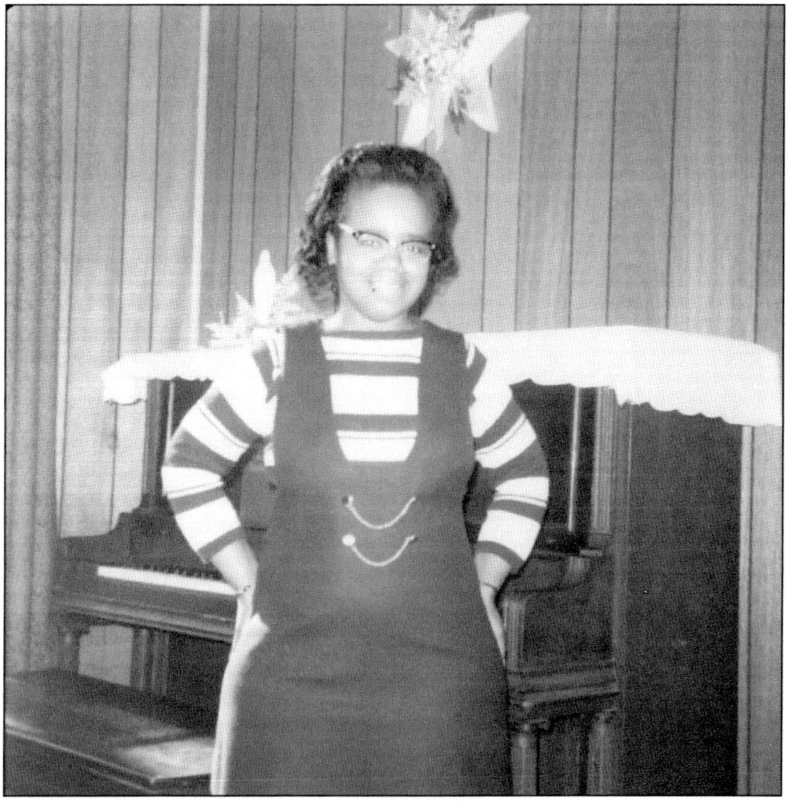

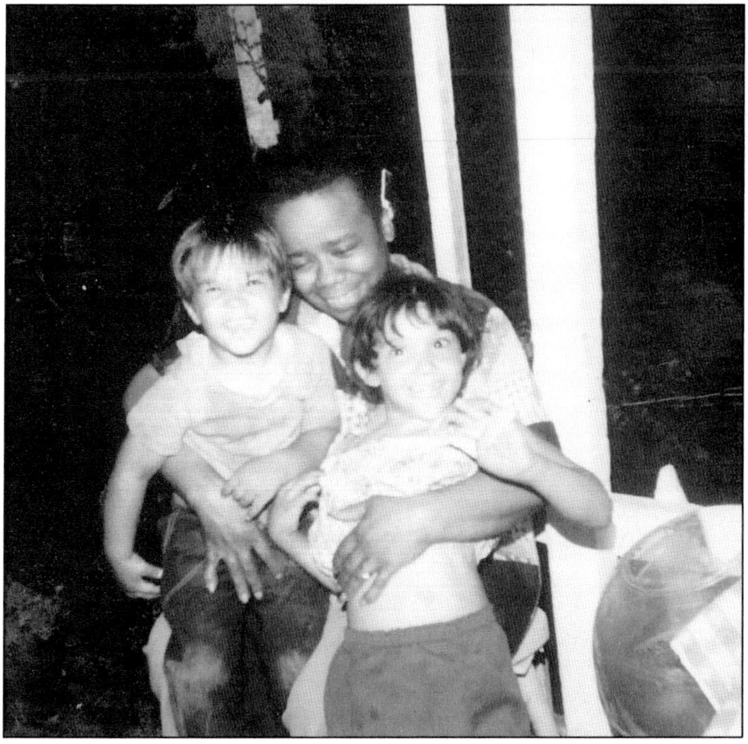

Mildred Grace McDonald loved all children. Scott and Christine McDonald are pictured with her here in November 1980.

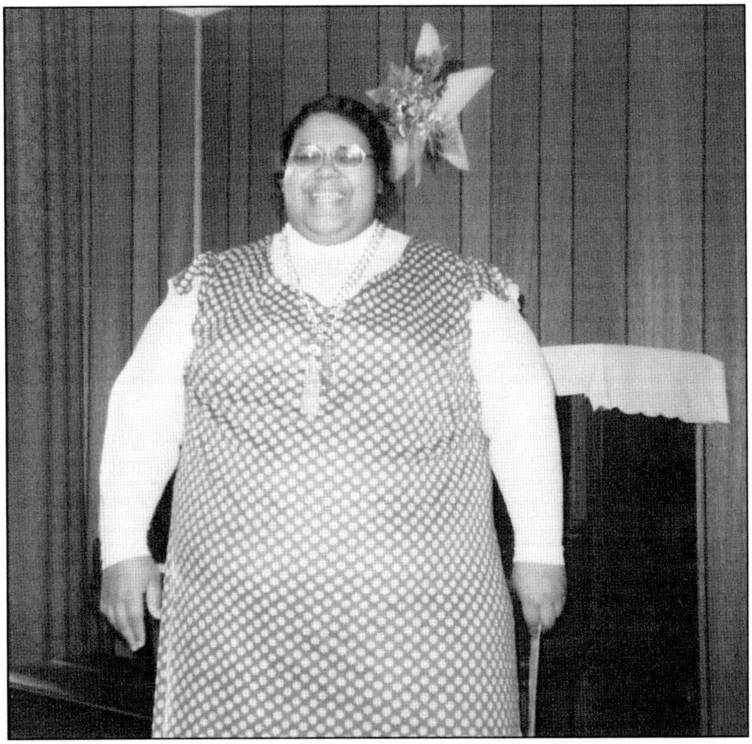

Janet McDonald worked as a social worker in the child abuse and neglect division of the Department of Health and Human Resources. This photo was taken in the early 1960s.

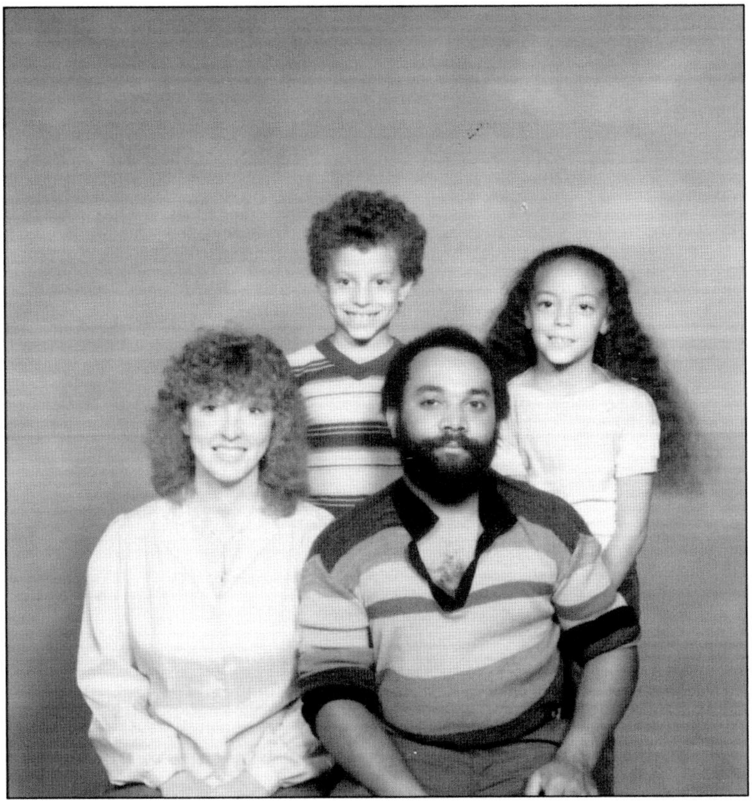

Shirley and Marcus McDonald are pictured here with their children Regan Jefferson (left) and Devon Beckner (right) in the 1970s. Shirley was an excellent cook and assisted with many church activities.

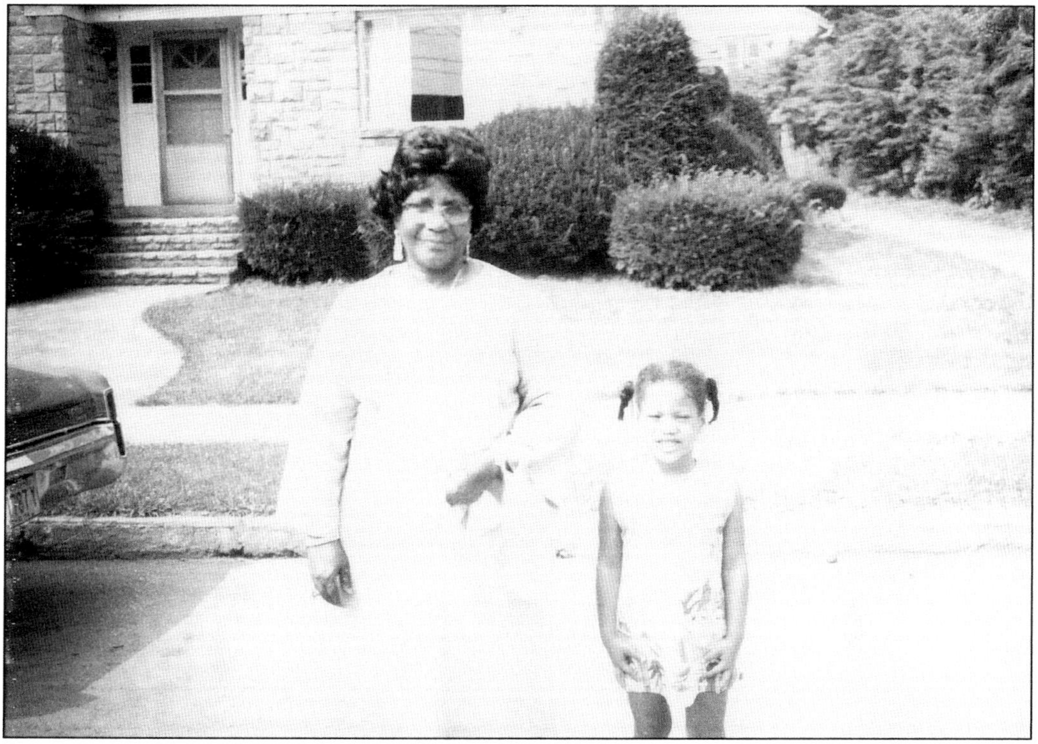

Margaret Copney and Roxanne Smith stand on Brown Avenue for this 1960s snapshot.

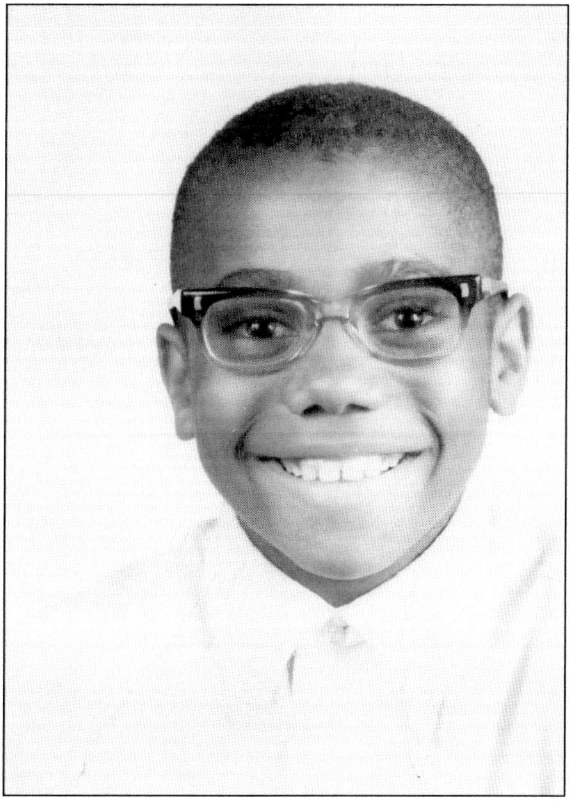

Here we see Frank Goines in his May 1978 school photograph.

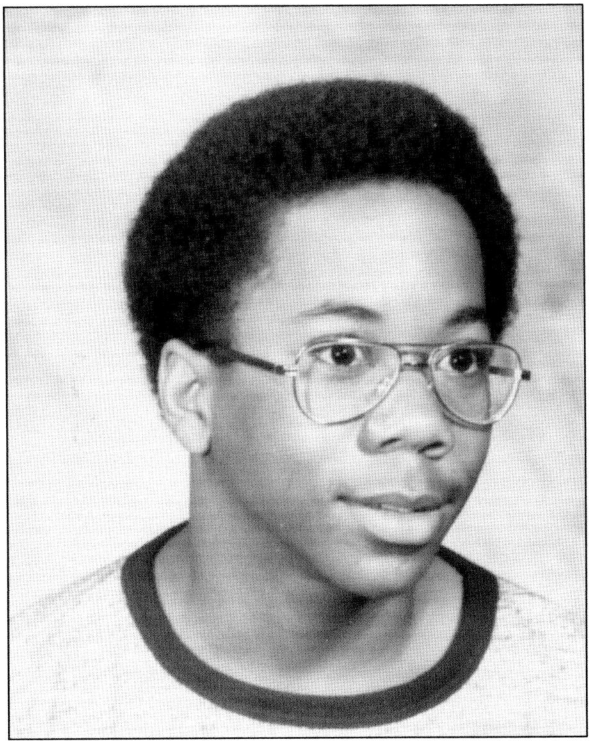

Gregory McDonald, pictured here, was graduated from KHS. He worked for Charles Baker Construction Company building houses and was also employed at Big Bear Lake. He married Lisa Williams.

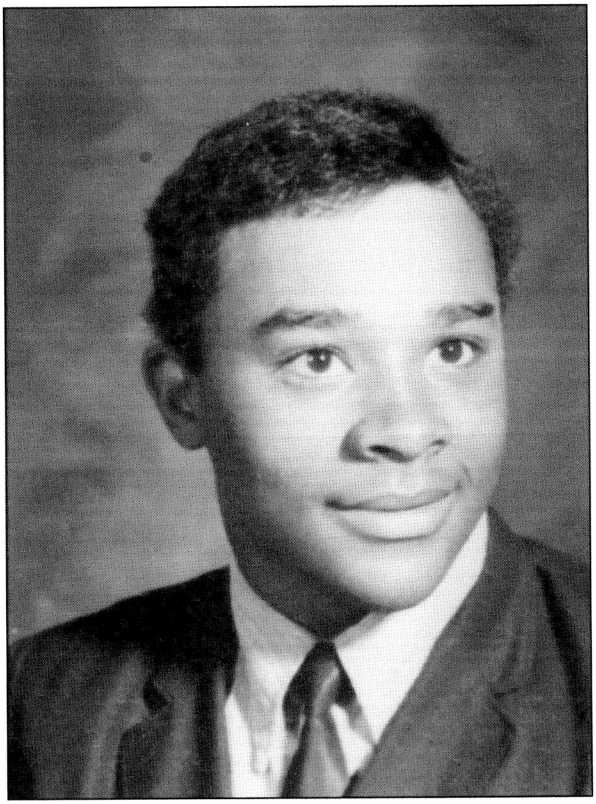

Roger Dale McDonald looks smart in his jacket and tie. Roger was also graduated from KHS, in 1970. He attended West Virginia State College and Institute and achieved a position to help train juniors for the rangers in the ROTC College Military Program. He completed a four-year program in auto mechanics and was the first graduate of KHS to attend this college. He was a "B" student in ROTC. He recently received a 25-year service award from Ashland Petroleum Oil Co. in Columbus, Ohio, where he is a floor supervisor.

Russell Goines Jr. smiles for his school portrait.

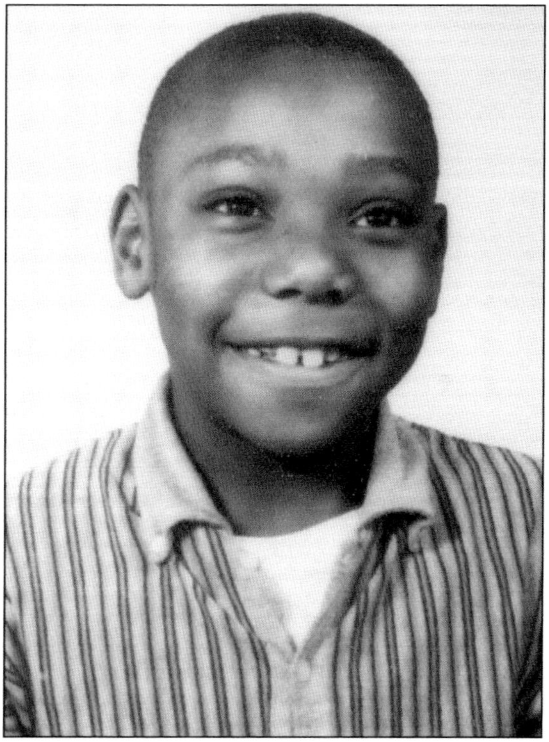

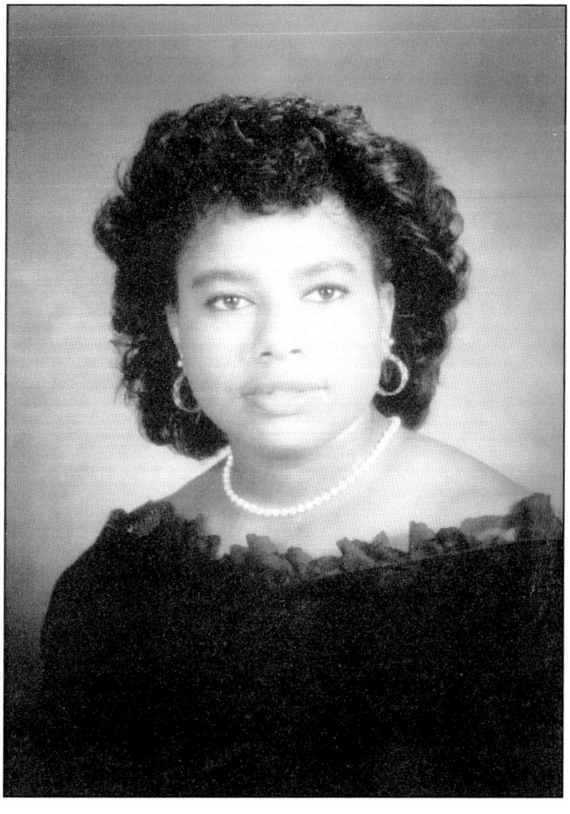

Annie Jo Crawford poses for this beautiful picture. She worked as a nurse.

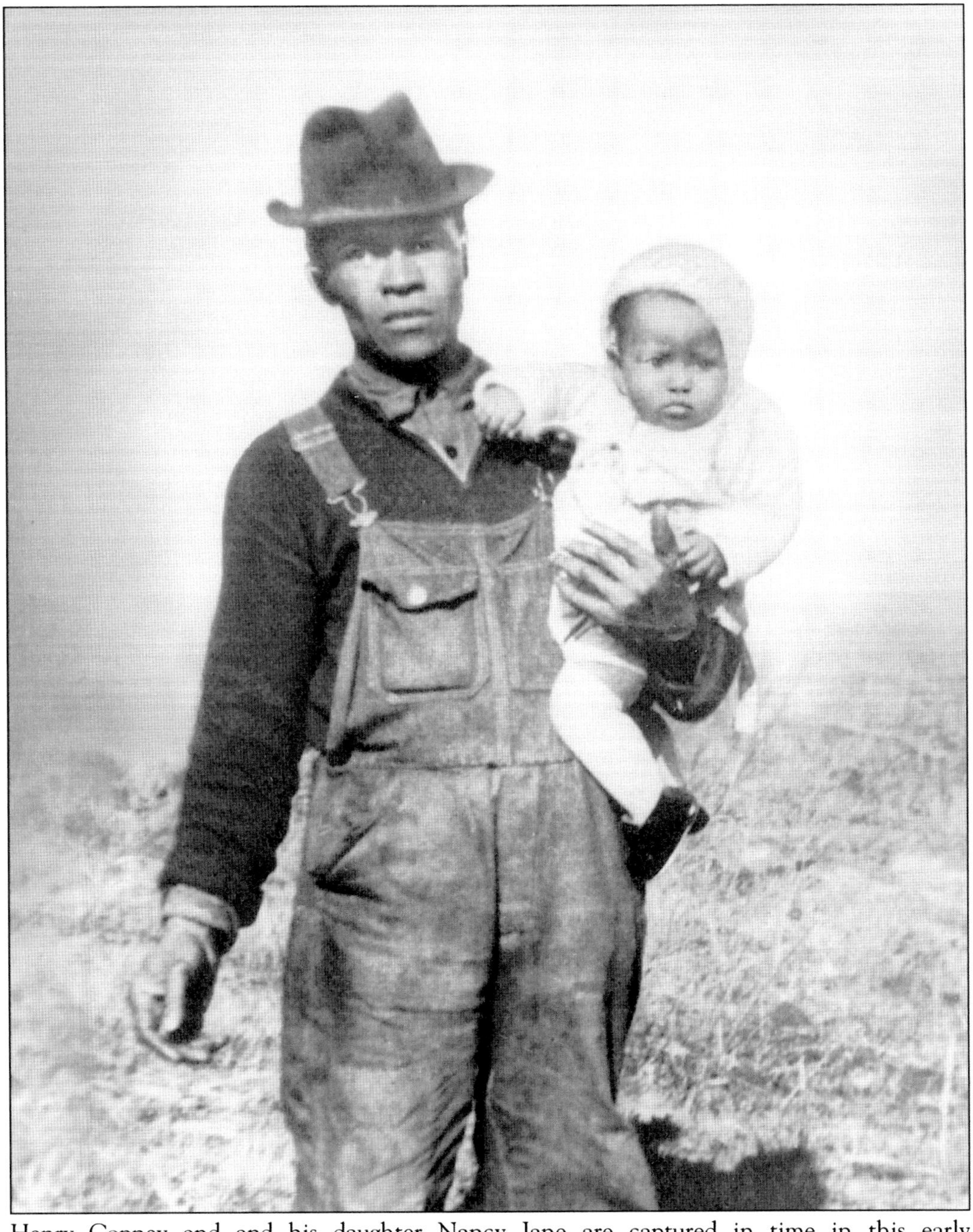

Henry Copney and and his daughter Nancy Jane are captured in time in this early 1940s portrait.

Two

SERVING THEIR COUNTRY

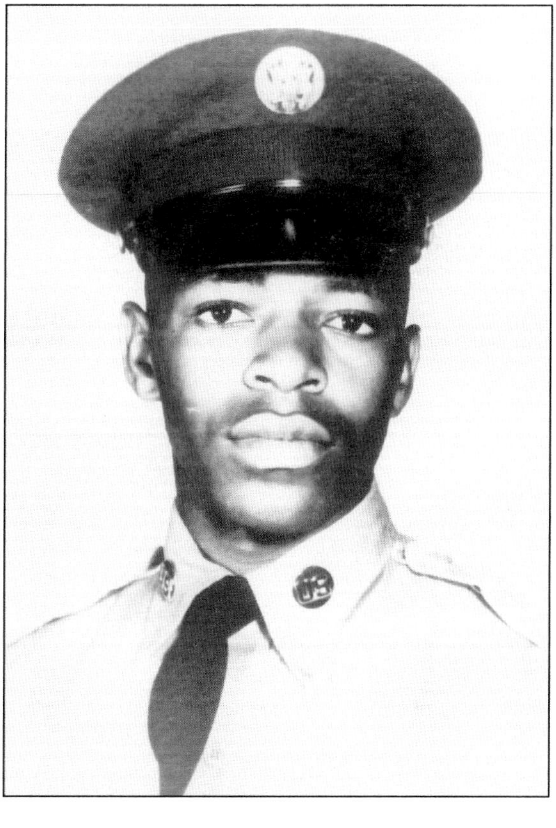

Melvin Eugene Copney served in the U.S. Army and is pictured here in the 1960s.

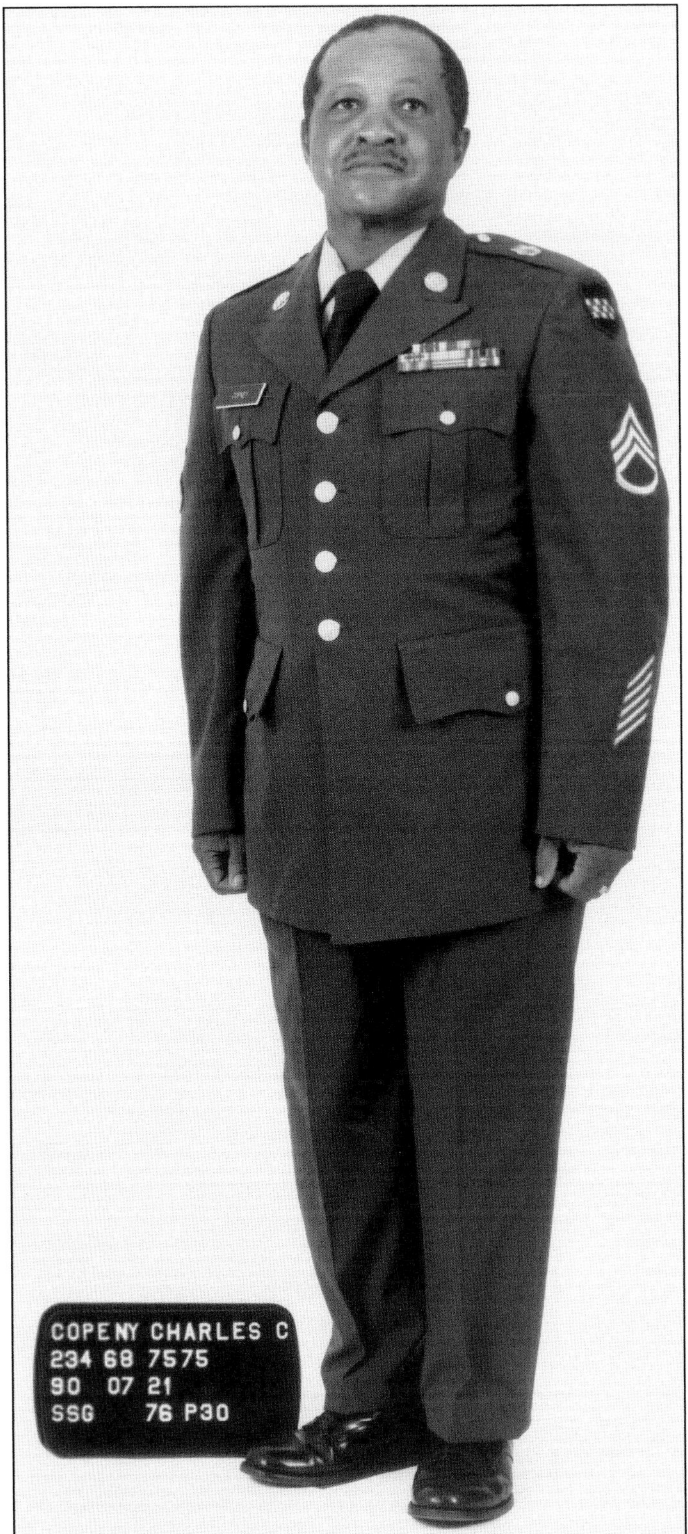

Charles Cramer Copney served in the U.S. Army from 1960 until his retirement in the 1980s.

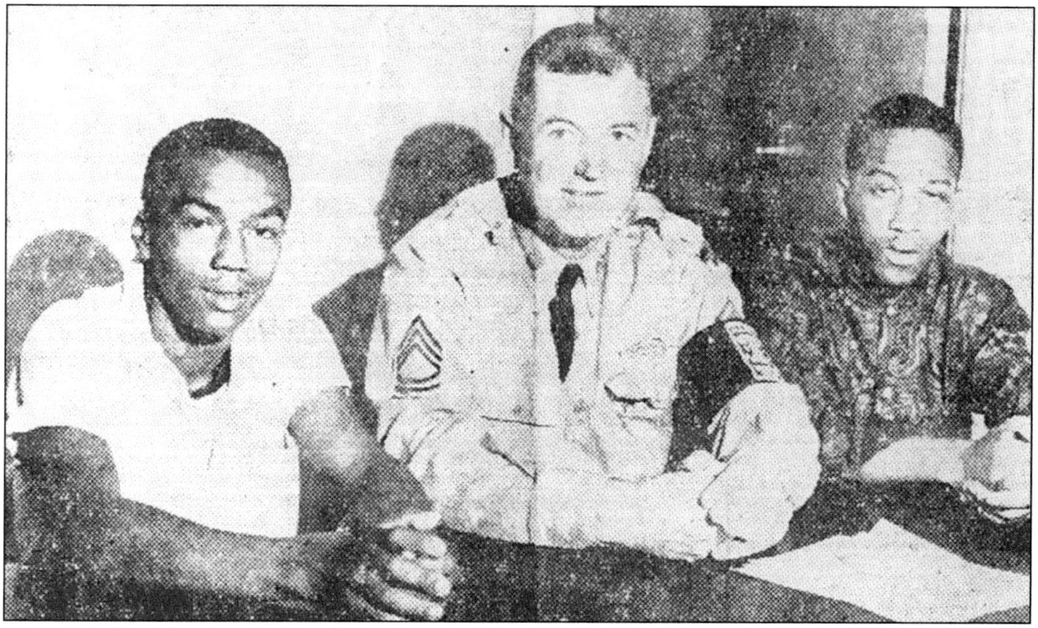

Maj. Sgt. Joseph Sherron sits between twin enlistees, Joe and Jim Page, sons of Mr. and Mrs. Joseph D. Paige of Kingwood. The identical twins enlisted in the army for three years and were sent to Fort Jackson, South Carolina, for basic training. This picture was taken in May 1957.

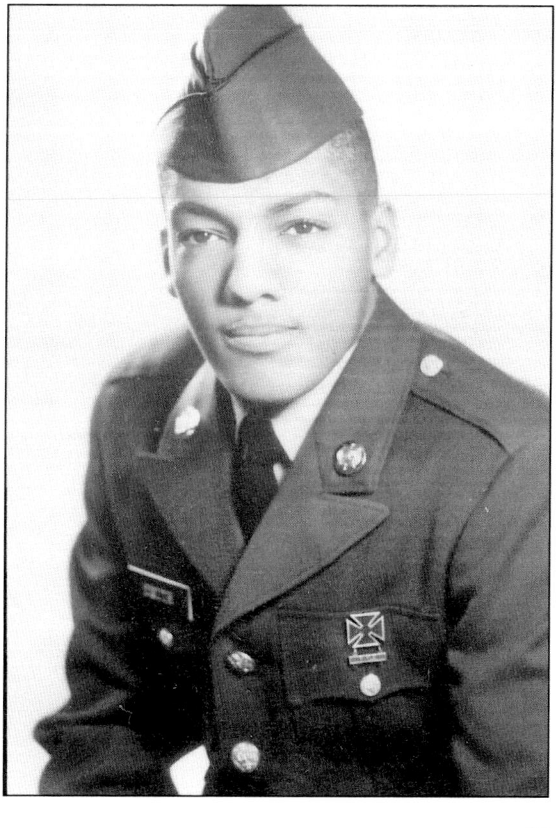

Once out of high school, Leonard G. Smith, at right, enlisted in the U.S. Army in 1963. He was sent to Ft. Gordon, Georgia, for communications school. His specialty was cryptography. The army afforded him the opportunity to travel to exotic places such as Germany, Denmark, and France. He joined an American and French band in Paris called the Diplomats and was the drummer for a year.

After his enlistment was over, Leonard decided to move to Washington, D.C. He worked 19 years for the Department of Veterans Affairs. He held several project manager positions such as pharmacy and alcohol and drug abuse. He was project leader of the first automated National Wheelchair Games starting in 1985 and remained so until he left the program in 1988. He currently holds a senior management position at the IRS. He is an active member of the 2,000-member Maple Springs Baptist Church where he serves as chairman of the Board of Trustees.

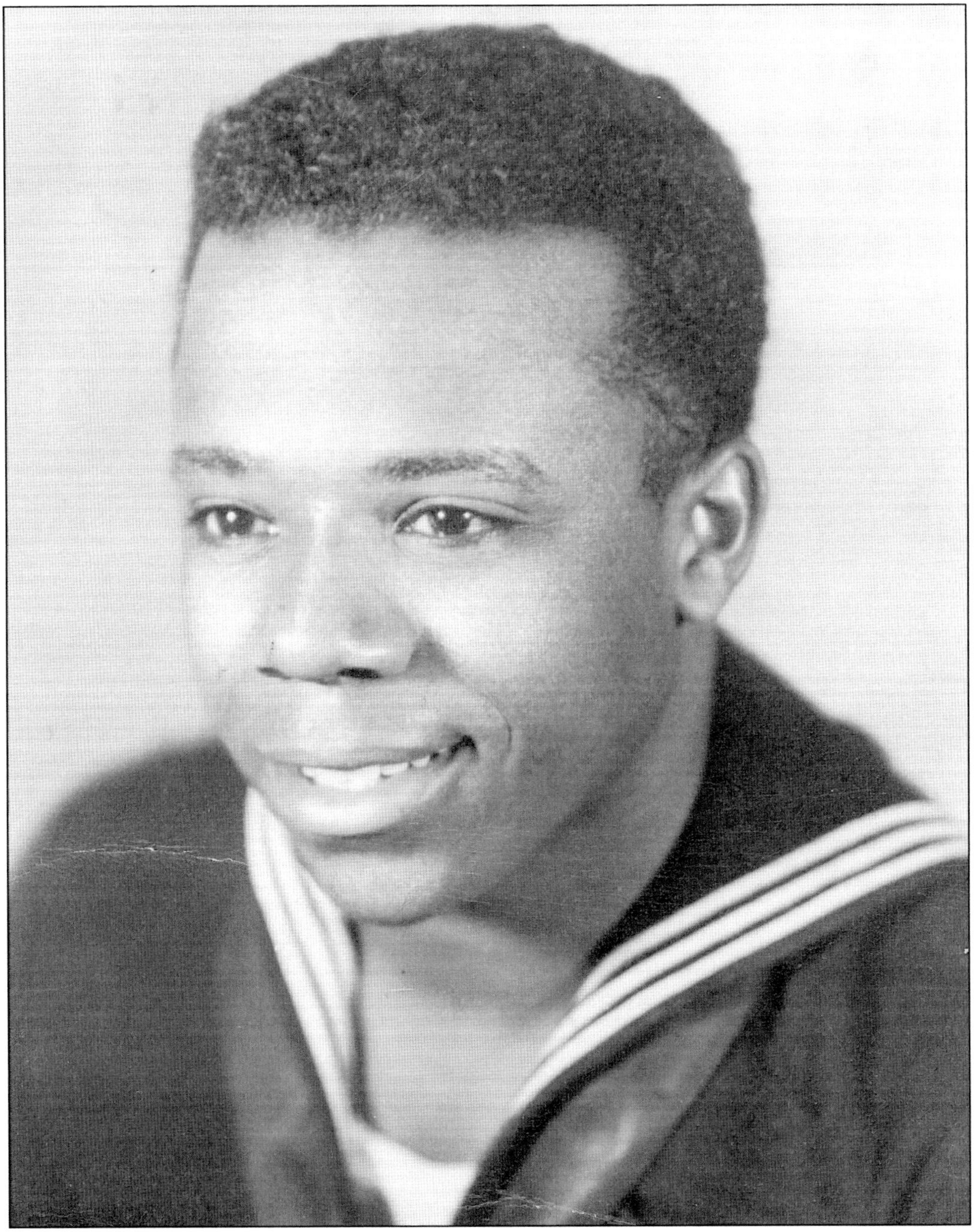

Jesse McDonald Jr. graduated from Beverly Hill Elementary School in May 1939 and from Monongalia High School in Westover in May 1943. Jesse was drafted into the Navy on November 4, 1944, when he was 18 years old. He was sent to boot camp in Great Lakes, Illinois, and afterwards attended U.S. Institute Navy Training School, in Hampton, Virginia, from which he graduated on June 5, 1945. After a short trip home, Jesse was sent to Norfolk, Virginia, to board the U.S.S. *Albemarle*, which would later be stationed on both the Pacific and Atlantic Oceans. While aboard, Jesse qualified for three medals: American Erea, Asiatic Pacific, and Victory. He was honorably discharged on July 5, 1946, in Shoemaker, California.

Jesse McDonald Jr. served in the U.S. Navy during the 1940s.

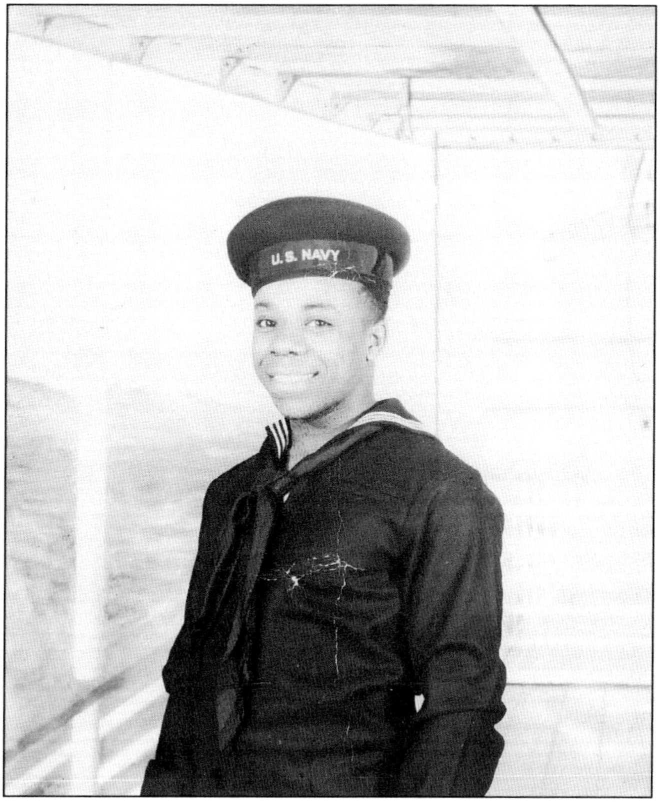

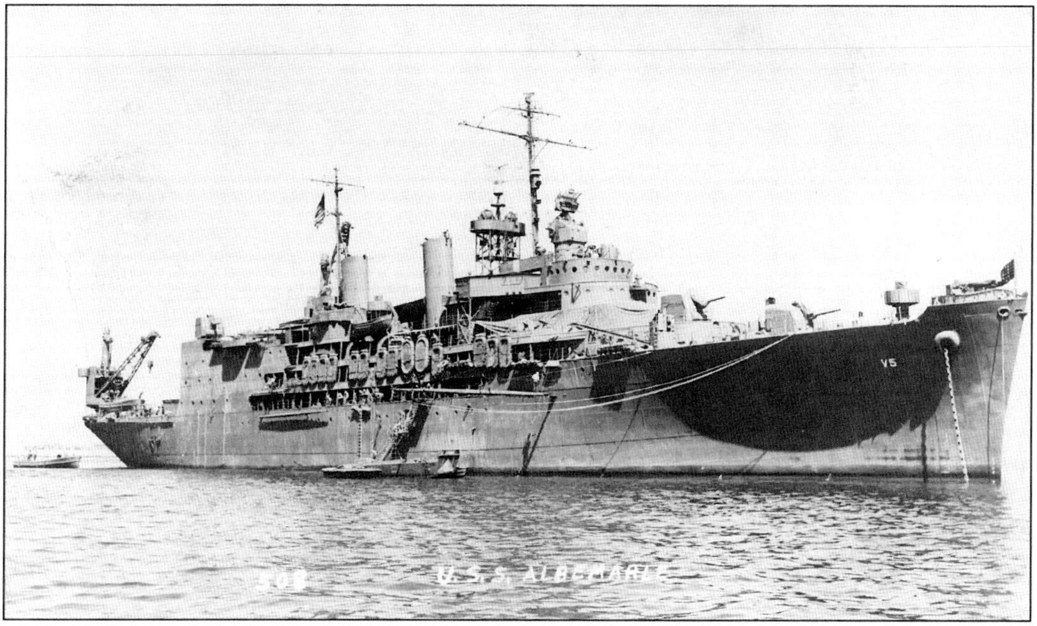

McDonald served on the USS *Albemarle*, an impressive looking ship seen here in the 1940s.

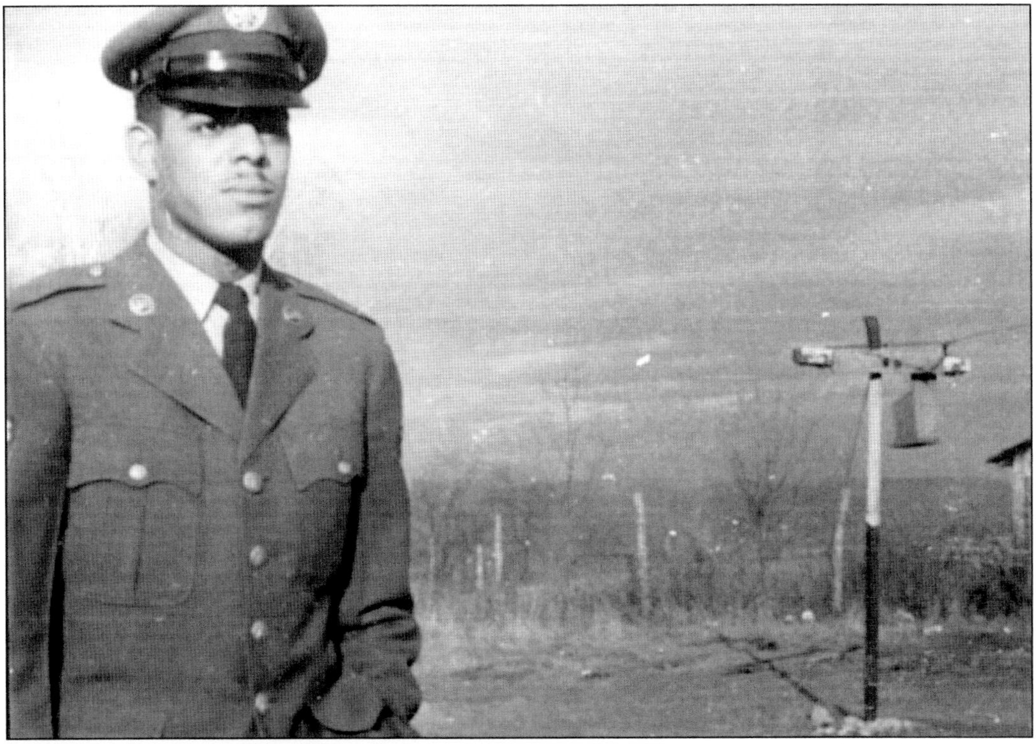

This picture of a uniformed Reginald Williams was snapped on a very overcast day.

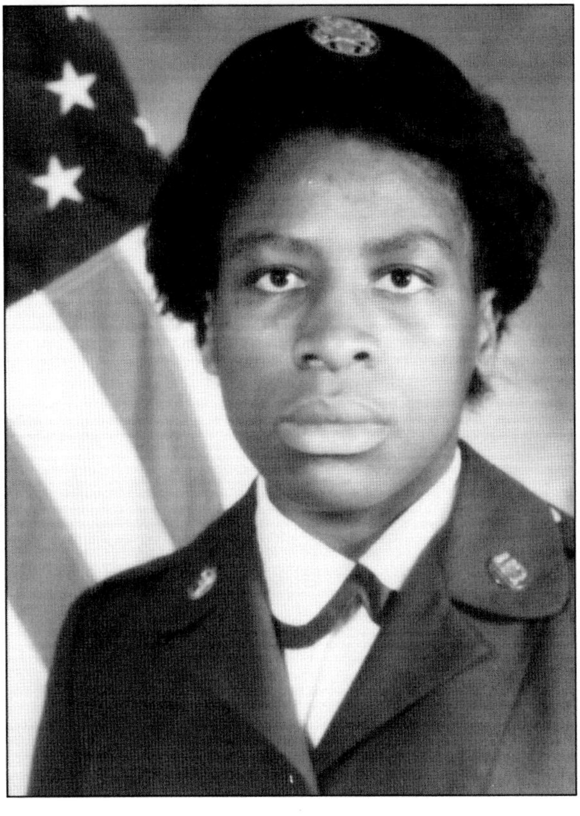

Rhonda Crawford served in the military just like her male counterparts from Preston County.

Calvin Lawerence McDonald joined the U.S. Army at the age of 17 and retired at age 38. During his military career, he served several years in Germany.

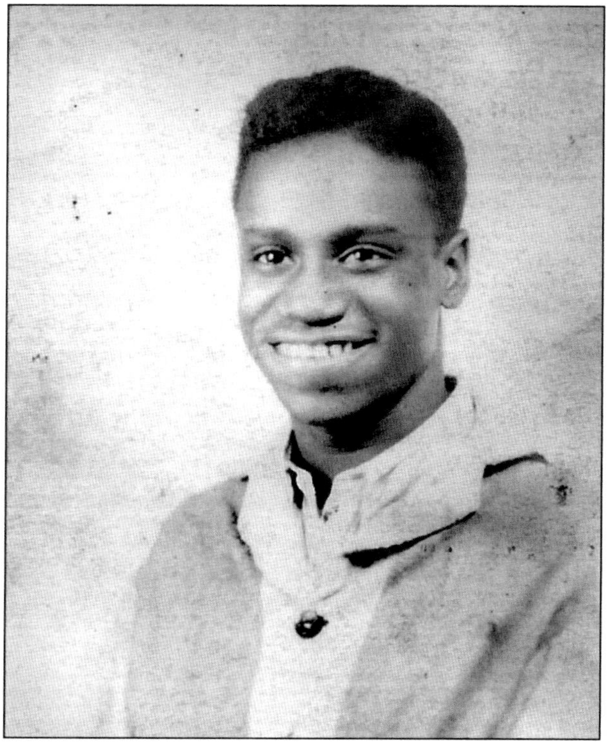

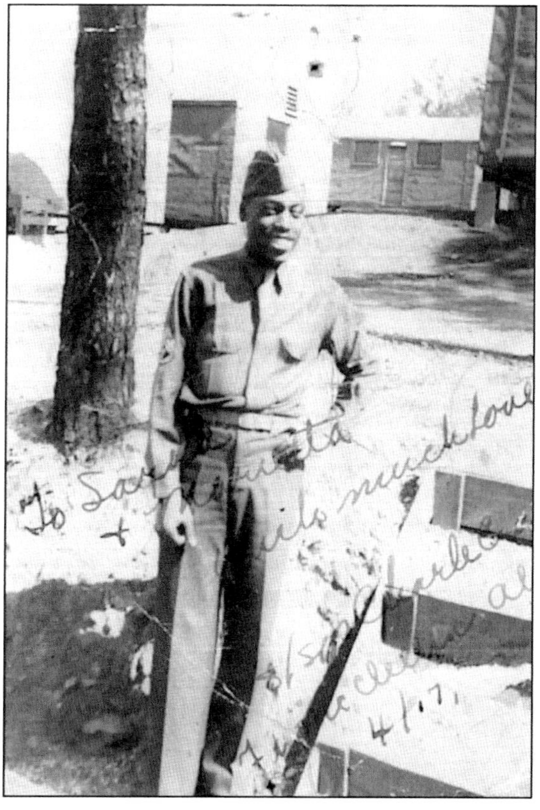

Charles Cranford, pictured here in uniform, was the only male teacher at Beverly Hill Elementary School in the school's history. This picture was taken in the 1930s at Fort McClellan in Alabama and is dedicated "To Sarah + Marietta with much love."

Honorable Discharge from the Army of the United States

TO ALL WHOM IT MAY CONCERN:

This is to Certify, *That* Robert Flippen, #4044046, Prvt. Co. "M" Development Battalion No. 3,160 Depot Brigade,

as a Testimonial of Honest and Faithful Service, is hereby Honorably Discharged from the military service of the United States by reason of Demobilization telegram A. G. O. November 15th. 1918.

Said Robert Flippen *was born in* Connellsville, *in the state of* Pennsylvania *When enlisted he was* 31 *years of age and by occupation a* Miner *He had* Brown *eyes,* Dark *hair,* Dark *complexion, and was* 5 *feet* 4 *inches in height.*

Given under my hand at Camp Custer, Michigan, *this* 27th *day of* November *one thousand nine hundred and* Eighteen

F. Goedeck, Major,
10th. Inf
Commanding.

ENLISTMENT RECORD

Name: Robert Flippen (4044046) *Grade:* Private

Enlisted August 5th., 19 18, *at* Kingwood, West Va.

Serving in First *enlistment period at date of discharge.*

Prior service: None

Noncommissioned officer: No

Marksmanship, gunner qualification or rating: None

Horsemanship: Not Mounted

Battles, Engagements, Skirmishes, Expeditions: None

Knowledge of any vocation: Miner

Wounds received in service: None

Physical condition when discharged: Good

Typhoid Prophylaxis completed: August 20th. 1918

Paratyphoid Prophylaxis completed: August 20th. 1918

Married or Single: Married

Character: Very Good

Remarks: No A. W. O. L.

Signature of Soldier: Robert Flippen

Malolen Lerknen, 1st. Lieut.

Commanding Co. M. Det. En.#3.160 D. Brgd.

STATE OF WEST VIRGINIA,

Preston *County Court, Clerk's Office,* April 5th 19 19.

The foregoing Discharge, with the enlistment record thereto, was this day admitted to record in said office.

Teste: E. C. [illegible] *Clerk.*

Robert Flippen, an army private, was honorably discharged from duty on November 27, 1918. He was 31 years old when he enlisted only a few months before and listed his occupation as that of a miner.

Daniel Young smiles brightly in this uniformed portrait. A 1960 graduate of Kingwood High School, Daniel made a career as a tennis instructor, and he also founded the National Tennis Teacher's College. After graduation, he was invited to try out with the Cleveland Indians baseball team's minor league club, but he failed to make the cut. He then joined the military service and later worked at the General Accounting Office in D.C. and the San Diego County Sheriff's Department.

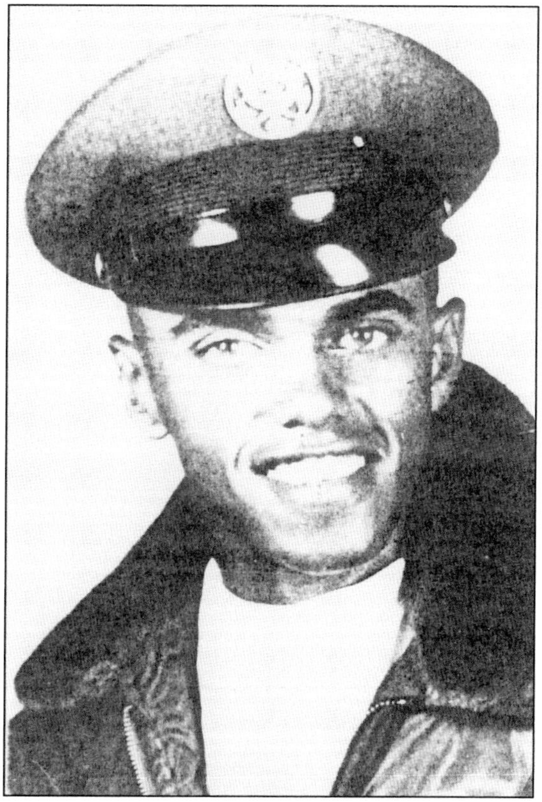

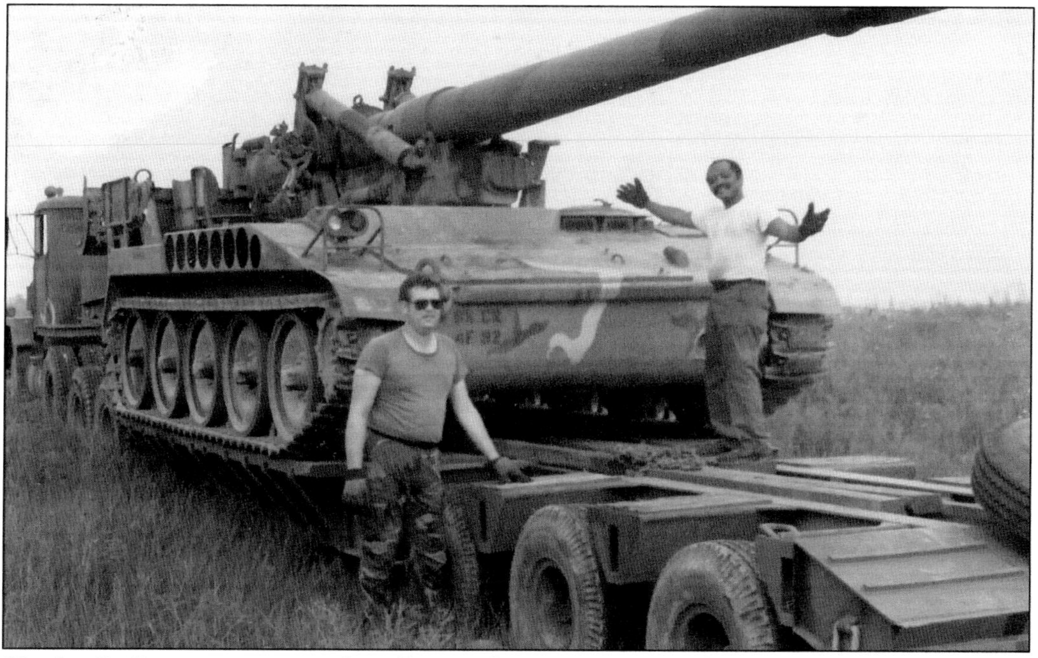

Charles C. Copney, a reservist from Fayette County, participated in an engineering exercise in Honduras, where he assisted in the final phase of the three-year road project. This picture was taken in February 1988.

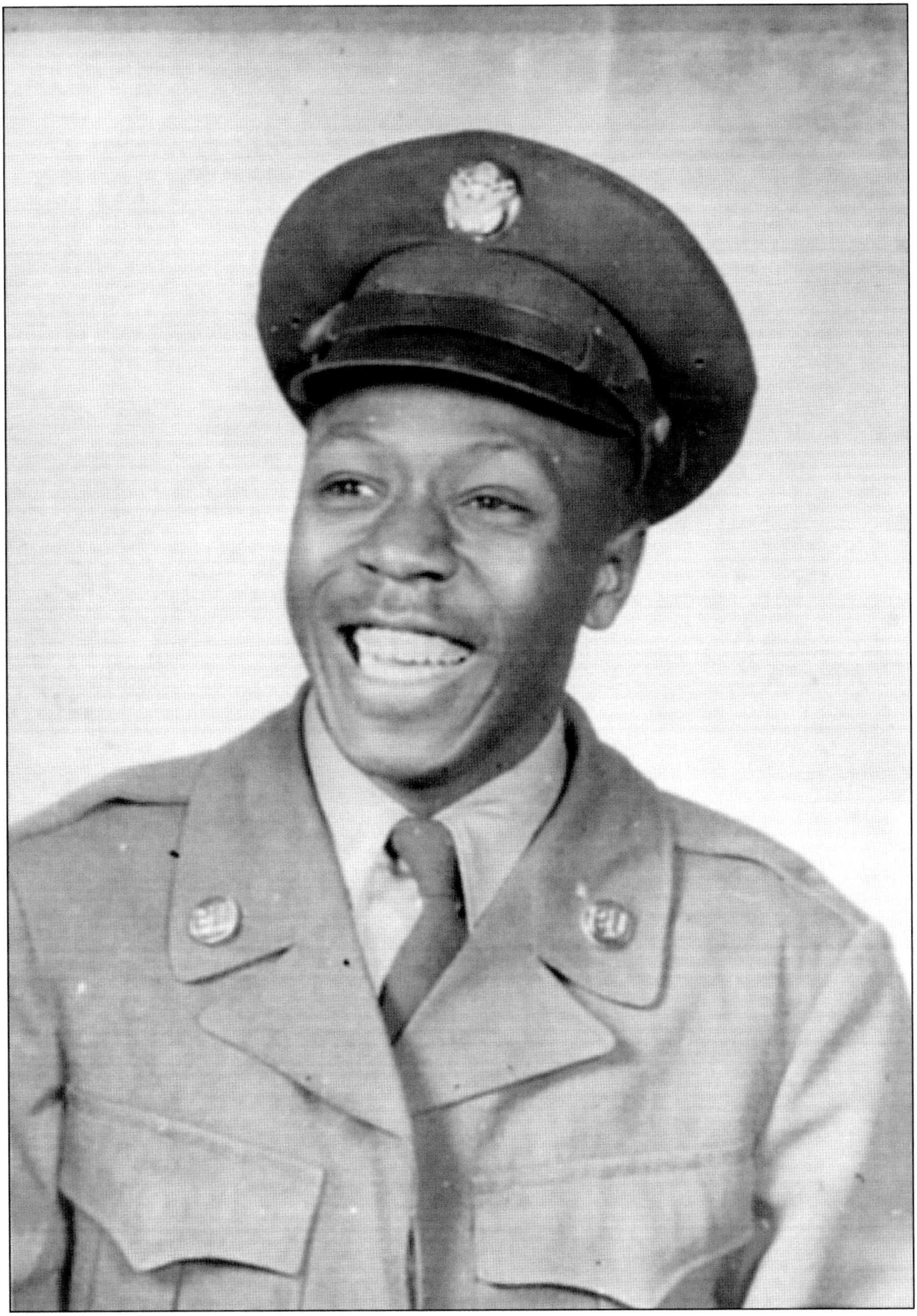

Ray Franklin Copney, also a soldier in the U.S. Army, is pictured here smiling broadly in the 1950s.

Three

At Work, School, and Play

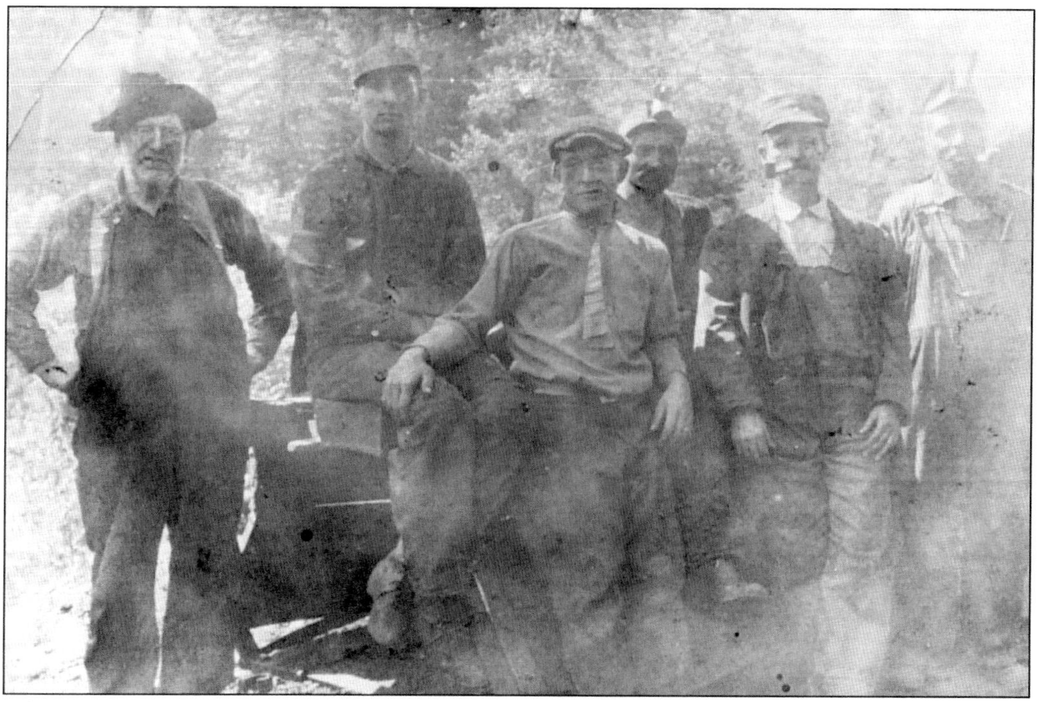

John Henry Younger, pictured on the far right at the old Irona Coal Company near Kingwood, was born on March 7, 1874, in Irontown to Joseph and Ann Younger. Before John Younger's time, slaves had been brought from Virginia to work in the iron and coal industry in West Virginia. The other workers pictured are, from left to right, Brice Mannings, Clay Wilson, W.G. Williams Sr., and two unidentified men.

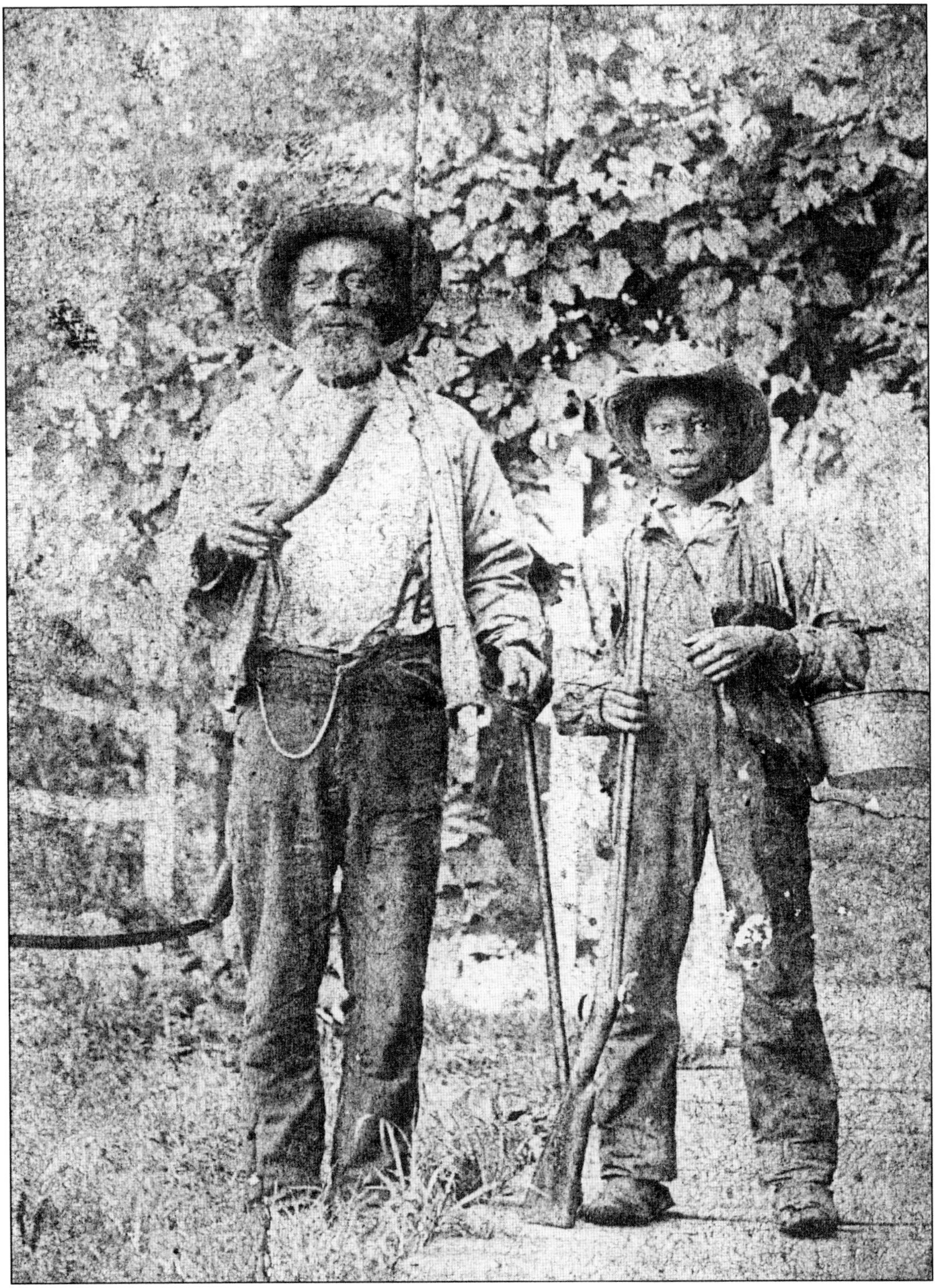

Joseph Whitley Sr. and son Joseph Jr. paused for this picture in the late 1800s. As their equipment suggest, the two were preparing to go hunting and blackberry picking.

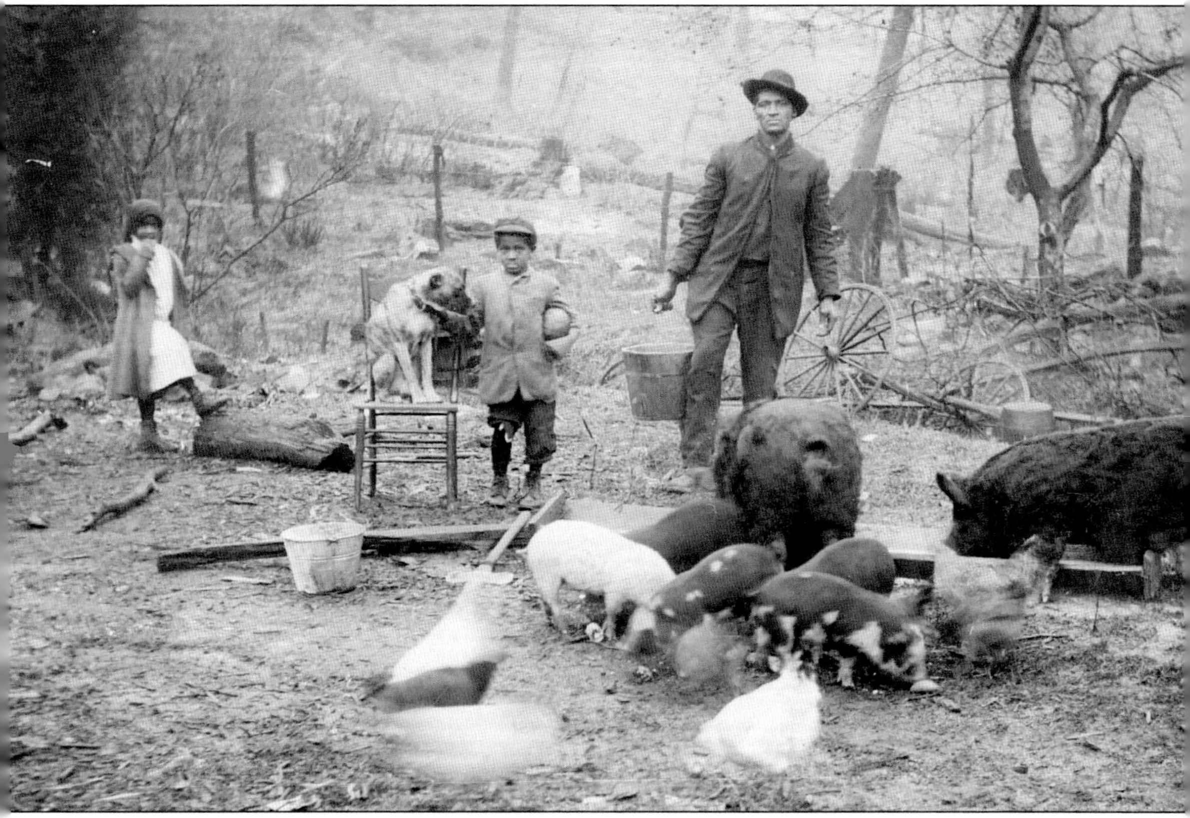

Samuel Younger is pictured here at work with his daughter Pauline on the far left and his son Emery, holding a ball under his arm. Samuel is busy feeding the pigs that he raised on Tunnelton Street in Kingwood.

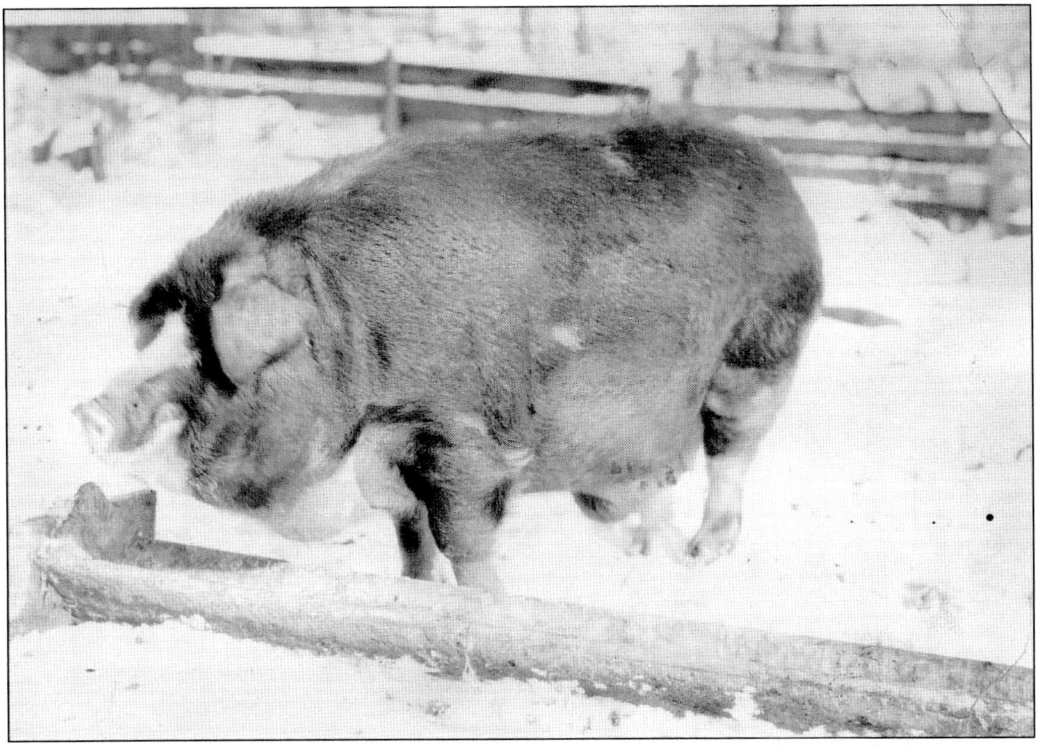

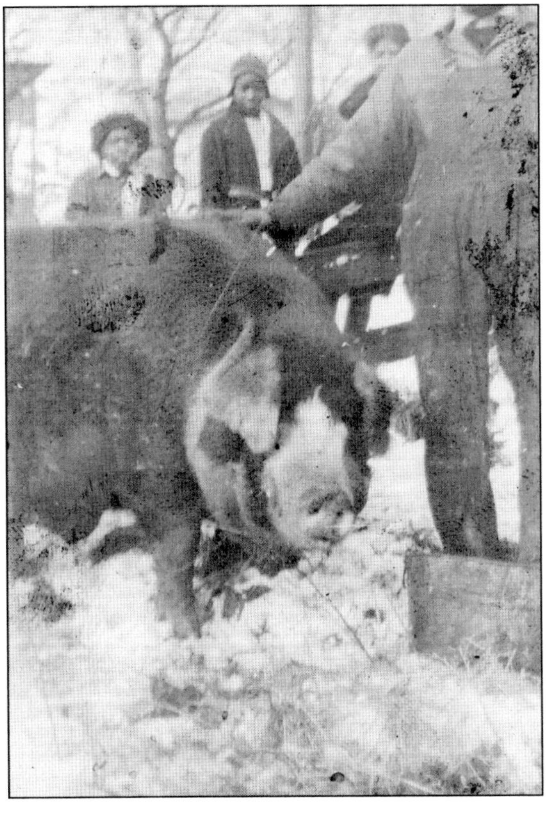

This early 1900s photograph shows one of the largest hogs ever raised by Sam Younger. This incredible creature weighed over 1,000 pounds dressed.

Showing off his prize hog to his niece Margaret Younger and daughters Pauline and Helen in the early 1900s, Sam Younger stands close enough to the animal that its immense size is even more apparent.

The men seen here are busy loading hogs onto a truck to take across the Tunneston Street woods to be butchered. The truck, owned by Sam Younger, had a nickname. When it was running, Sam called it a "Republican;" when it broke down, he called it a "Democrat."

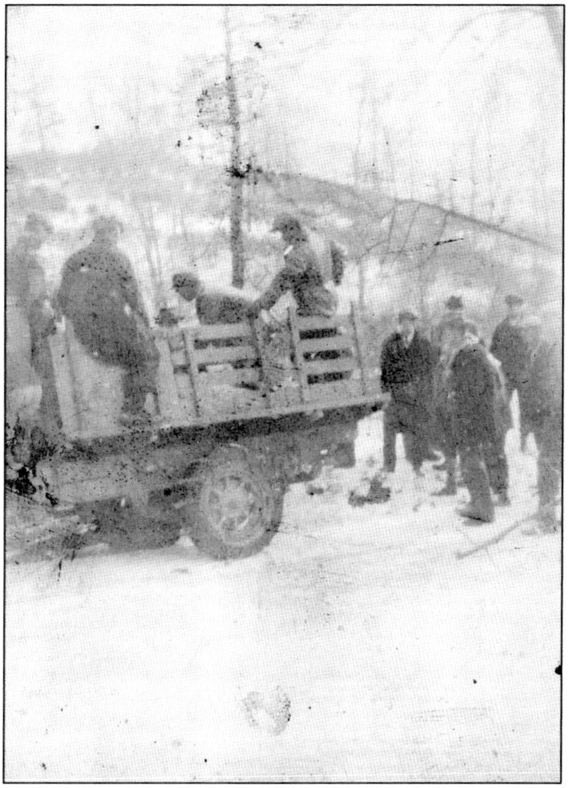

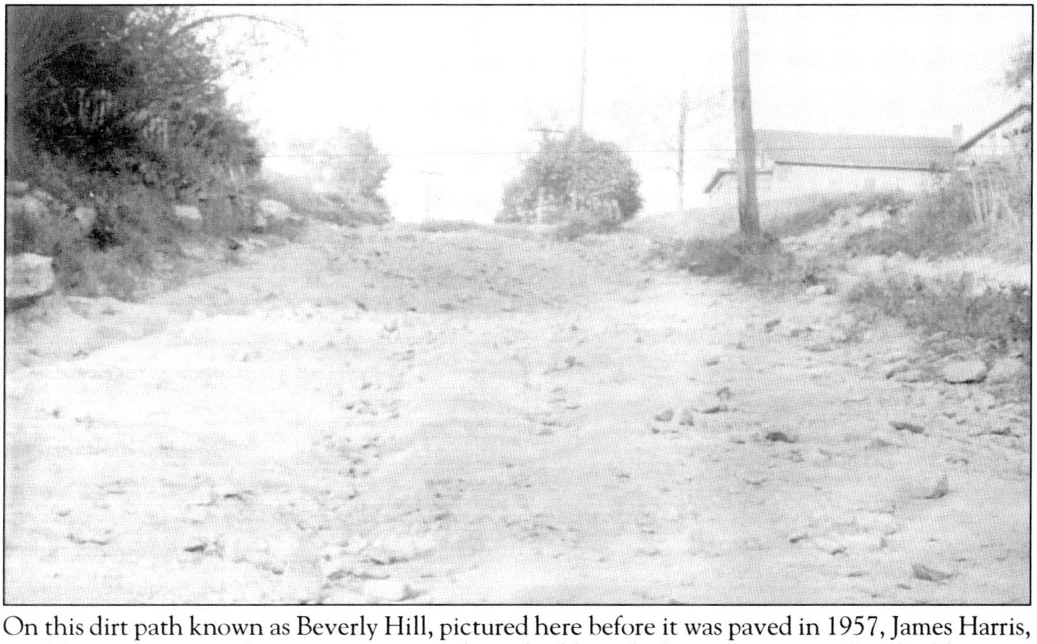

On this dirt path known as Beverly Hill, pictured here before it was paved in 1957, James Harris, an African-American businessman, owned two buildings before integration. One building was a general store where food, candy, ice cream, and a little bit of everything was sold. The other structure was used for social gatherings such as dances. In the 1960s, this second structure was rented as apartments.

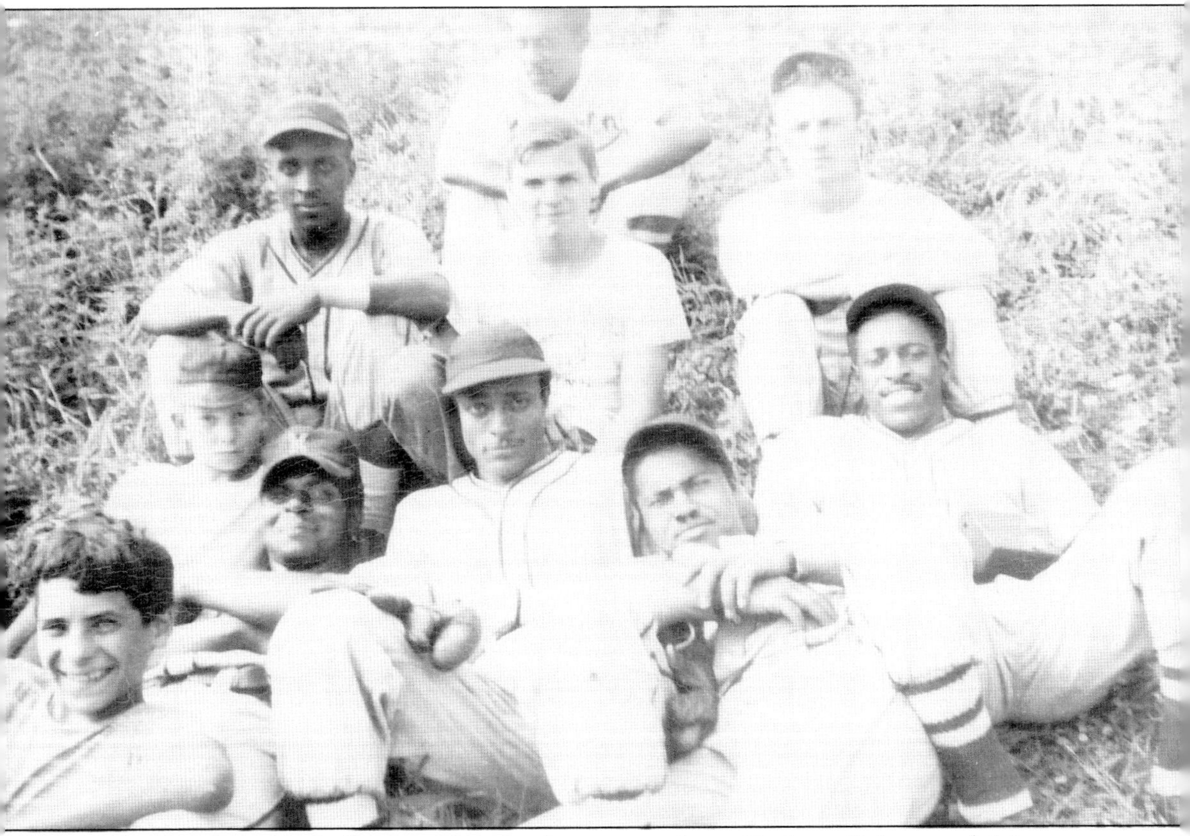

The Bombers baseball team played other teams from Grafton, Kaiser, and Morgantown in the 1940s. Posing here are, from left to right, (front row) Frank Cavalier (bottom left), unidentified bat boy (above Frank), Calvin Kidd, John Hall, Richard Lewis, and Buddy Walker, (back row) Bill Younger, unidentified bat boy, Milton Metheny, and Earl Barnett (sitting behind everyone).

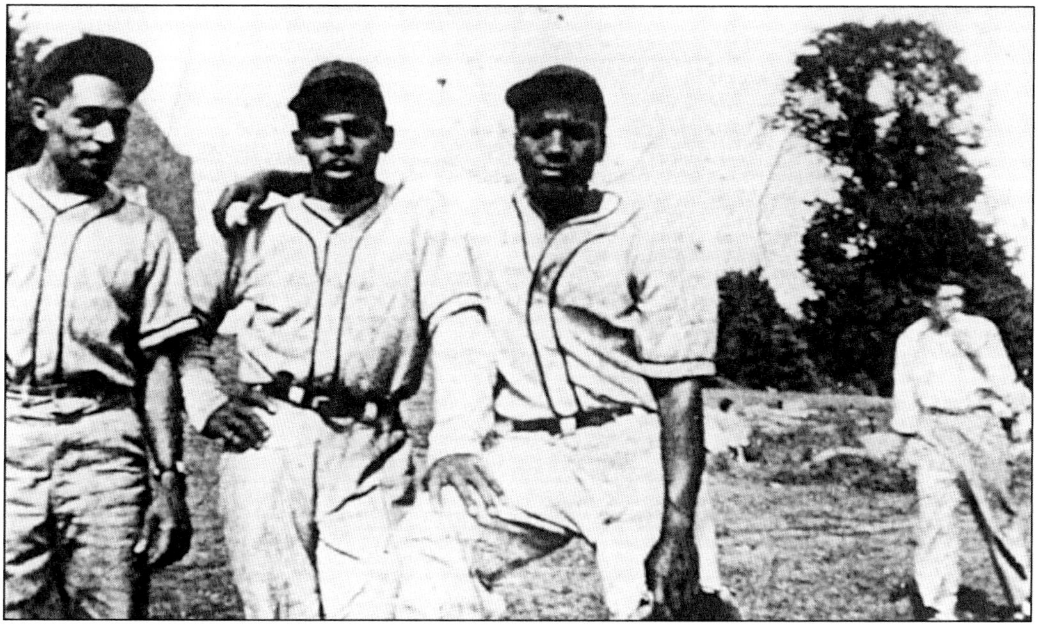

Three Bombers teammates, from left to right, Earl Barnett, Bobby Barnett, and Cornelius Smith, posed in uniform for this snapshot.

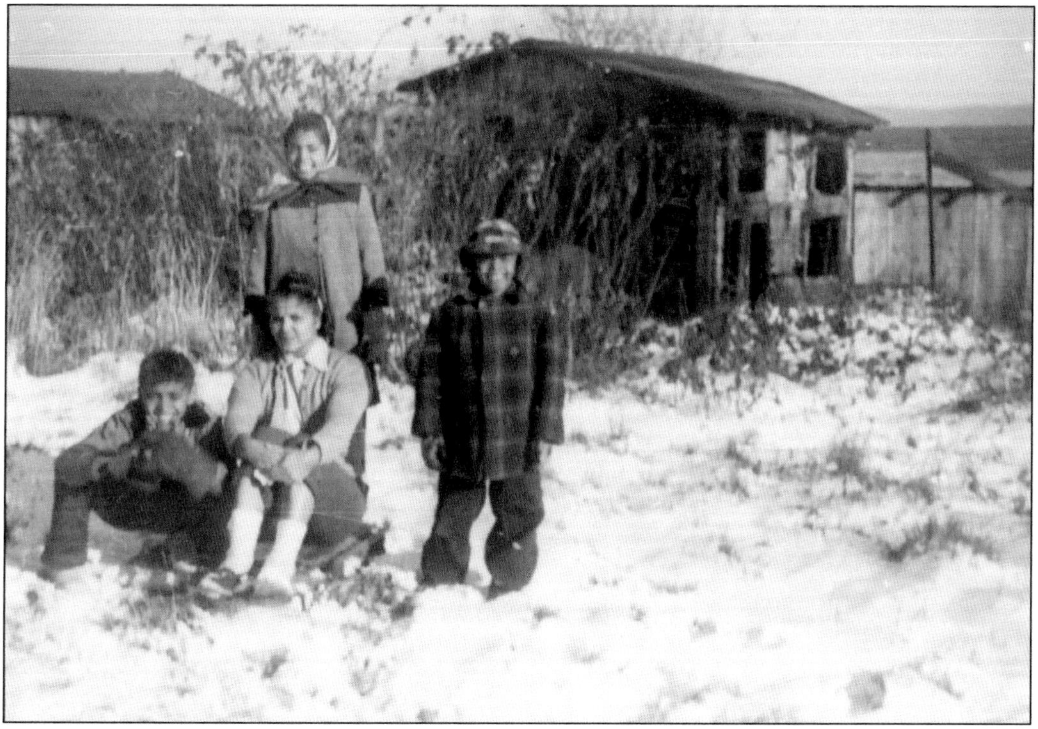

Danny, Alice (sitting in center), Calvin, and Carolyn Young pause from playing in the snow for this picture. The only one missing from the group is Alice's husband and the children's father, Herbert, who was hospitalized at Denmar Sanitarium.

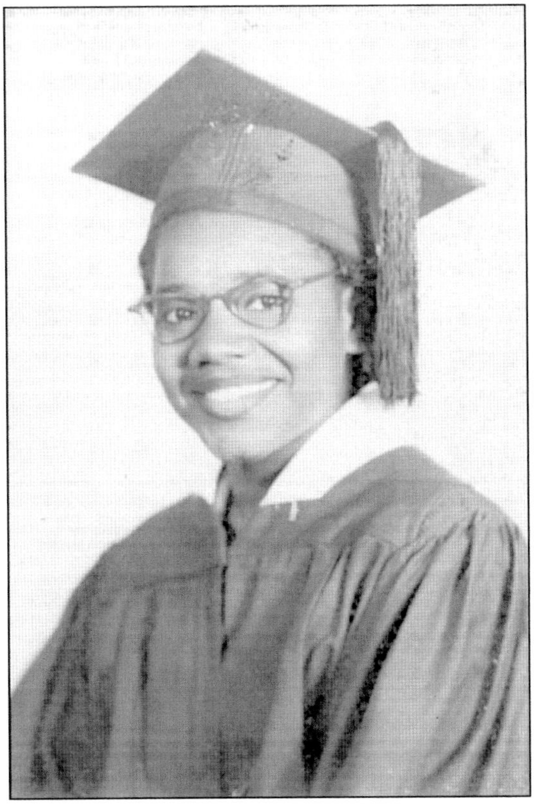

Sarah McDonald is also pictured here in cap and gown for her Monongalia High School graduation photograph.

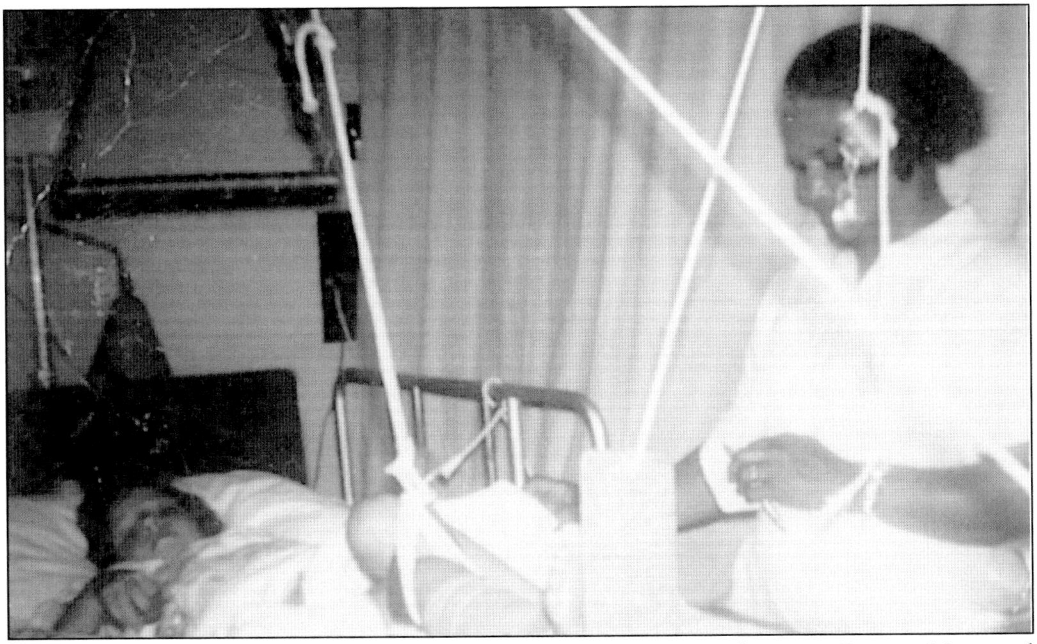

In this picture, Alice Young cares for a young patient, Cindy Kay Anderson, at Preston Memorial Hospital on July 12, 1965.

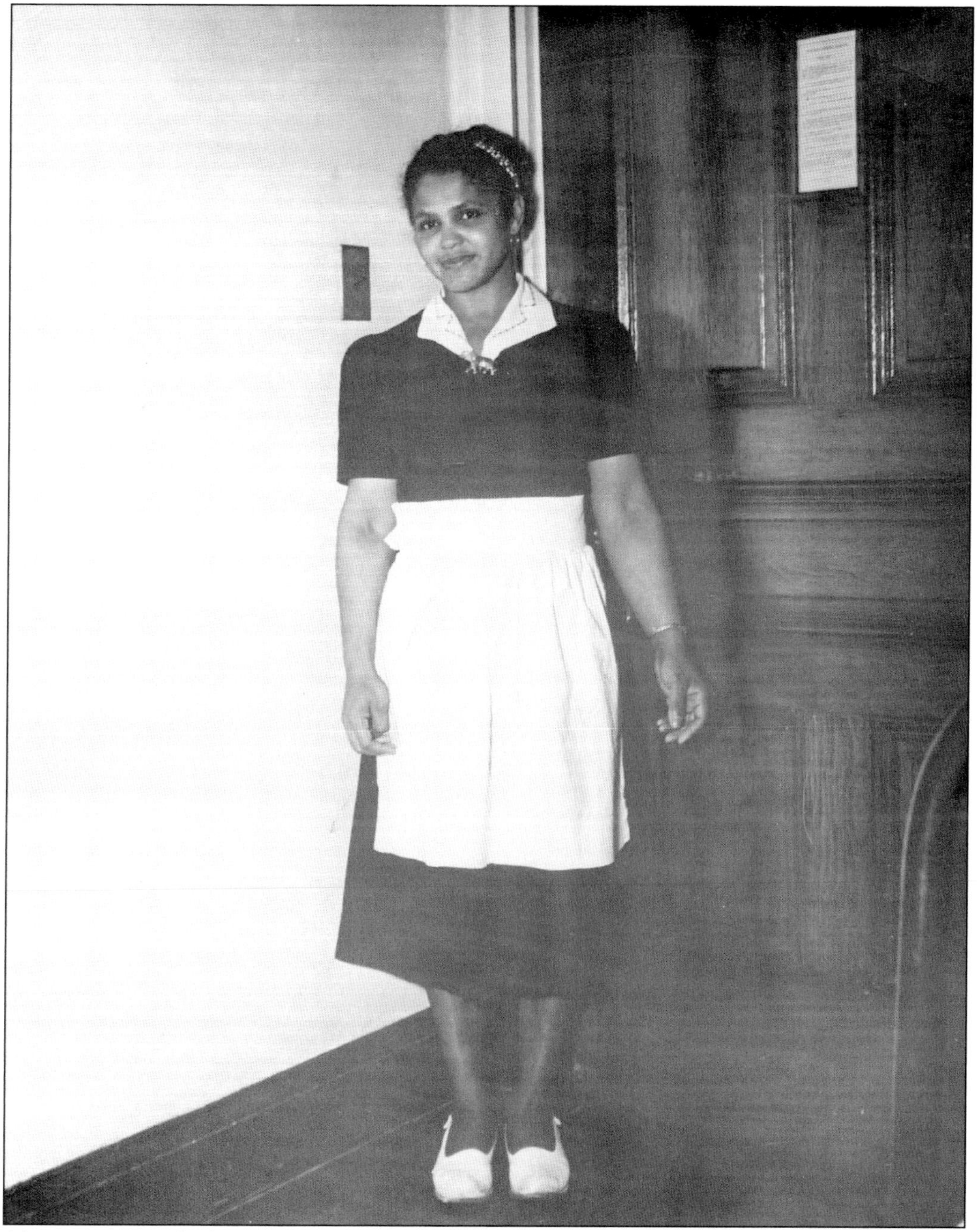

Alice Young worked as a nurse's assistant at John Hopkins Hospital in Baltimore, Maryland. This picture shows her in the early 1950s.

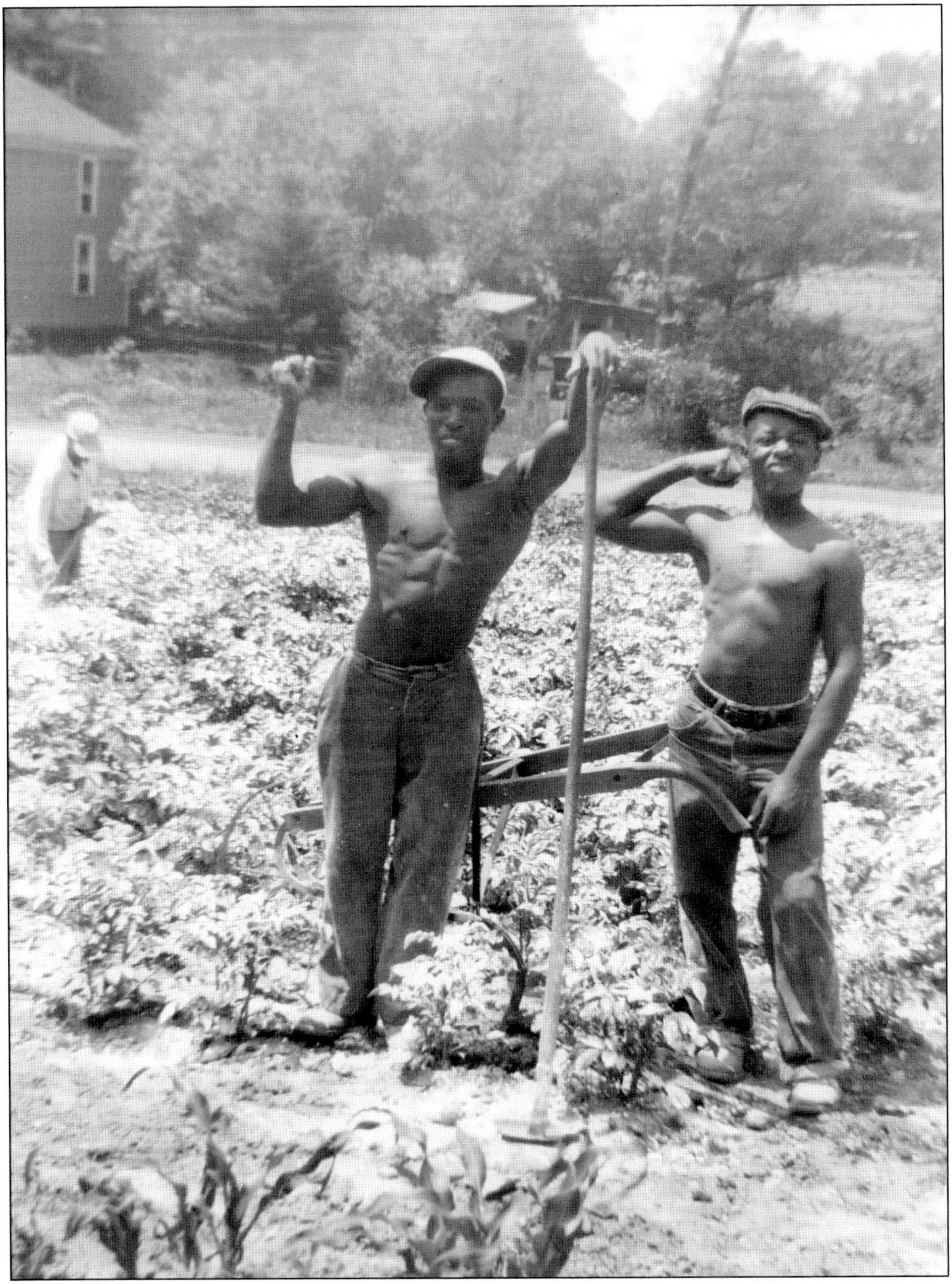

This 1958 picture shows Henry Copney, in the background, hoeing potatoes in the family garden. His sons Charles (left) and Melvin are spending their time showing off their muscles for the camera. The majority of the vegetables the family ate were raised in this garden by Henry Copney. In 1994, a house was built for Henry's elderly widow on the spot where this garden once was.

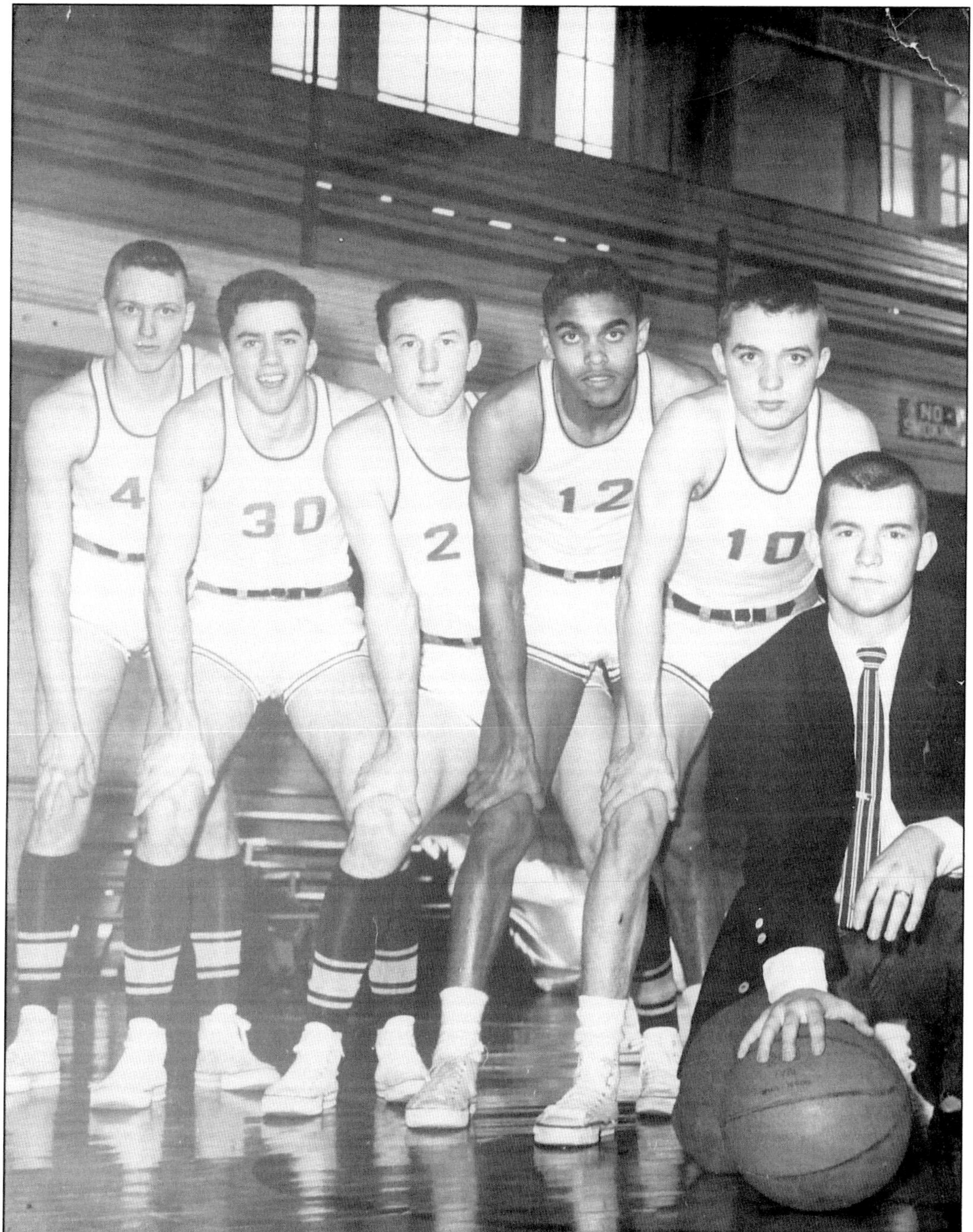

With Daniel Young in the #12 uniform, the Kingwood High School basketball team members pose for their yearly picture.

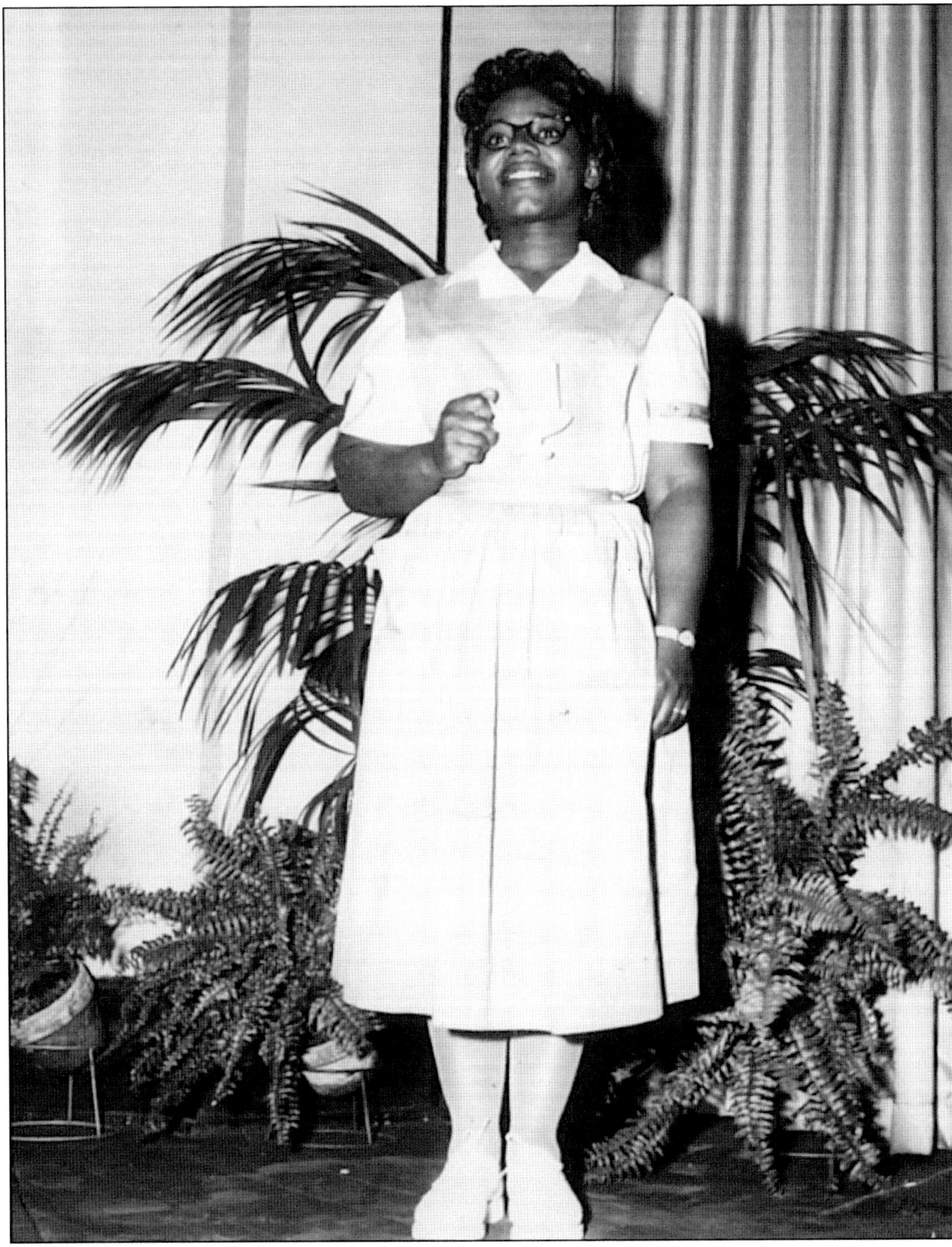

Sarah McDonald was a nursing assistant and LPN at Preston Memorial Hospital in the 1960s. McDonald also served as a constable.

Crystall Hall Patterson (left), a social security employee counselor and soon to be lawyer, had her picture taken here on May 11, 1991, with her sister, Connie Hall Grant, the executive director of family services in Monongalia County.

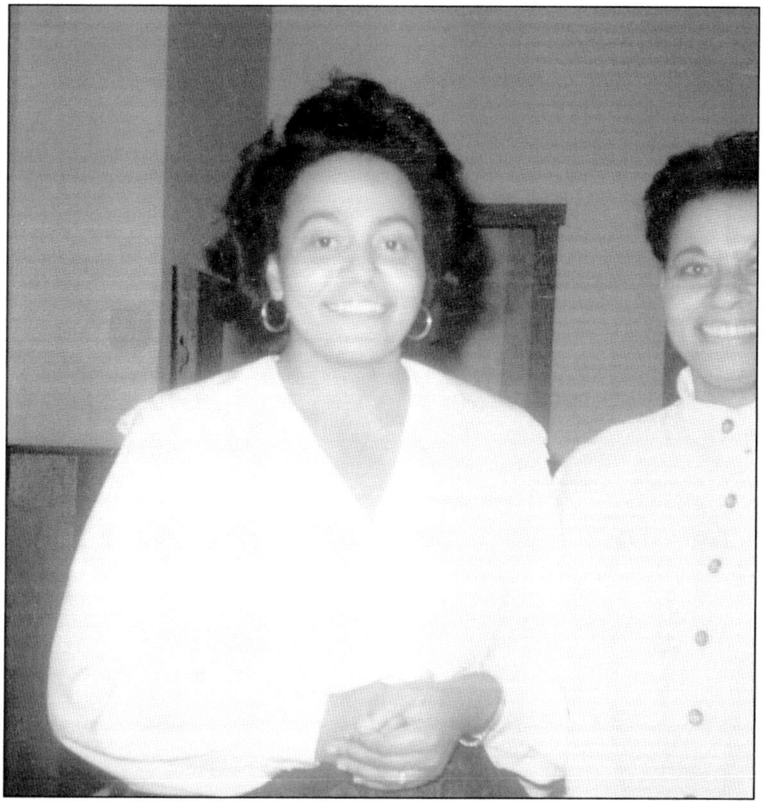

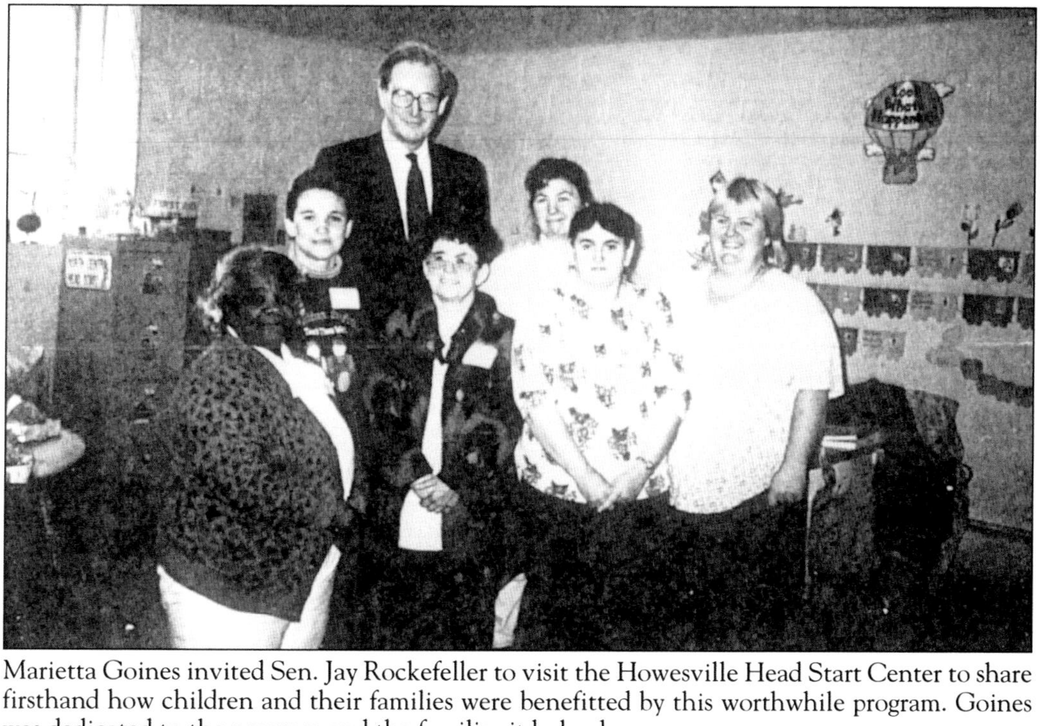

Marietta Goines invited Sen. Jay Rockefeller to visit the Howesville Head Start Center to share firsthand how children and their families were benefitted by this worthwhile program. Goines was dedicated to the program and the families it helped.

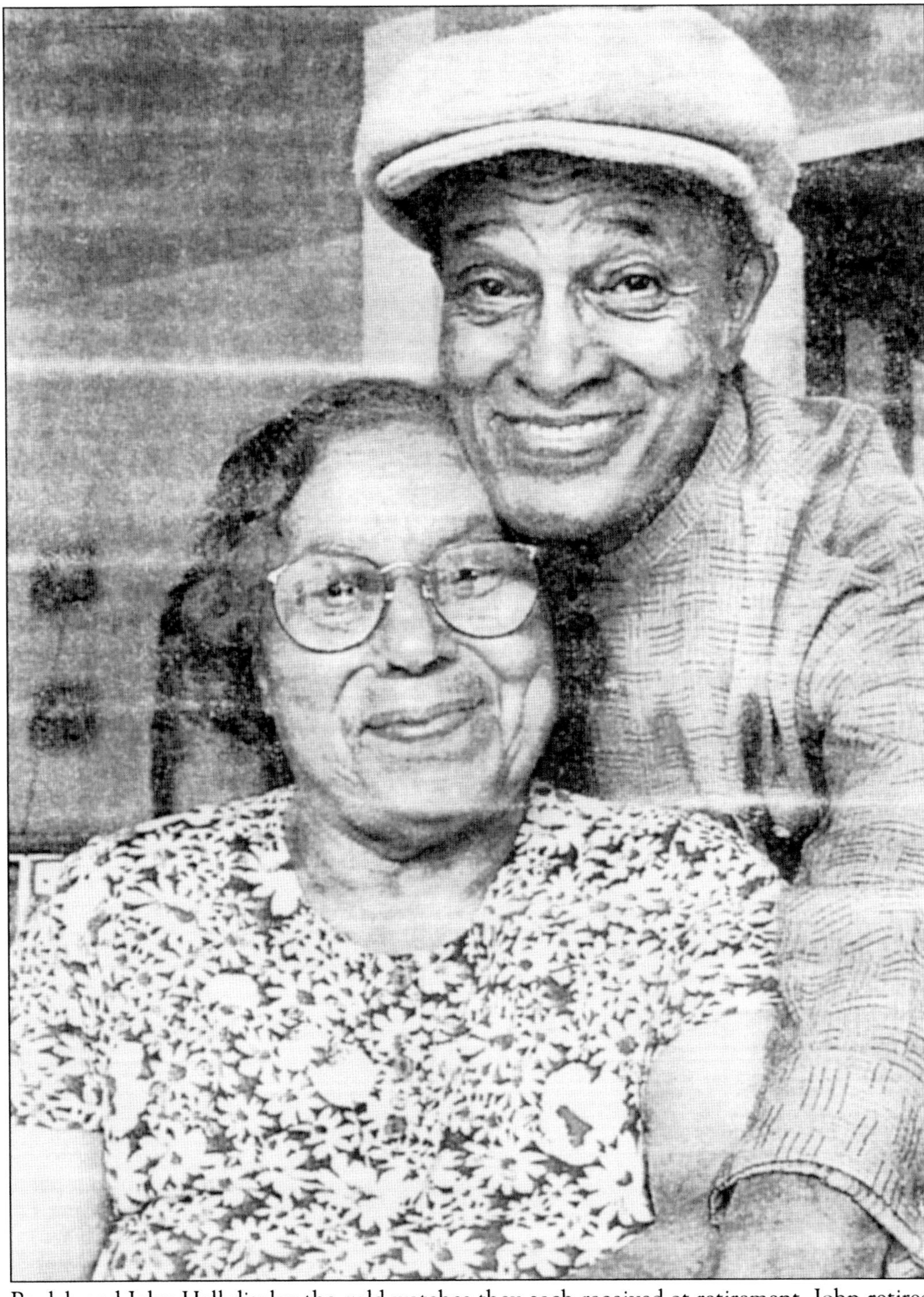

Beulah and John Hall display the gold watches they each received at retirement. John retired in January of 1970 from the Baltimore & Ohio Railroad and retired again on December 31, 1996, from the Albright power plant. Beulah retired in 1994 after 20 years at Ruby Memorial Hospital. This photograph was taken on January 27, 1997.

Mary Ashby Younger and Mrs. Julius James are seen in this unusual photograph in which Mrs. James got a chance to show off her musical skill on the saxophone.

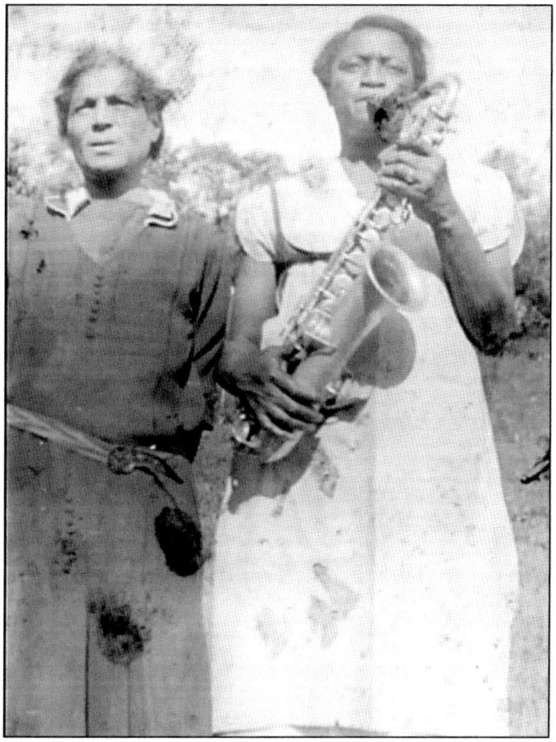

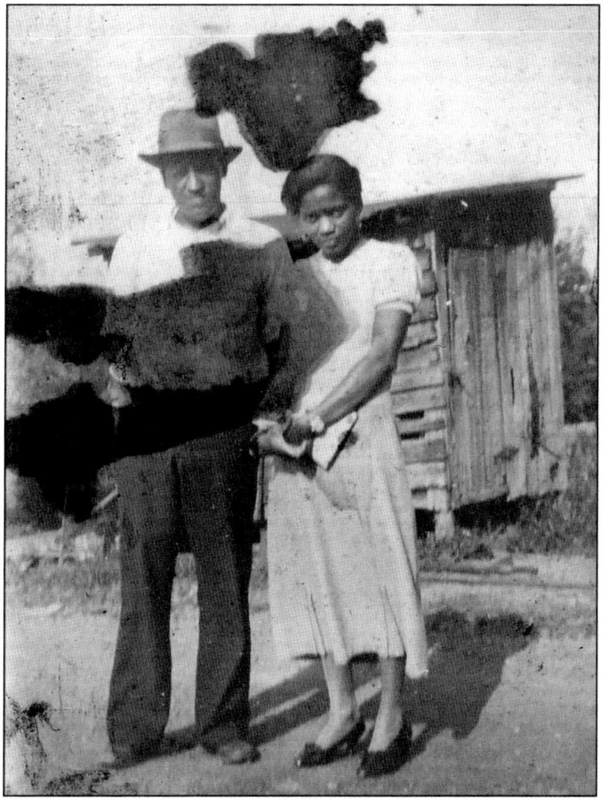

Emery and Rheta Lewis Younger are pictured here. Rheta Younger was a school teacher. The couple was married some time around the 1920s.

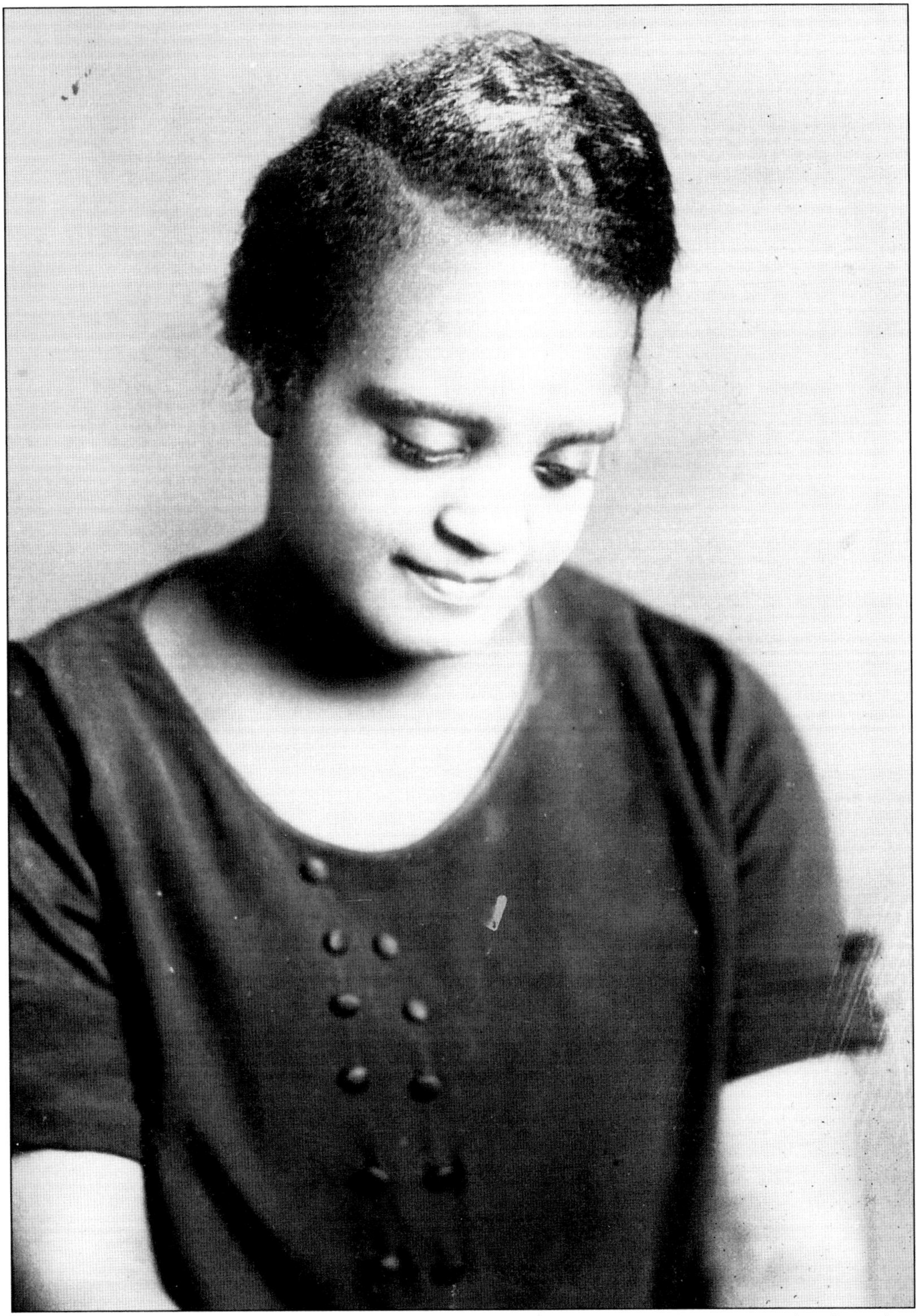

This demure portrait is of Hazel Robinson, who was employed as an elementary school teacher in the 1920s.

Attending an Eagle Club event are Lucien Randell (Hattie Barnett's brother) and John Hall.

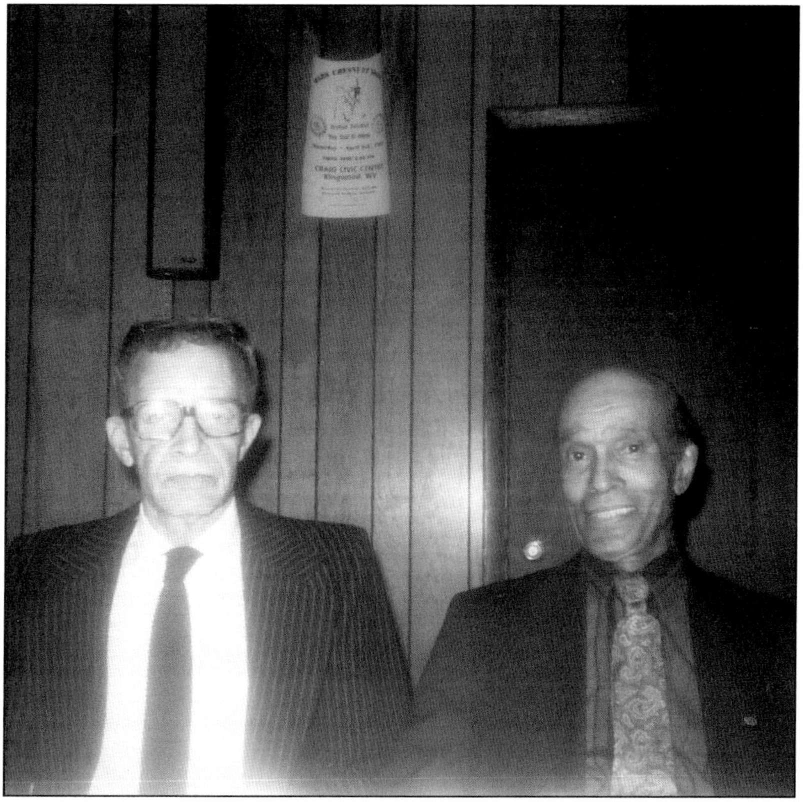

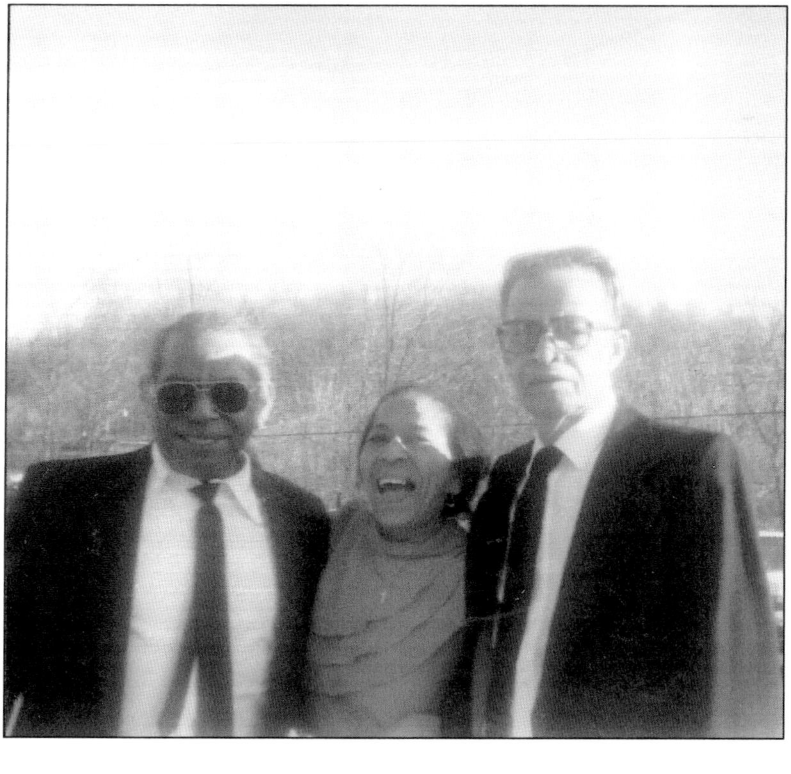

Here, Robert Barnett (right) and Florence Garrett (middle) join Lucien Randall for the repast at the Eagles Club.

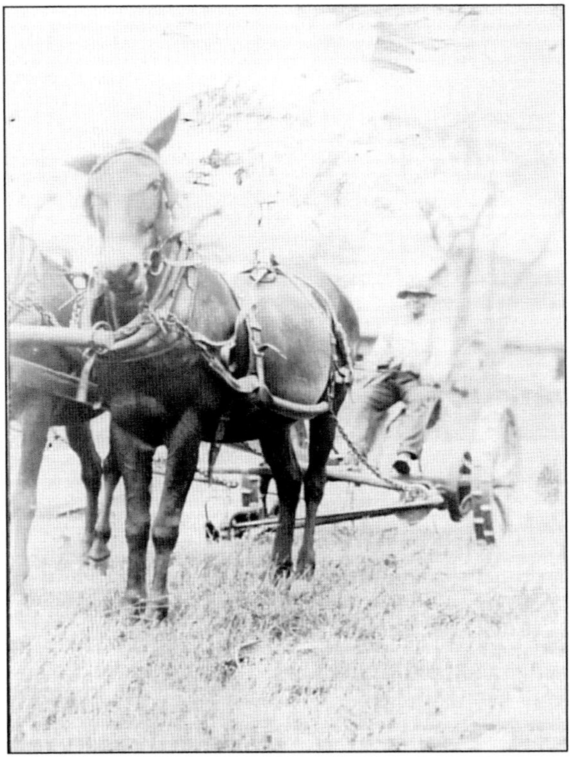

Henry Younger is pictured here plowing his garden.

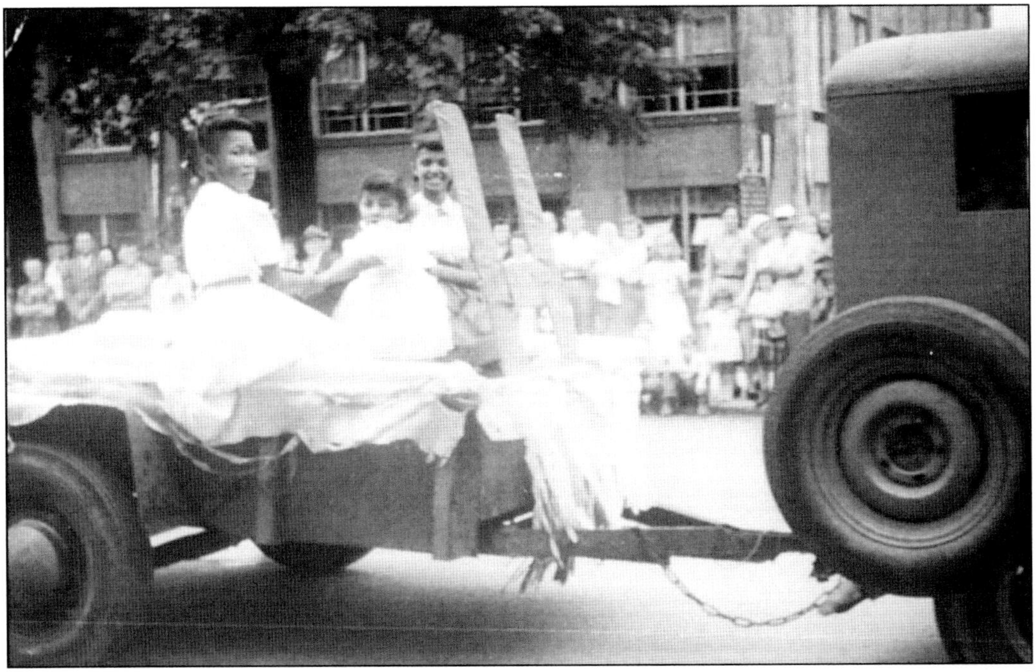

This scene comes from the Buckwheat Festival Days in September 1954, and the float pictured is the 4-H float. Riding on the float are, from left to right, Carol Paige, Connie Hall, and Carolyn Young.

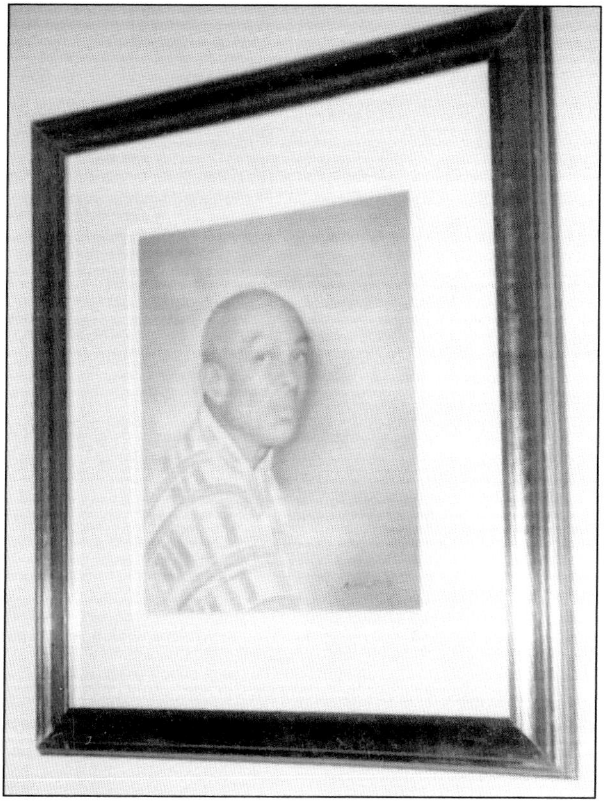

D.C. (Duke) Spencer served two terms as constable for the Kingwood District of Preston County. Below is promotional material used in his campaign. Spencer was married to Lula Ann Younger Spencer.

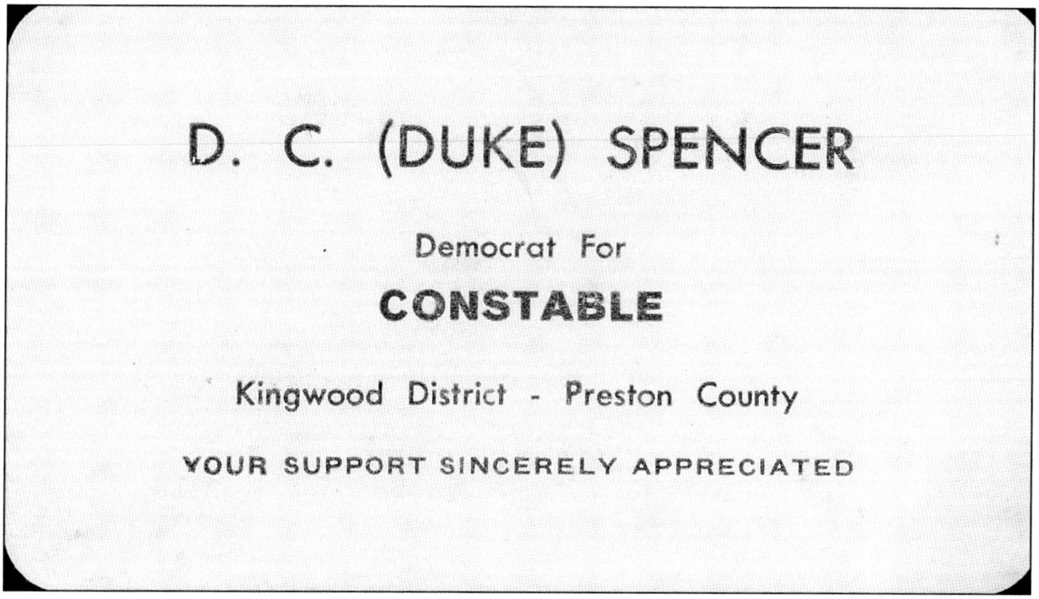

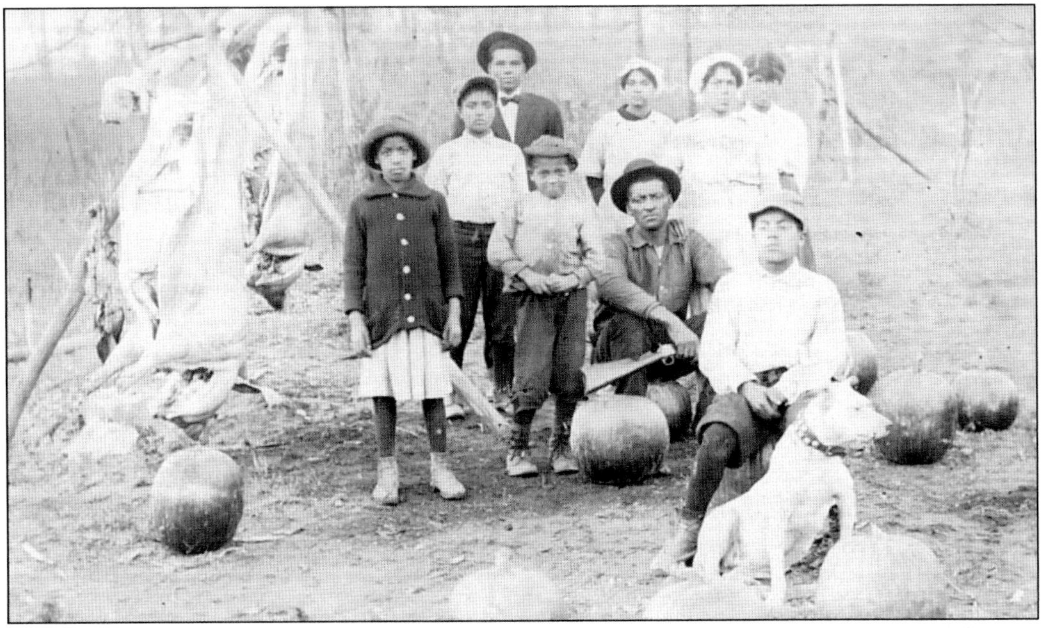

Samuel Younger and his large family, surrounded by pumpkins, take a break during butchering time to have their picture taken. Members of the family are, from left to right, Pauline, Joseph, George Ashby (brother of Mary Ashby Younger, in back), Emery, Sam (with shotgun), Mrs. George Ashby (in back), Mary (Sam's wife), Helen, and Charlie (in front).

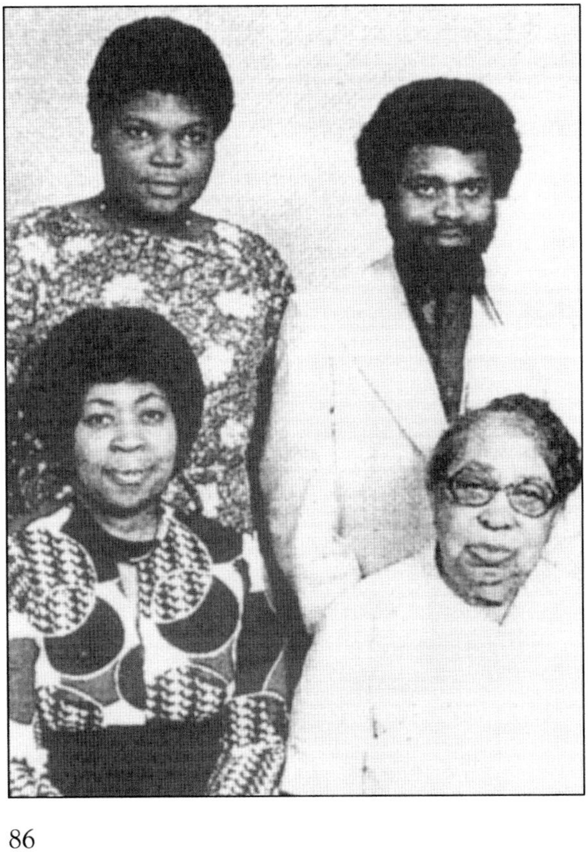

Pictured here are Angela, Michael, Ruth, and Mrs. Hattie Barnett in 1978. Angela has served as president of the PTA and is involved in several activities in the community. Michael is a local D.J. on WFSP Radio. He also owns Barnett Enterprise, Inc. and has served in the military. Ruth is an elementary school teacher, as well as a member of the Reading Council, and she was recently nominated to Who's Who of America by the Denver Tunnelton students. Ruth is a member of the Wesley United Methodist Church Administrative Board and is a wonderful gospel singer.

Russell Goines Jr. was named "Mr. Football" and posed for this regal portrait in May 1970.

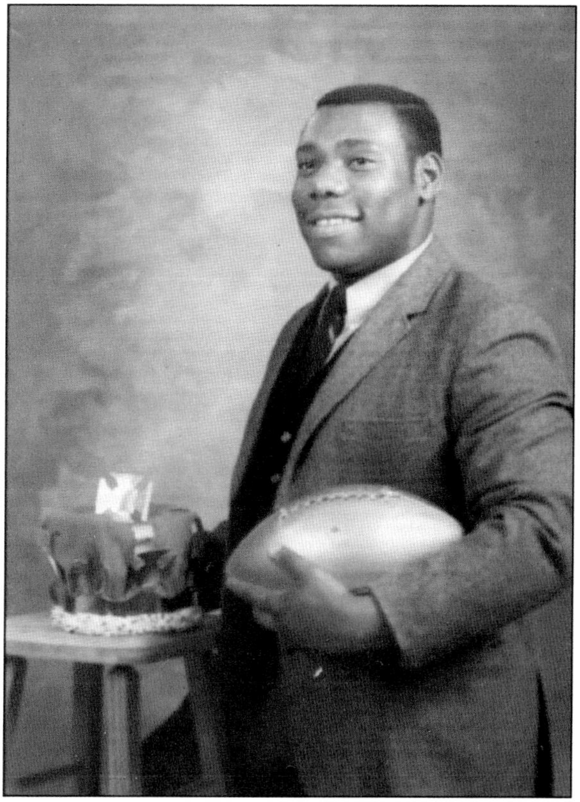

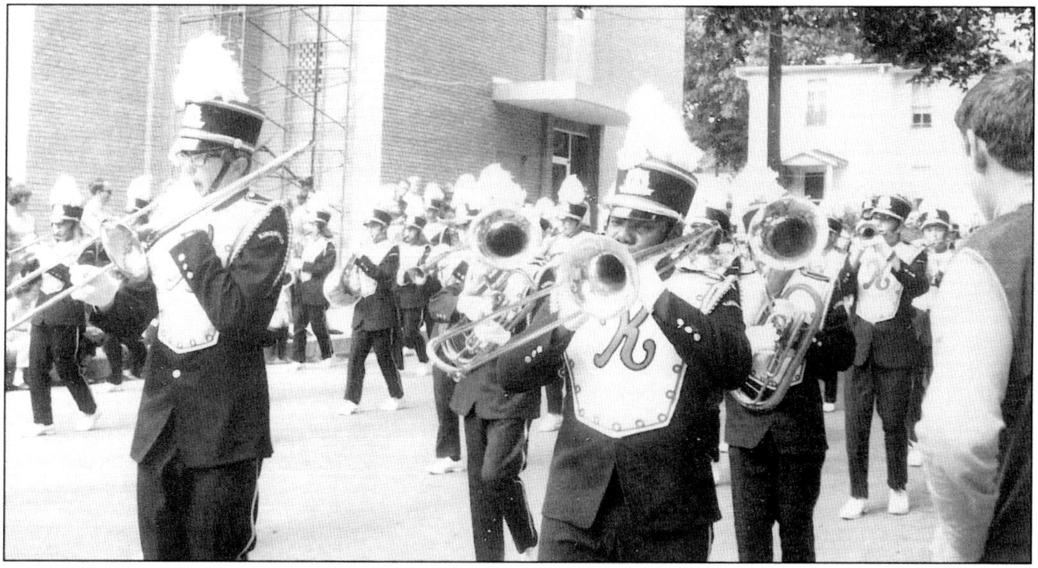

Russell Goines Jr., on the extreme right playing a trombone, and the rest of the Kingwood High School band are pictured here marching down Tunnelton Street.

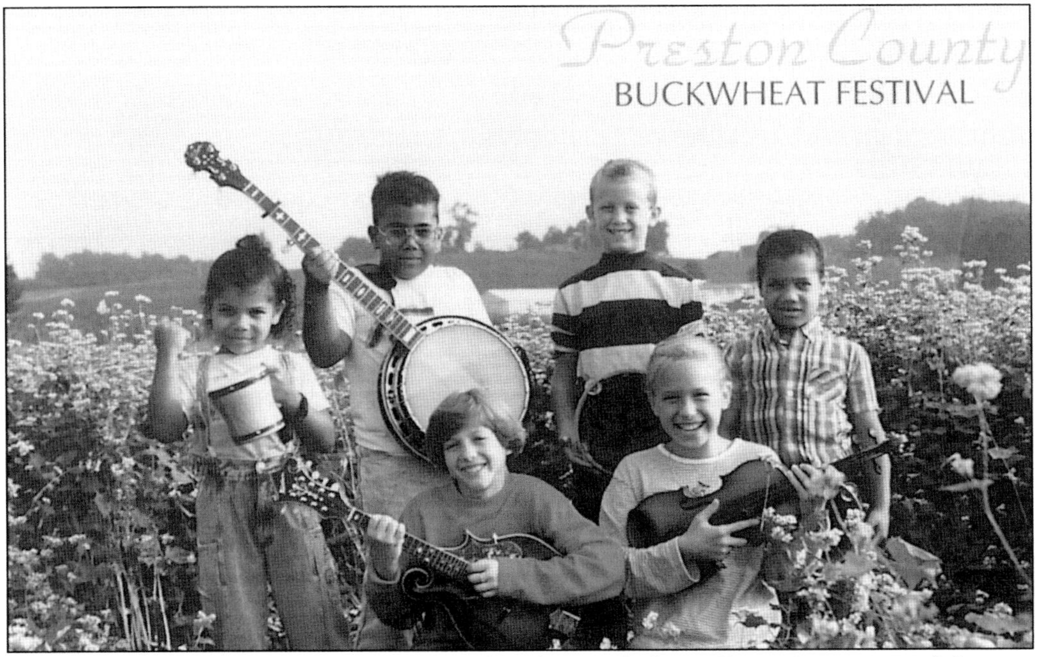

These young Prestonians are tuning up for the Buckwheat Festival, an annual harvest homecoming, featuring traditional music, arts and crafts, parades, exhibits, and Preston County's renowned Buckwheat Cakes and Sausage dinners. The festival is a volunteer effort and begins on the last Thursday in September. The children pictured are, from left to right, as follows: (front row) Alyssa Schooley and Kelly Calvert; (back row) Jessica Goines, Frank Goines II, Ryan Schooley, and Nathaniel Goines.

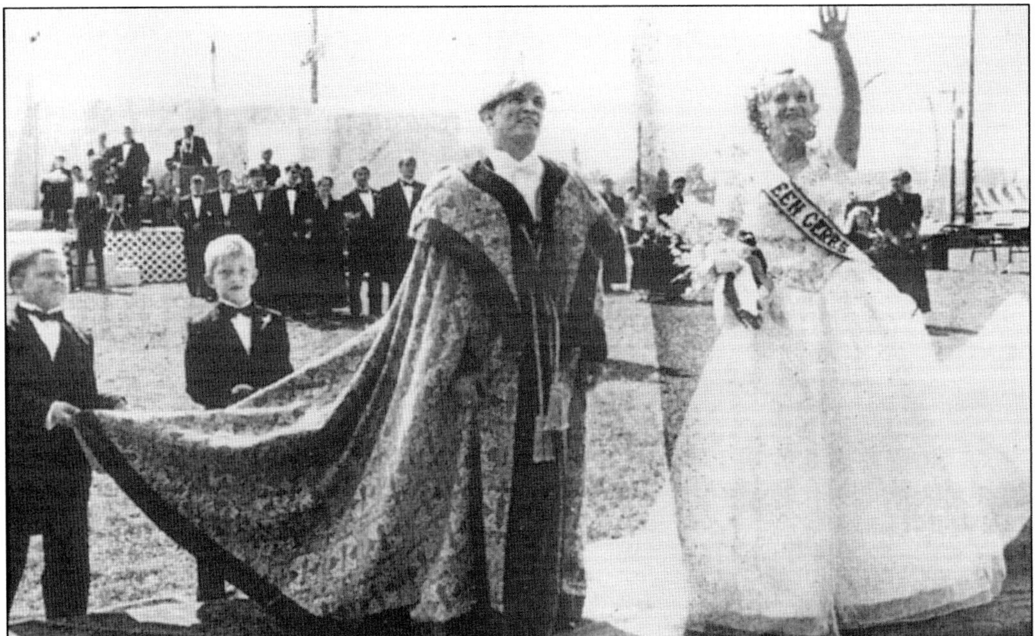

Michael L. Barnett II is pictured here as the Train Bearer to King Buckwheat Ronald Lynn Feather on September 29, 1995. Barnett is the second black train bearer in the festival's history.

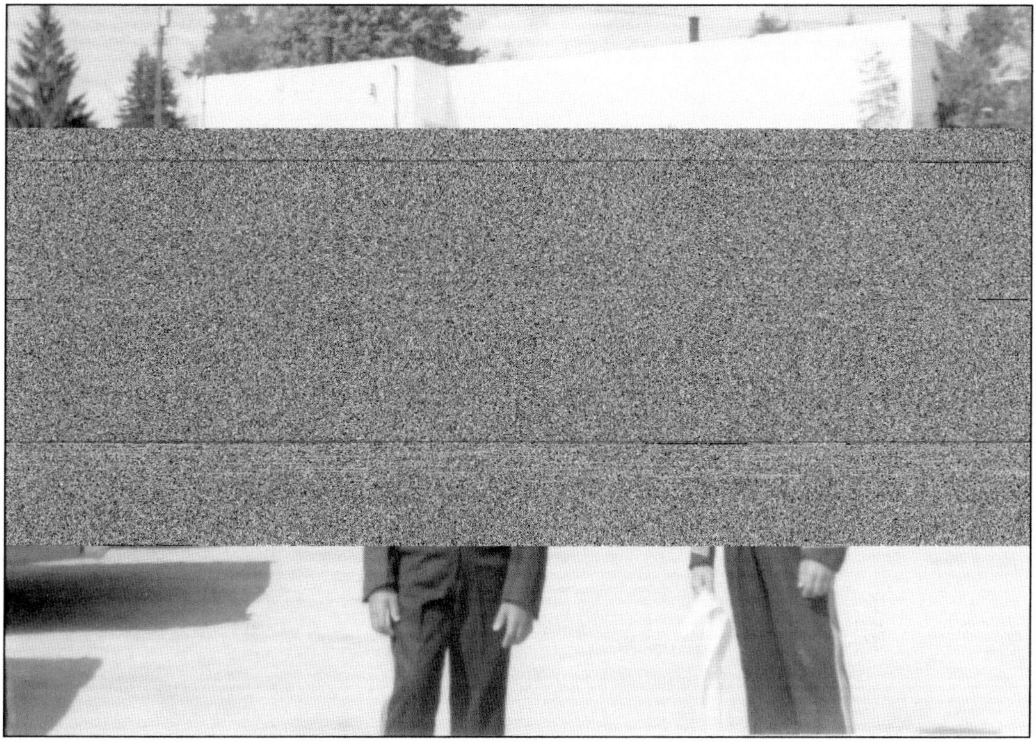

Frank Goines and Marcus McDonald participated in the Kingwood marching band and competed in this 1970 music festival.

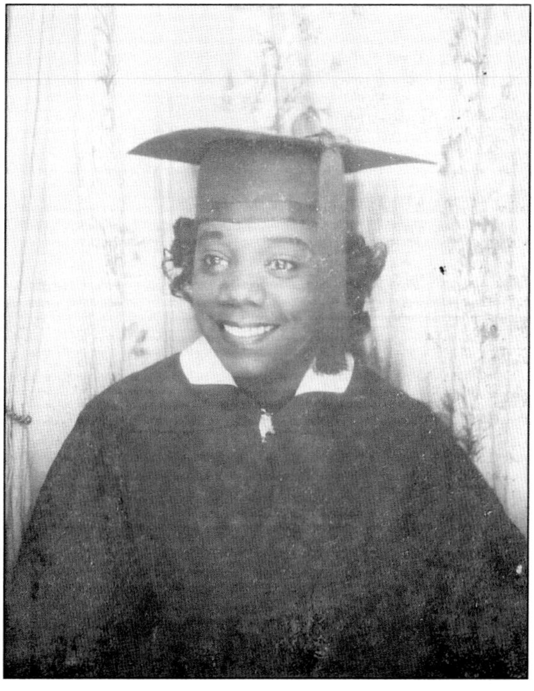

Marty Etta McDonald of Kingwood carried off major honors at Monongalia High School in June of 1949. She was the valedictorian of her class and won three separate scholarships offered by the Aubrey Toller Post, American Legion; the Civics Booster Club; and the Woman's Club. Miss McDonald was the first student from Preston County to win these honors.

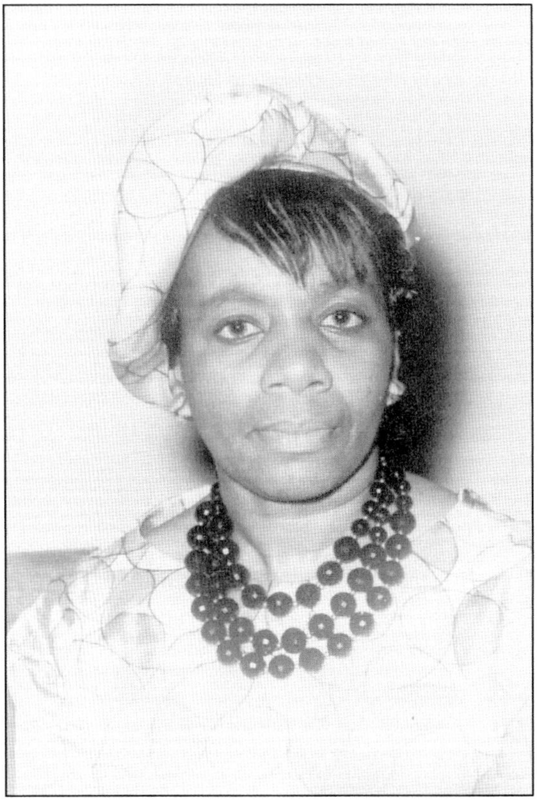

Mabel Younger Jackson was the first African American in Preston County to graduate from high school and college and become the first African-American school teacher from Preston County. Jackson was also one of the first crossing guards hired by the Chicago Police Department when the position was opened to civilians. Jackson regularly served as a volunteer at Salem House, delivering food to shut-ins; taught Sunday school for over 40 years (she even picked up some of the children); and chaired the Sick Committee's delivery of flowers to the sick and shut-ins every Sunday. For over 20 years, Jackson has also volunteered at the Atlas Center where she served senior citizens in the Golden Diners luncheon program for Chicago's Department of Aging and Disability. She was named to Chicago's Hall of Fame in May 1988 when she was 72. The ceremony was conducted by Eugene Sawyer, acting mayor of Chicago, in City Council Chambers.

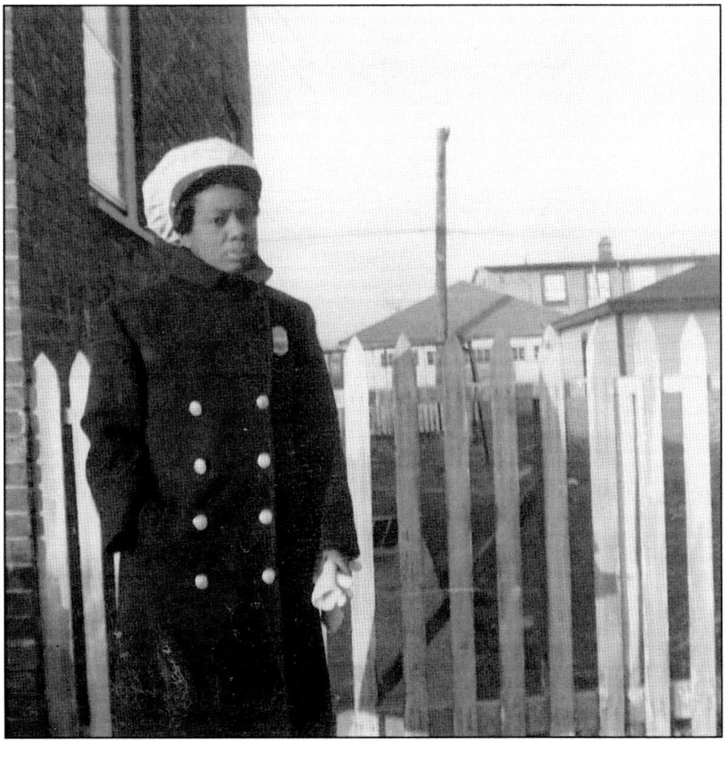

Mable Younger Jackson is seen here working as a Chicago crossing guard on January 2, 1956.

Melvin Eugene Copney graduated from high school in 1960.

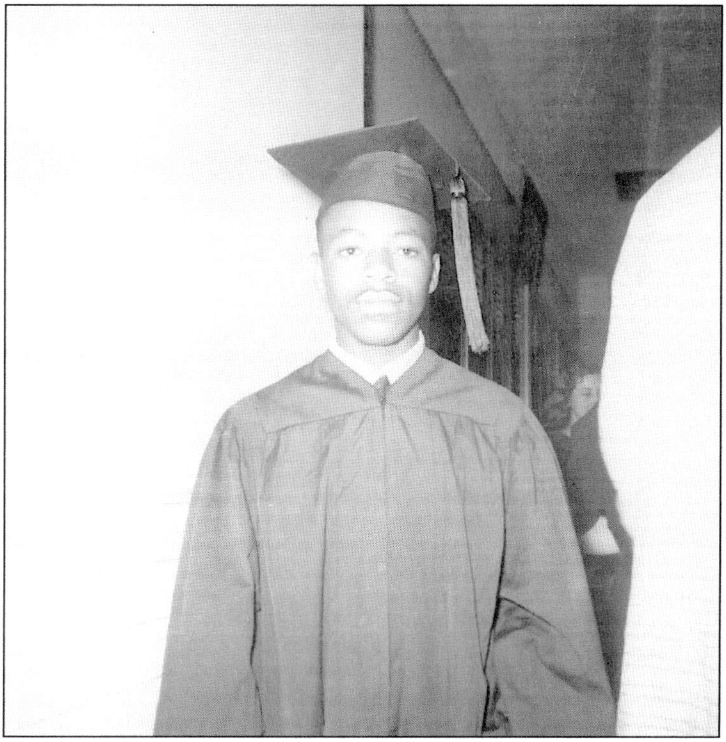

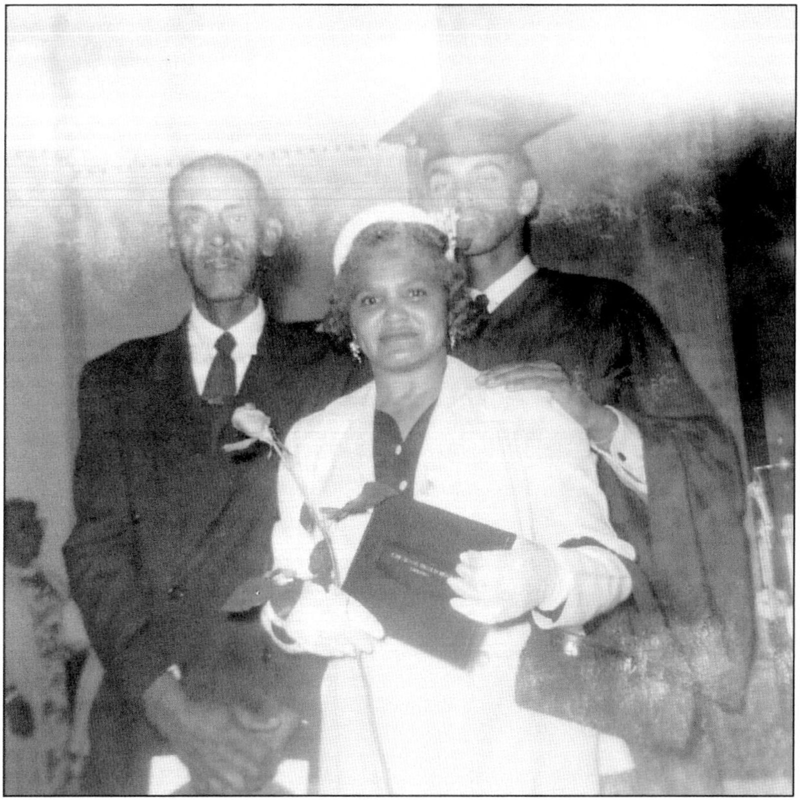

Daniel Young, another 1960 graduate, poses with his proud parents, Herbert and Alice Young.

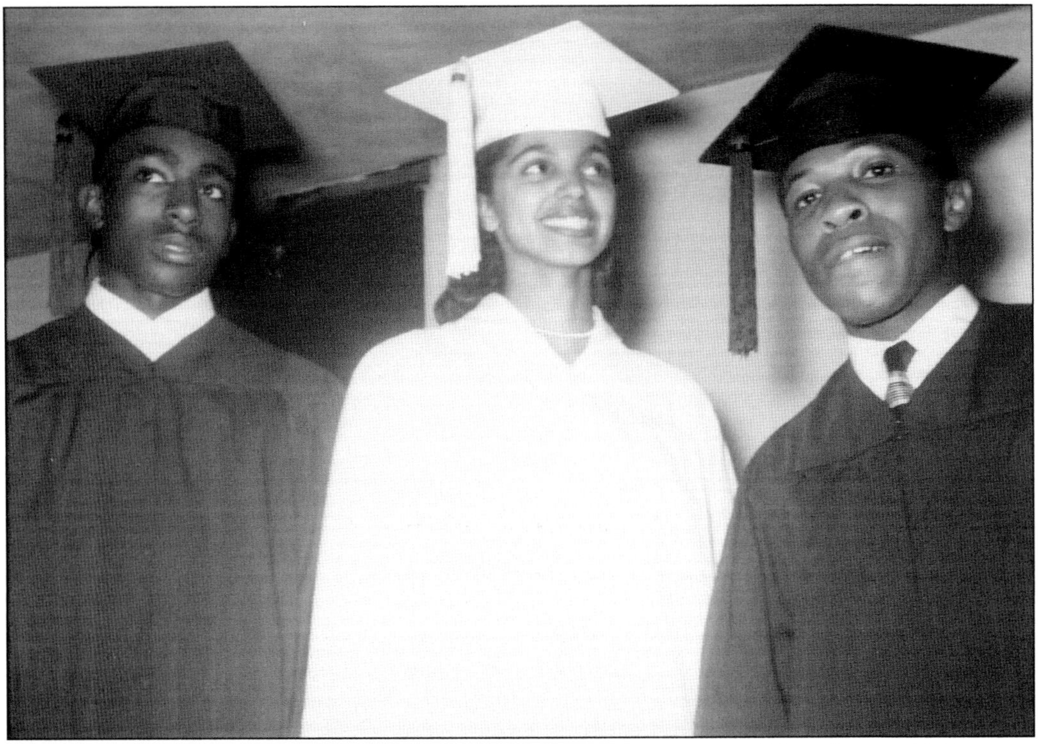

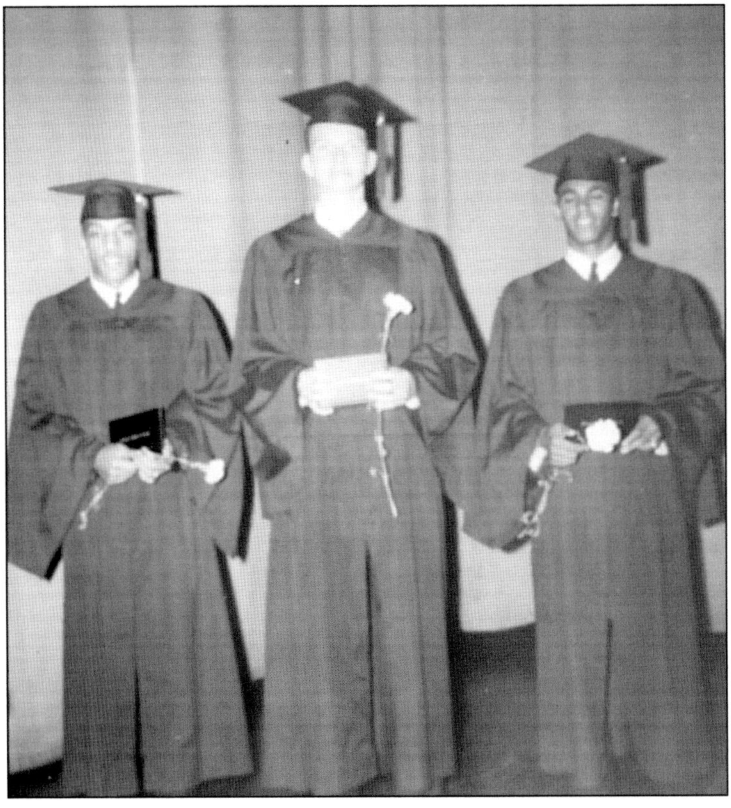

These happy 1961 graduates are, from left to right, Robert Spencer, Carolyn Young, and Charles Copney.

Pictured from left to right are Leonard Smith, unidentified, and Calvin Young as they pose for another graduation picture with their diplomas in hand.

This adorable school photo is of Marcus McDonald, an avid motorcycle enthusiast and member of the Motorcycle Club in Fairmont, West Virginia. Marcus was employed by Preston Memorial Hospital in December 1991 and, later, was made manager of Preston Laundry in Terra Alta.

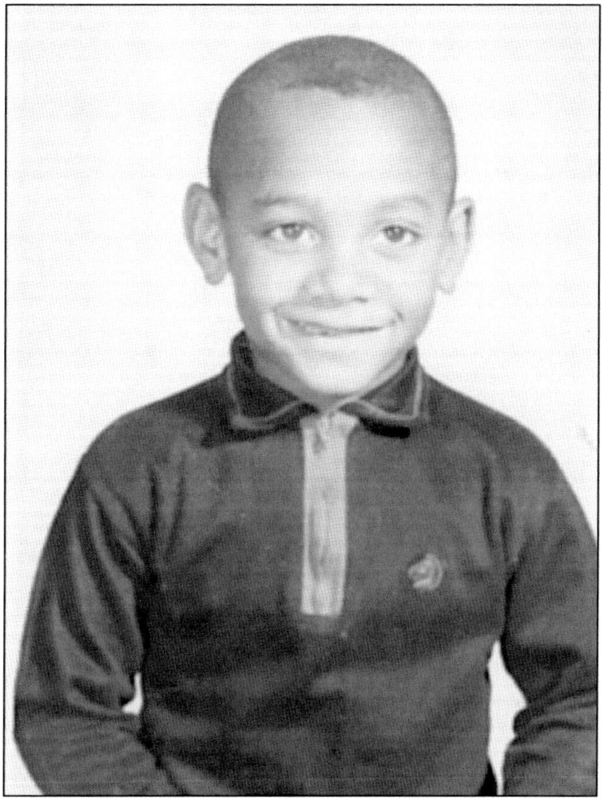

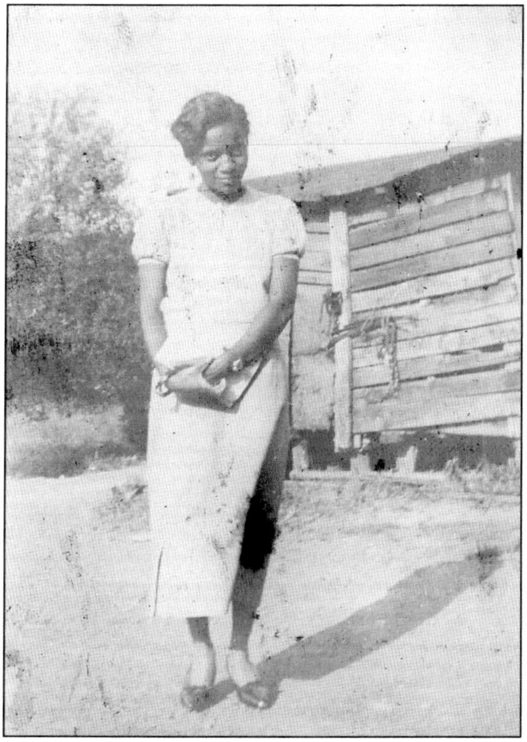

Rheta Lewis Younger was an elementary school teacher in Preston County in the 1920s and '30s.

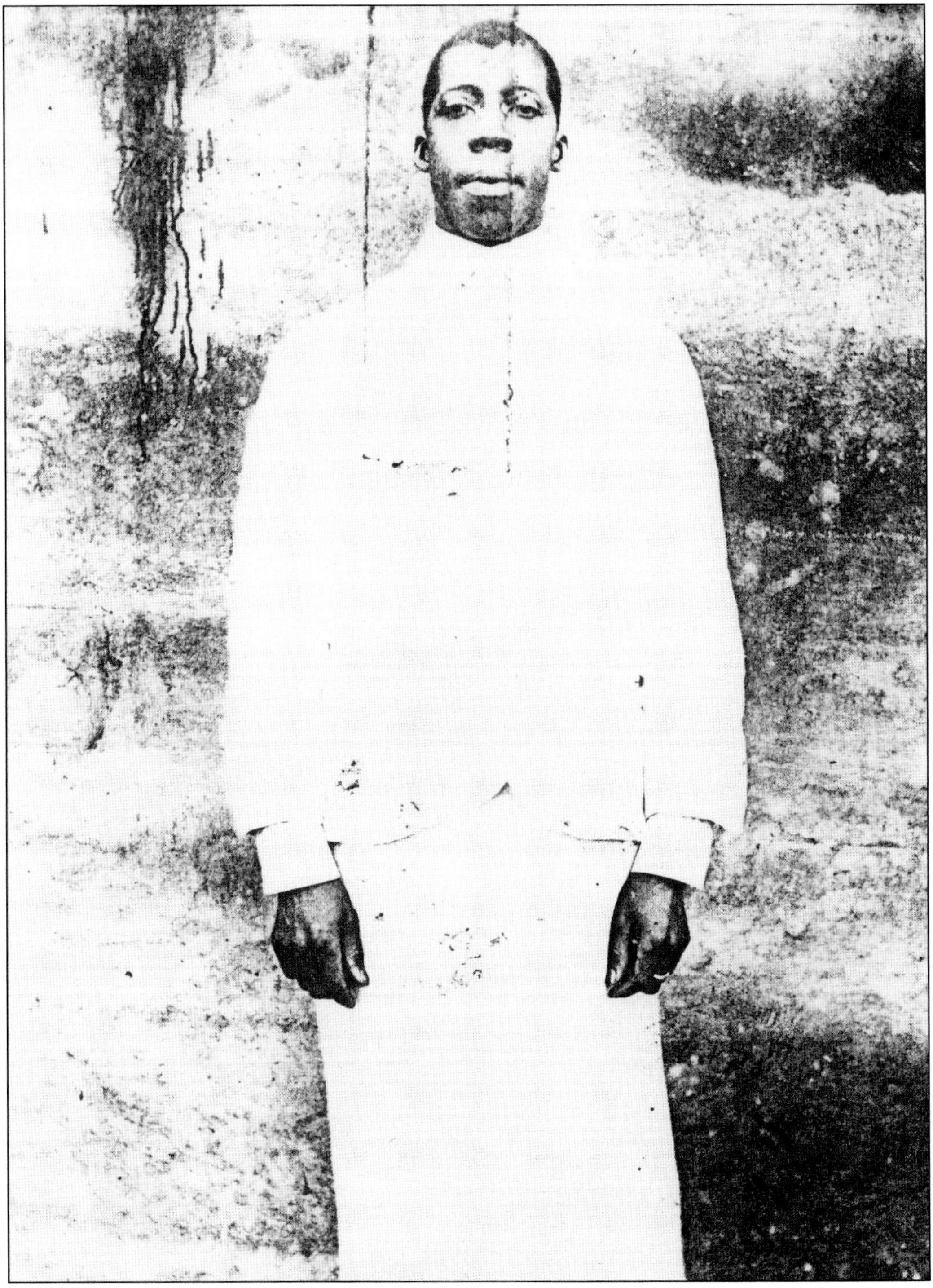

This gentleman, whose name was Edmond, worked as a cook. He posed in his white uniform in the early 1900s.

Carolyn McDonald was a drum majorette at Central Preston High School.

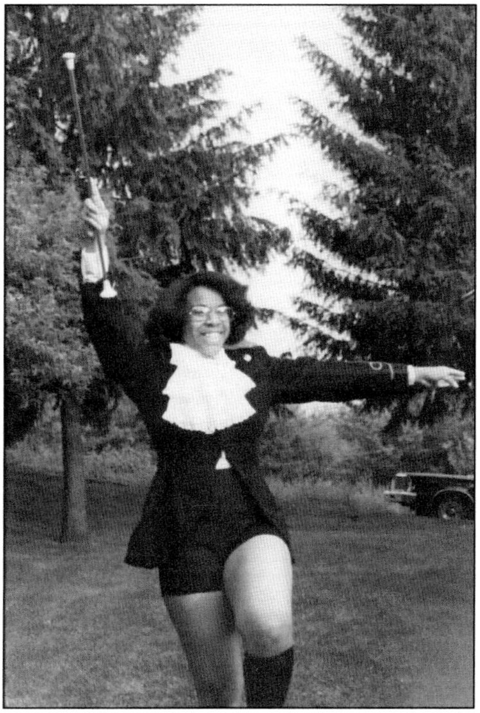

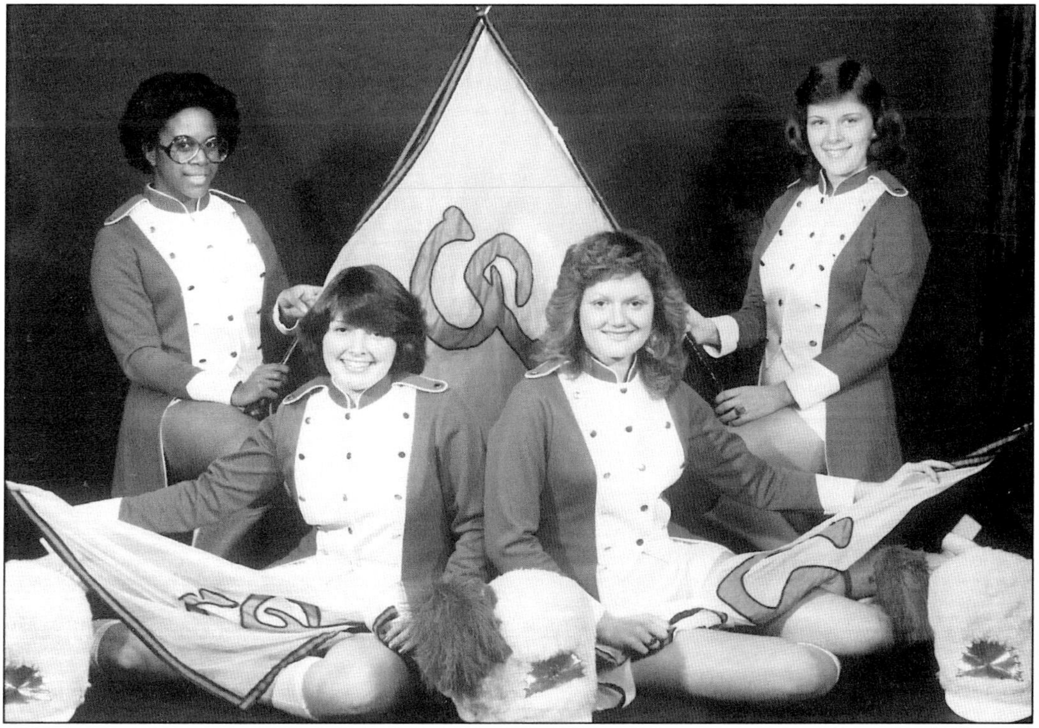

Carolyn McDonald (left) and her fellow Central Preston flag twirlers posed for this school-spirited photograph in the 1980s.

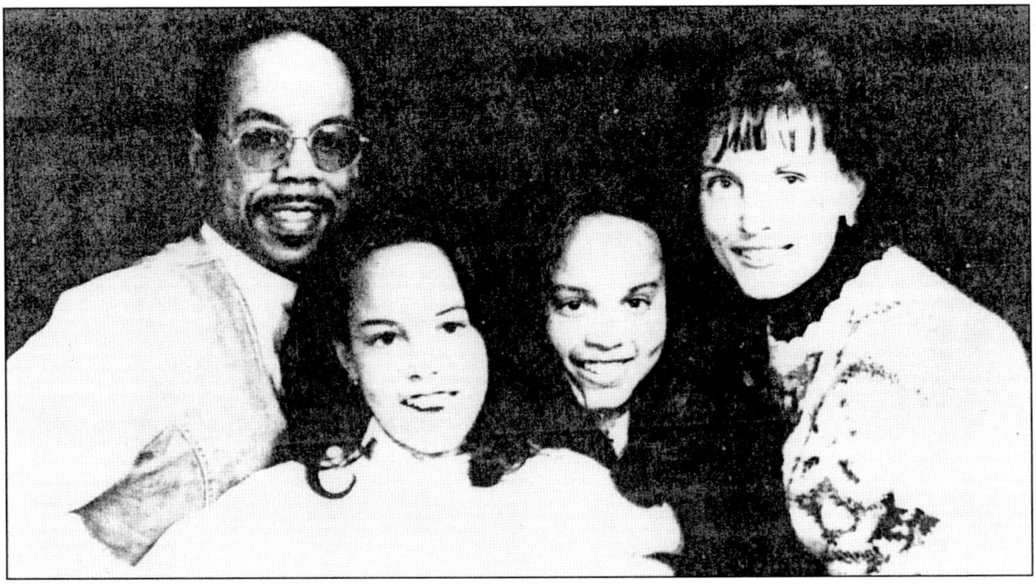

Pictured here are David, Jackie, Natasha, and Cecelia McDonald. David began working at Fibair on December 18, 1978. He helped design the flower bed at Love Chapel, and every spring, he cleans and replants flowers in memory of Mildred Grace McDonald. He worked with the Central Preston Marching Band for two years. Cecelia is also involved in the school as a cheerleading coach and team mom for the Stags and Wildcats. Both daughters are active in cheerleading and teeball. Jackie takes tumbling classes at WV Gymnastics Training Center in Morgantown, West Virginia.

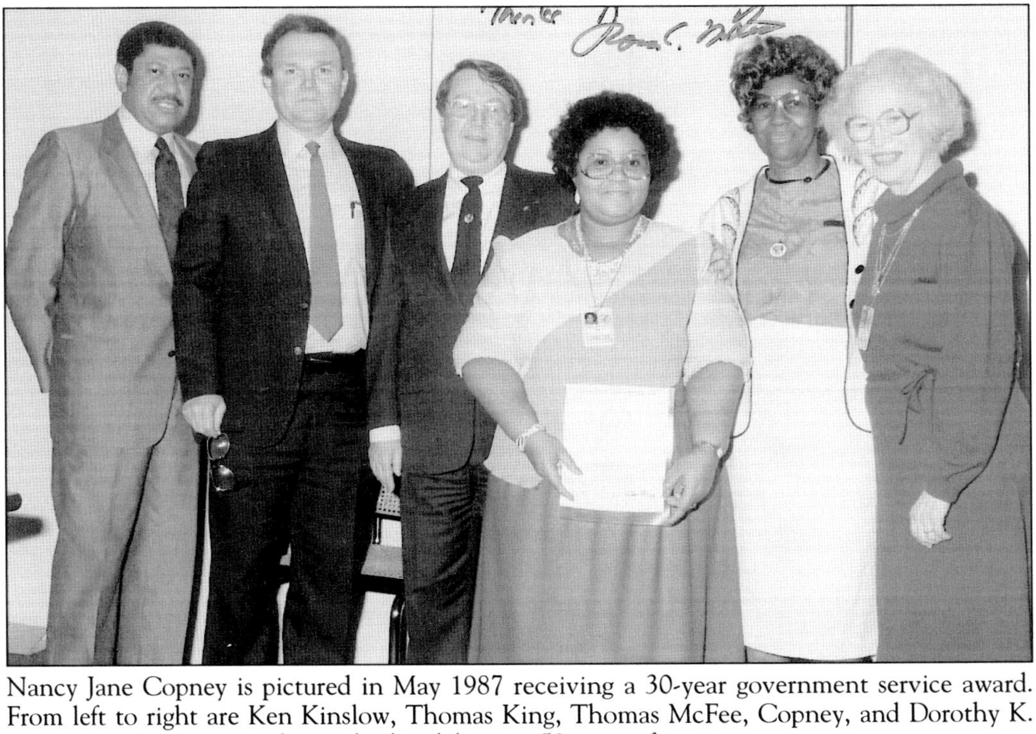

Nancy Jane Copney is pictured in May 1987 receiving a 30-year government service award. From left to right are Ken Kinslow, Thomas King, Thomas McFee, Copney, and Dorothy K. Dunn and Mrs. Mason, who are both celebrating 50 years of government service.

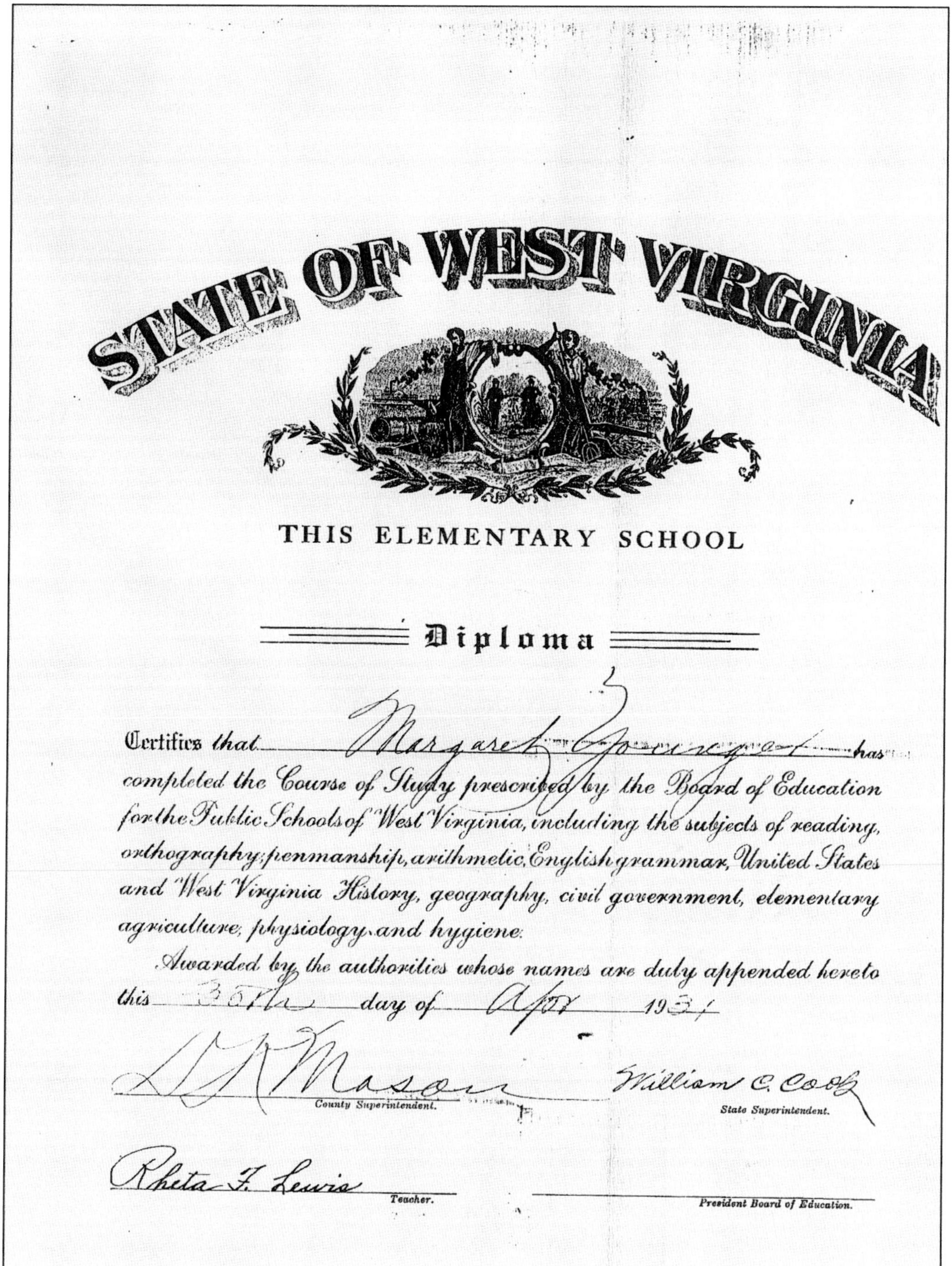
STATE OF WEST VIRGINIA

THIS ELEMENTARY SCHOOL

Diploma

Certifies that Margaret Younger has completed the Course of Study prescribed by the Board of Education for the Public Schools of West Virginia, including the subjects of reading, orthography, penmanship, arithmetic, English grammar, United States and West Virginia History, geography, civil government, elementary agriculture, physiology and hygiene.

Awarded by the authorities whose names are duly appended hereto this 30th day of Apr 1931

W. K. Mason
County Superintendent.

William C. Cook
State Superintendent.

Rheta F. Lewis
Teacher.

President Board of Education.

This diploma was awarded to Margaret Younger Copney when she graduated from elementary school in 1931.

BOOK 315 PAGE 103

THIS DEED, made this 19th day of August, 1954, by and between The Board of Education of the County of Preston, State of West Virginia, a statutory corporation, party of the first part, GRANTOR, and, John Henry Younger, Jesse McDonald, Jr., and Henry Copney, Trustees of the Love Chapel Methodist Church, Kingwood, West Virginia, and their successors as trustees, parties of the second party, GRANTEES.

WHEREAS, the GRANTOR has heretofore ascertained that the Beverly School property situate in the Town of Kingwood, Preston County, West Virginia, is no longer needed for school purposes, and the said GRANTOR has complied with the provisions of Chapter 18, Article 5, Section 7 of the West Virginia Code, relating to the disposal of school property, and pursuant to said statute held a public sale of the said building and land at the front door of the Court House of Preston County, West Virginia, on July 17th, 1954, and,

WHEREAS, at a subsequent meeting of The Board of Education of the County of Preston held on August 4th, 1954, the said Board of Education duly accepted a bid from the said GRANTEES for said school property in the amount of FOUR HUNDRED FIFTY DOLLARS ($450.00), and the deed for the said property was ordered to be made.

NOW, THEREFORE, WITNESSETH: That for and in consideration of the sum of FOUR HUNDRED FIFTY DOLLARS ($450.00) cash in hand paid, and other good and sufficient considerations, the receipt of all of which is hereby acknowledged, the said GRANTOR does hereby sell, grant and convey unto the said GRANTEES, with covenants of SPECIAL WARRANTY, all its right, title and interest in and to the

This is the deed to the Beverly Hill Elementary School, which the trustees of the Love Chapel Methodist Church in Kingwood purchased from the Preston County Board of Education on July 17, 1954. The property was awarded to the church for the price of $450. Nan S. Armstrong was the last teacher at Beverly Hill before integration; she taught from 1947 to 1953.

BOOK 315 PAGE 104

-2-

Beverly School property, consisting of the improvements and land, all situate in the Town of Kingwood, Kingwood District, Preston County, West Virginia, and more particularly bounded and described as follows:

Beginning at the corner of what was formerly the Schaeffer and Conn property at a stake where said properties adjoin the right-of-way of the West Virginia Northern Railroad and running with the Conn line to "Indian Creek"; thence with said "Indian Creek" 150 feet to a stake; thence from said stake N. 185 feet to the West Virginia Northern Railroad; thence with said railroad right-of-way, 150 feet to the place of beginning, and being the same lot or parcel of land, a life estate of which was conveyed to the Board of Education of Kingwood District by Mrs. Israel Schaffer, by deed dated July 22nd, 1924, and now of record in the office of the Clerk of the County Court of Preston County, West Virginia, in Deed Book No. 167, at page 189, to which deed reference is hereby made.

It is the intention of the said Board of Education of Preston County, West Virginia, since there is no conveyance on record to the GRANTORS, for the school lot herein conveyed, other than the conveyance above mentioned, to also make this deed under the provisions of Chapter 18, Article 5, Section 6 of the said West Virginia Code, said Beverly School House and property having been held in the undisputed possession of the County Board of Education for the period of more than five years prior to the sale of said school property.

Witness the following signature and seal:

THE BOARD OF EDUCATION OF THE COUNTY OF PRESTON, STATE OF WEST VIRGINIA, a statutory corporation,

BY: Paul H. Whittaker (SEAL)
Its President

ATTEST: Paul W. Watson
Secretary

THIS DEED, made this 28th day of February, 1969, by and between the Board of Education of the County of Preston, State of West Virginia, a statutory corporation, party of the first part, the GRANTOR, and Ruth Whetsell Morris, party of the second part, the GRANTEE;

WHEREAS, the Grantor has heretofore ascertained that the Colored School Lot is no longer needed for school purposes, and the Grantor has complied with the provisions of Chapter 18, Article 5, Section 7, of the West Virginia Code, relating to the disposition of school property, and pursuant to said law, after due publication in the Preston County Journal, a weekly newspaper of general circulation in Preston County, West Virginia, held a public sale of said school property on the 23rd day of November, 1968, at which time the Grantee became the purchaser of said school property for the sum of Four Hundred Seventy-eight Dollars and Forty-one Cents ($478.41); and

WHEREAS, at a subsequent meeting of the Board of Education of said County of Preston, held on the 25th day of November, 1968, the said Board of Education duly accepted the Grantee's bid of Four Hundred Seventy-eight Dollars and Forty-one Cents ($478.41) for said school property and all right, title and interest owned by the said Grantor in the real estate, and the deed for said Colored School Lot was ordered to be made; and

NOW, THEREFORE, WITNESSETH: That for and in consideration of the sum of Four Hundred Seventy-eight Dollars and Forty-one Cents ($478.41), cash in hand paid, the receipt of which is hereby acknowledged, the Grantor does hereby grant, sell, convey and quit-claim unto the said Grantee, Ruth Whetsell Morris, all its right, title and interest in and to a certain lot or parcel of real estate known as the Colored School Lot, situate in the City of Kingwood, in the intersection of Beverly Street and McDonald Street, in Preston County, West Virginia, bounded and described as follows:

Beginning at a stone just to the left of the old road; thence S. 1° W. 2½ poles to a stone in lands formerly owned by J. R. Stone; thence S. 29° W. 6 poles to a dead WO corner of lands formerly owned by Stone and Heirman; thence N. 19° W. 5½ poles to a small WO; thence E. 7 poles to the place of beginning containing 28 poles, more or less, and being all the same real estate that was conveyed to the Board of Education of the Township of Kingwood, by Francis Heirman and Sarah M. Heirman, his wife, by deed dated the 20th day of September, 1870, which deed is of record in said Clerk's Office in Deed Book 30, at page 431.

There is excepted and reserved from this conveyance that portion of the above described lot that was consumed by the relocation and improvement of McDonald Street and Beverly Street.

There is a plat of record in said Clerk's Office in Deed Book 301, at page 374, showing the approximate location of said lot herein conveyed.

The Grantor makes no warranty as to its ownership in the subject real estate, and it is the intention of the Grantor to convey only such right, title and interest as it may have in the subject real estate.

This is the deed for a "Colored School Lot" in Kingwood that was transferred to Ruth Whetsell Morris for a bid of $478.41 on April 13, 1969. The house, which served as the elementary school, is still standing on the property and being lived in today.

DECLARATION OF CONSIDERATION OR VALUE

The undersigned Grantor, a political subdivision of the State of West Virginia, declares that this is a transfer from a political subdivision of the State of West Virginia, and is not subject to the excise tax on the privilege of transferring real estate, under the provisions of Chapter 11, Article 22, Section 1 of the West Virginia Code of 1961, as amended.

WITNESS THE following signature and seal:

THE BOARD OF EDUCATION OF THE COUNT[Y]
OF PRESTON, STATE OF WEST VIRGINIA,
a Statutory Corporation,

ATTEST:

Laurence Lash
Secretary

BY Kermit R. Ziner (SEA[L])
Its President

STATE OF WEST VIRGINIA,

COUNTY OF PRESTON, TO-WIT:

I, Beryl B. Cence, a Notary Public in and for the County and State aforesaid, do hereby certify that Kermit R. Ziner, who signed the writing above, bearing date the 28th day of February, 1969, for the Board of Education of the County of Preston, State of West Virginia, a statutory corporation, has this day in my said County, before me acknowledged the said writing to be the act and deed of said corporation.

Given under my hand this 3rd day of March, 1969.

My commission expires April 13, 1969.

Beryl B. Cence
Notary Public

This instrument was prepared by
Neil A. Reed, Attorney at Law
Kingwood, West Virginia 26537.

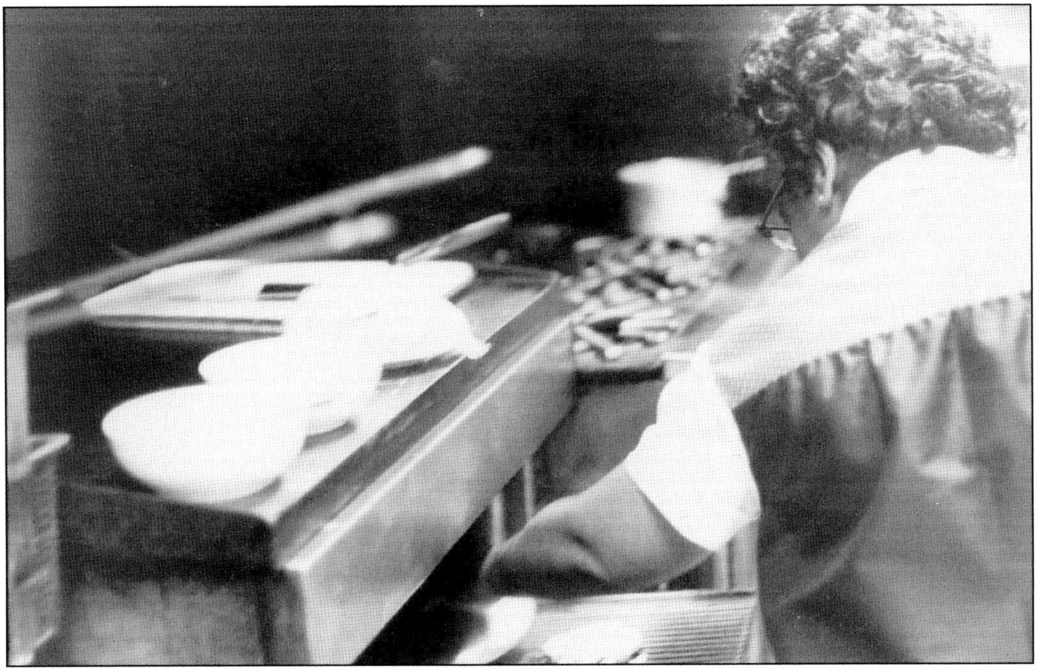

Mildred Grace McDonald was also a well-known cook, who was engaged in catering services and operated her own restaurant.

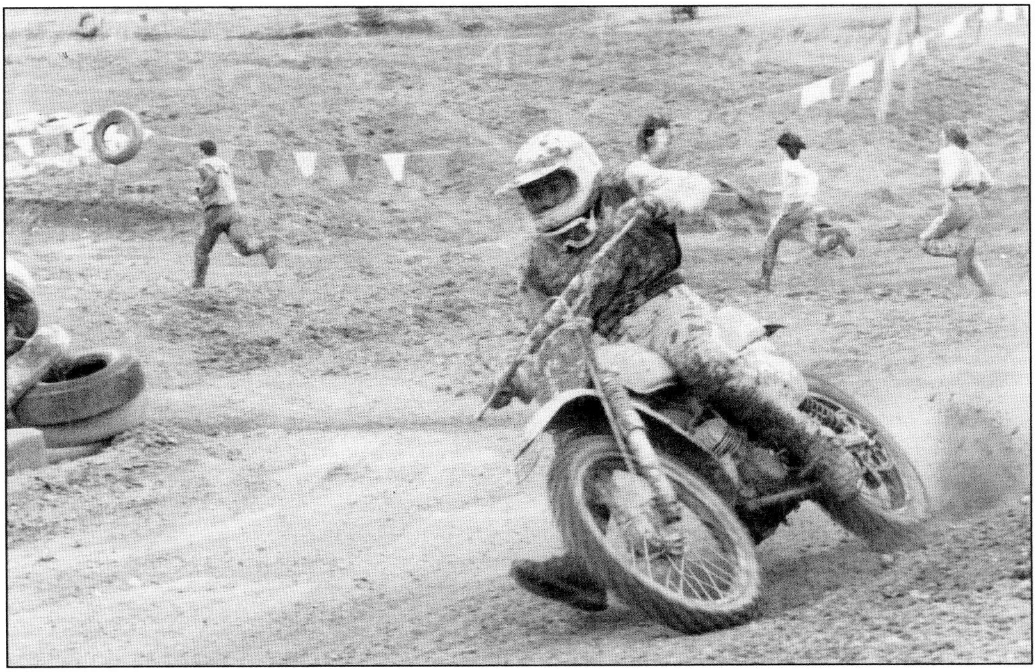

Frank Goines's favorite hobby was motor cross bike riding, and this action shot was taken of him in April 1978.

Four

Going to Church and Other Celebrations

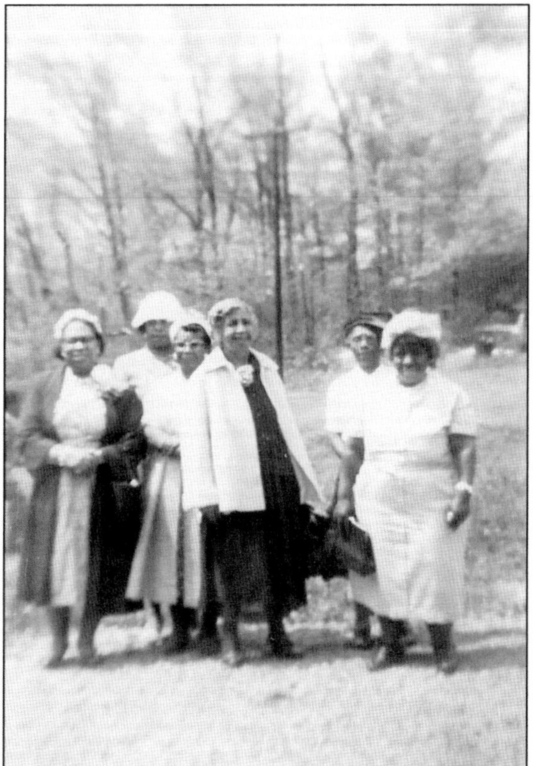

This picture of, from left to right, Mrs. Hattie Barnett, Mrs. Grace Younger, Mrs. Margaret Copney, Mrs. Nan S. Armstrong, Mrs. Lula Whitley, and Mrs. Laylor McDonald was taken on Mother's Day in May 1958 following church services.

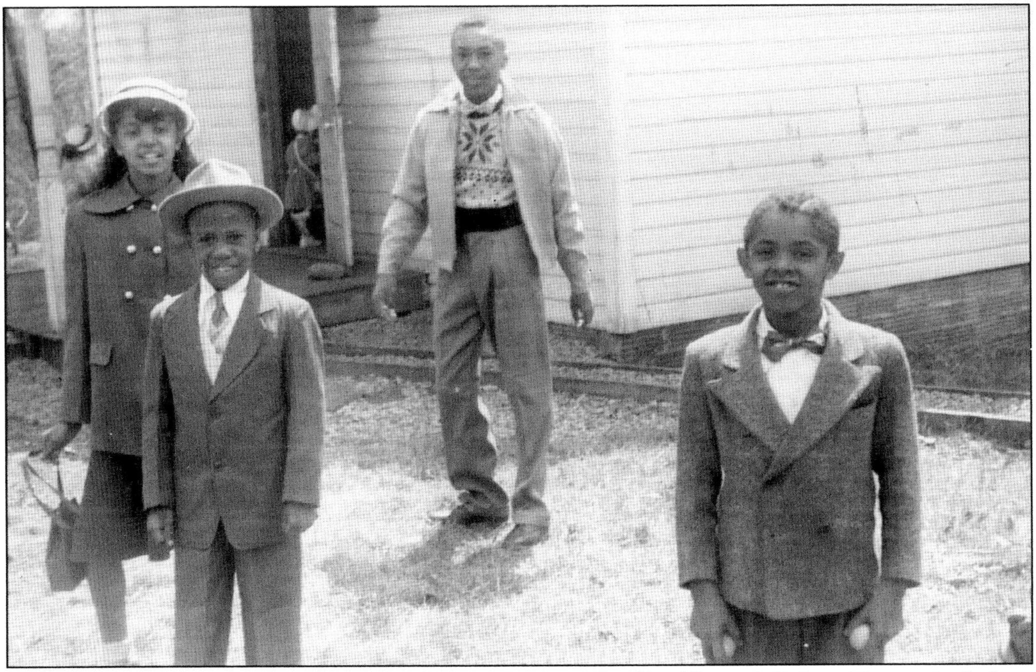

Carolyn Young, James "Peewee" Smith, Joseph Paige Jr. (back), and Calvin Young had their picture snapped while they were in their Sunday best on an Easter morning in the 1960s.

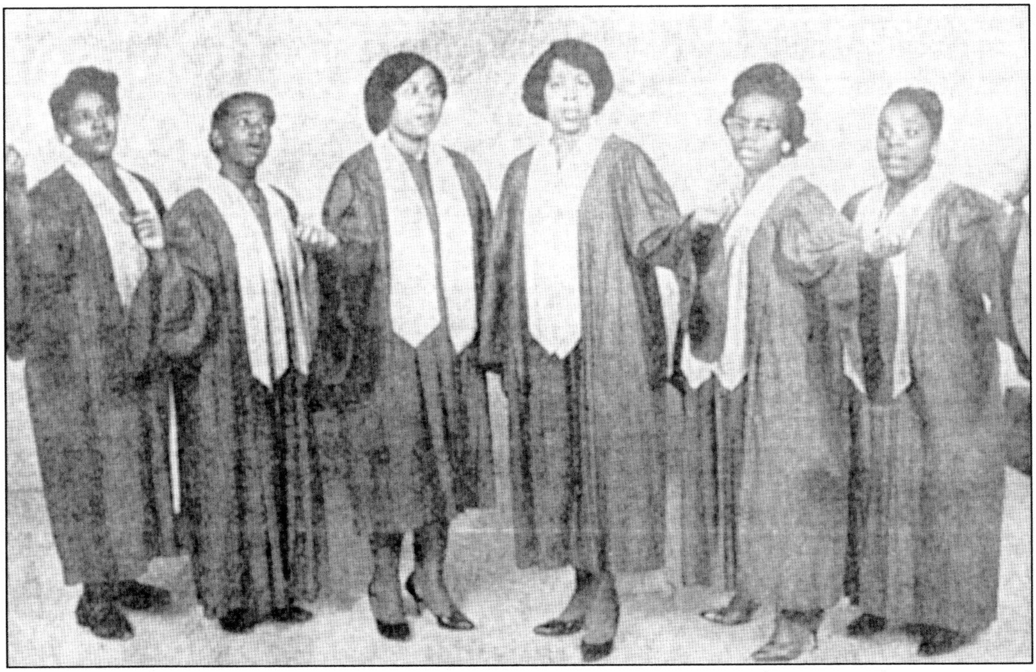

Love Chapel's choir once had 20 members, but, by the late 1960s, only six members remained in Kingwood. Pictured here from left to right, they are Louise McDonald, Sarah McDonald, Beulah Hall, Ruth Barnett, Grace McDonald, and Marietta Goines. Today, only three members, Louise McDonald, Beulah Hall, and Marietta Goines, are singing on a regular basis. They are joined on occasion by Ruth Barnett, who works as an elementary school teacher.

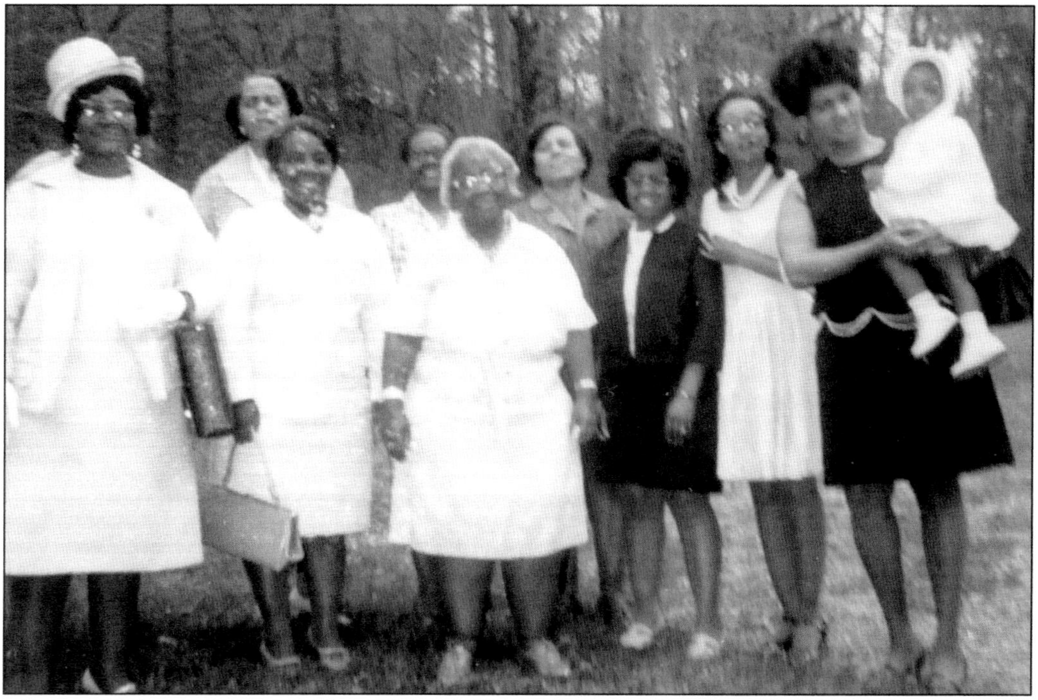

This group photograph was taken at the Easter services at Love Chapel in the early 1960s. The women pictured are, from left to right, (front row) Margaret Copney, Marietta Goines, Laylor McDonald, Grace McDonald, Loretta Etheridge, and Ruth and JoAnn Copney; (back row) Helen McDonald, Sarah Goines, and Beulah Hall.

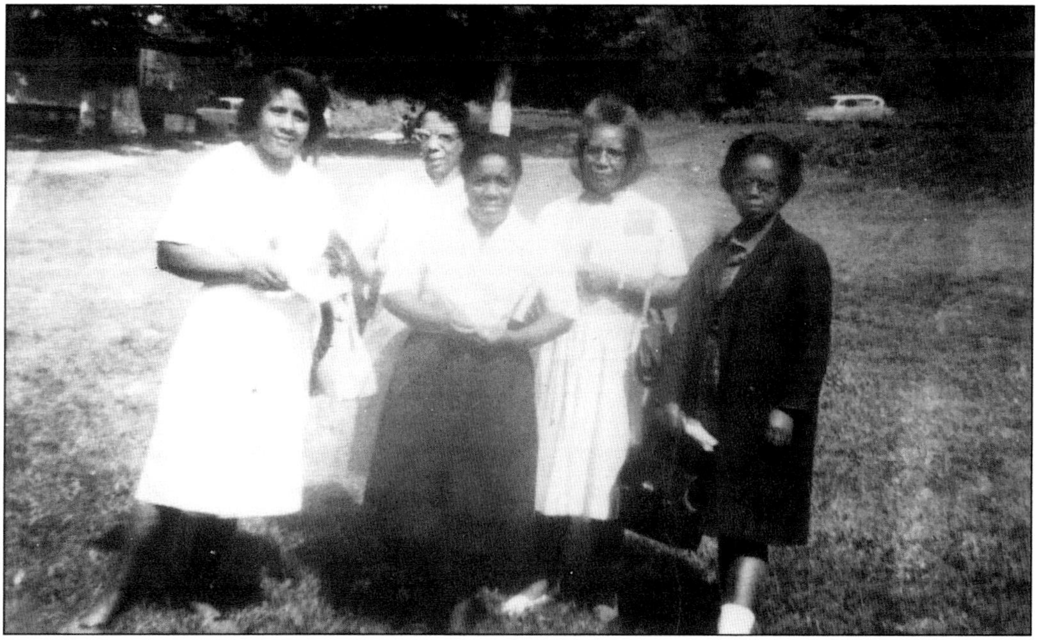

The staff of Love Chapel's Sunday School program are pictured here in 1966. They are, from left to right, Louise McDonald, Dorothy Smith, Marietta Goines, Margaret Copney (pianist), and Grace McDonald (superintendent).

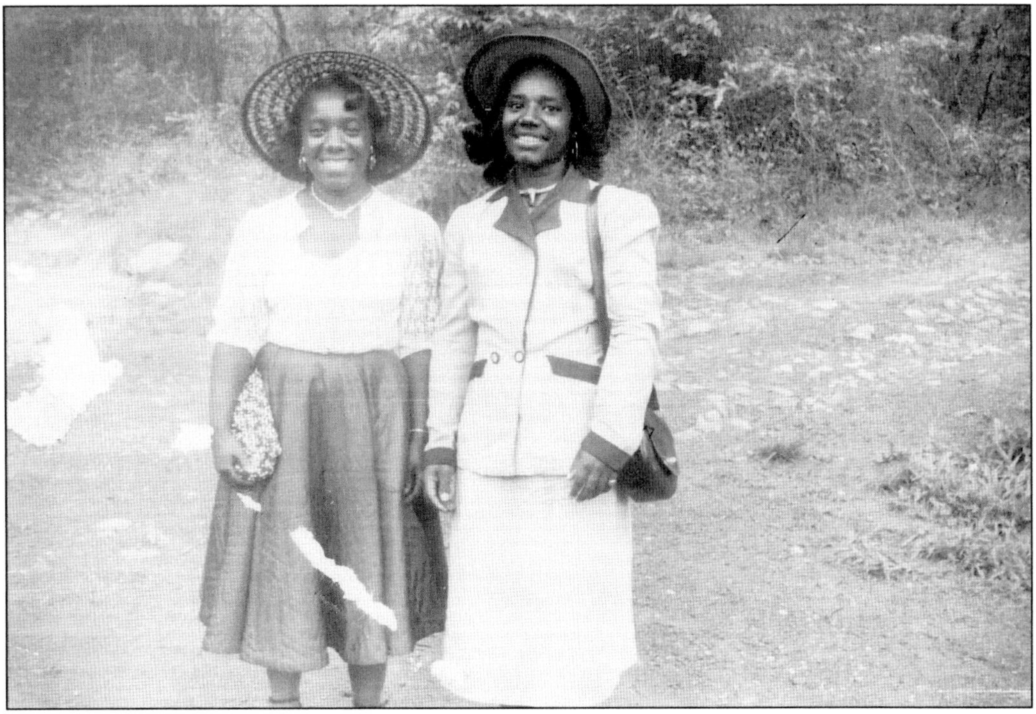

Sisters Sarah McDonald and Marietta McDonald Goines pause for this picture dressed as if on their way to Sunday church services.

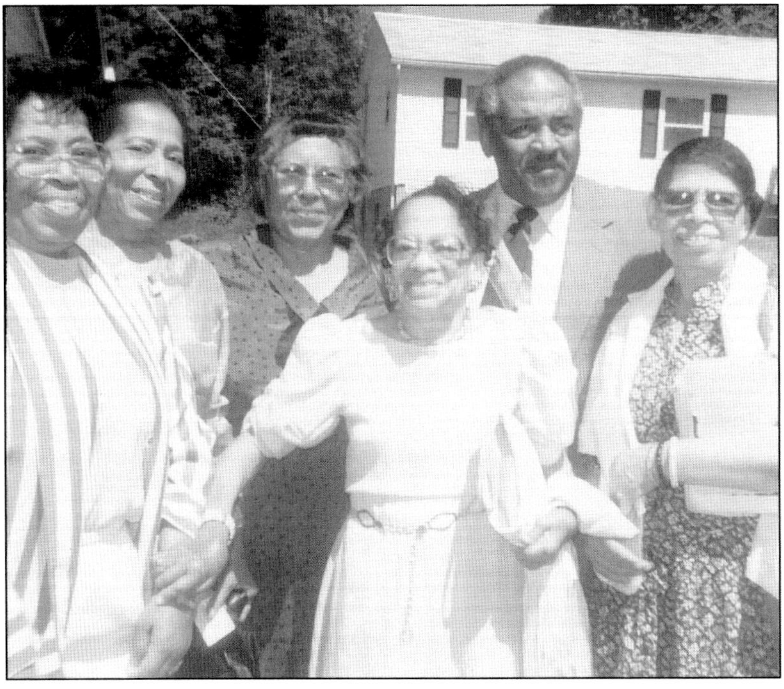

Attending services at Love Chapel Church in July 1988 are, from left to right, Ruth Barnett, Florence Barnett Garrett, Beulah Barnett Hall, Dorothy Lee Smith, William Younger Jr., and Viola Barnett.

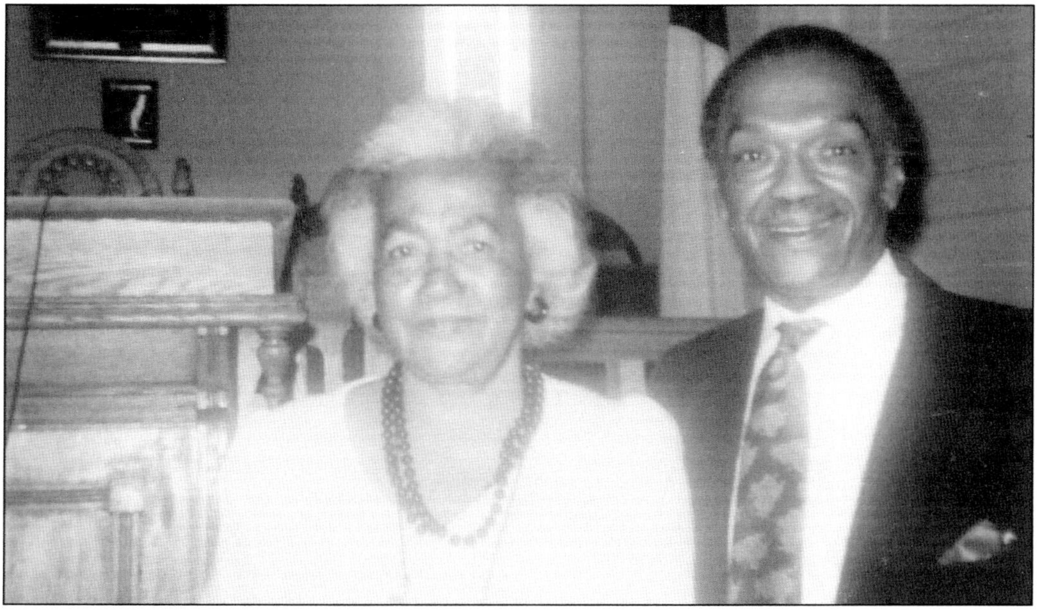

Evelyn Paige stands with her son Joseph D. Paige. Evelyn has appeared in many churches as a guest soloist.

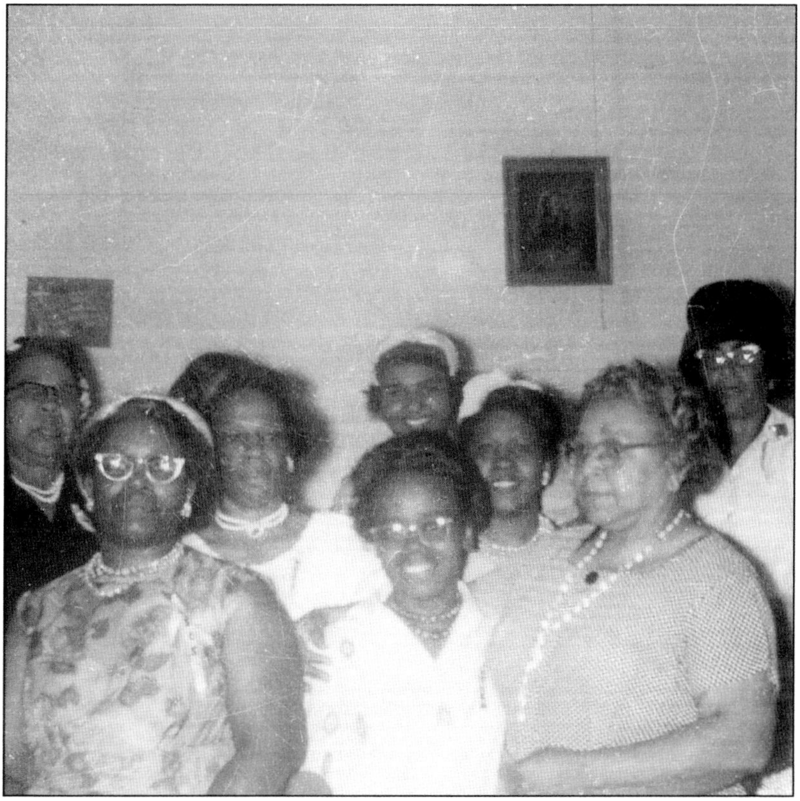

Attending church services at Love Chapel in the early 1960s are, from left to right, as follows: (front row) Margaret Copney, Grace McDonald, and Helen McDonald; (back row) Hattie Barnett, Dorothy Smith, Ruth Smith, Louise McDonald, and Grace Younger.

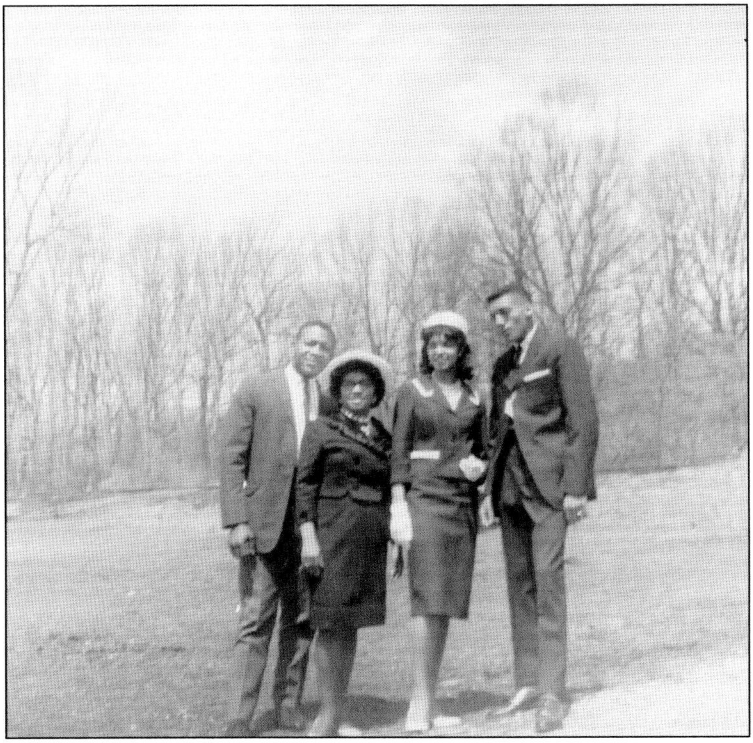

Charles Copney, JoAnn McDonald, Carolyn Young, and Leonard Smith were attending Easter services at Love Chapel in this early 1960s image.

The Reverend and Mrs. Ernest Jay Jr. are pictured here. Rev. Jay organized the first Foodshare distribution program at the Otterbein United Methodist Church in Kingwood on August 26, 1989. Foodshare is a regional self-help food program; churches, unions, and community organizations serve as host organizers. For $12 in cash or food stamps and two hours of volunteer service individuals may receive a total of $30 in food through the program. The local program is sponsored by Bethlehem, Love Chapel, and Otterbein Churches.

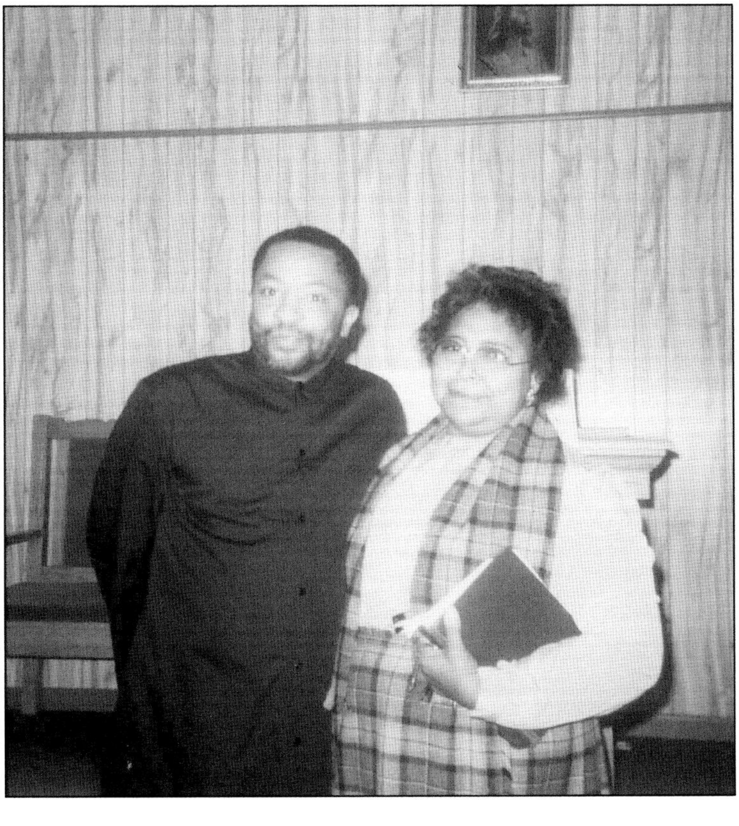

Lula Whitley is dressed up in this early 1940s photograph because she is on her way to church.

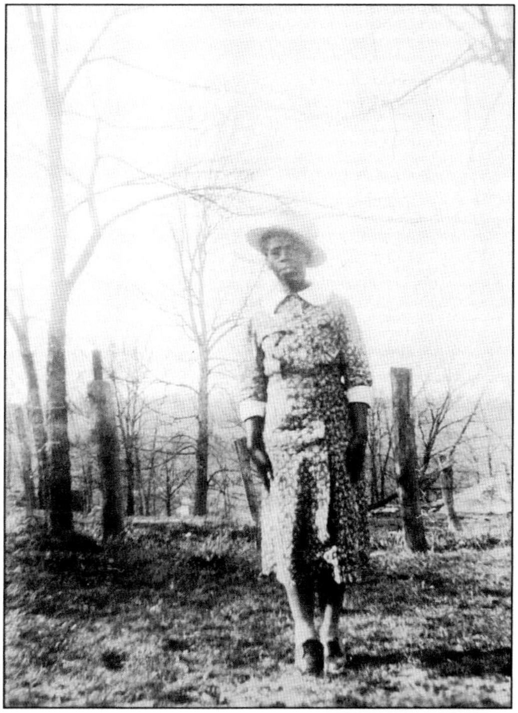

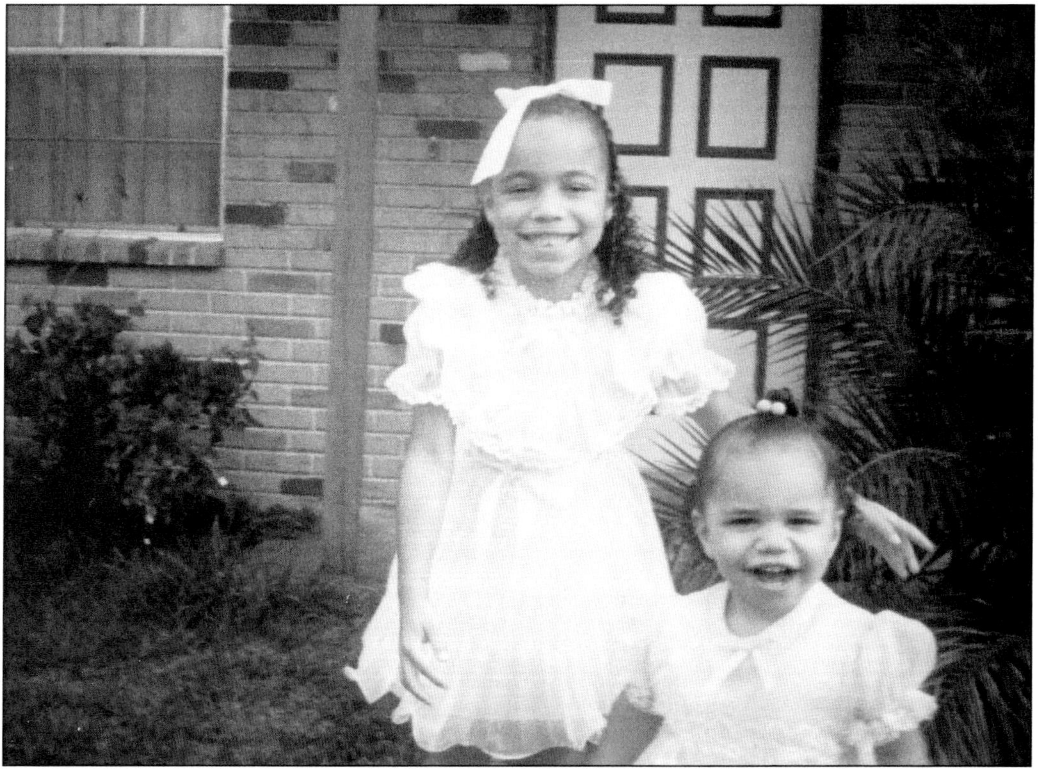

Brooke and Kinika Ford had this picture taken in their pretty Easter dresses and smiles in April 1985.

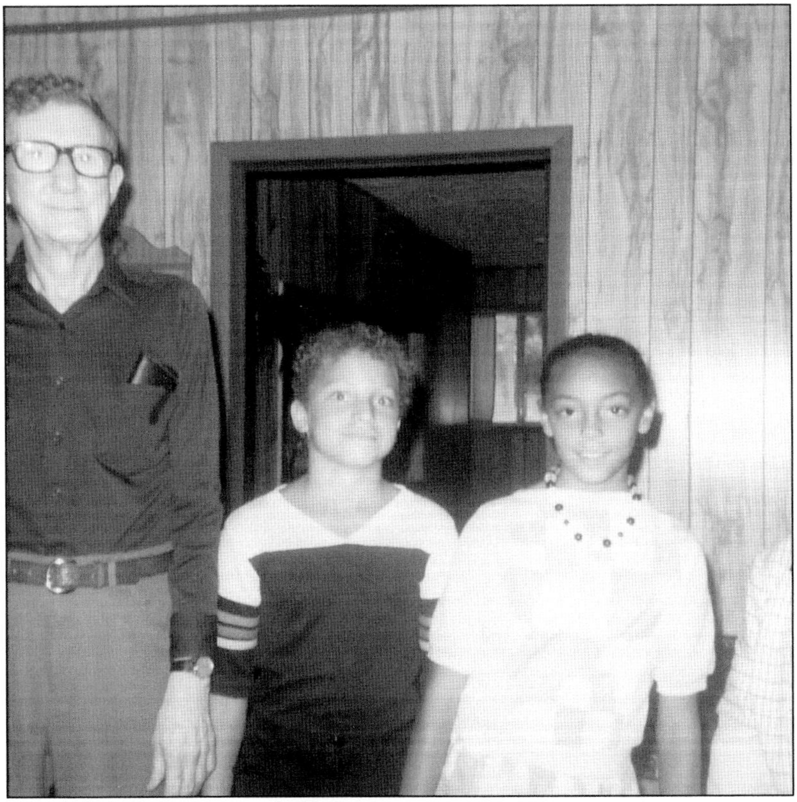

John Beckner, father-in-law of Marcus McDonald, attends church services at Love Chapel with his grandchildren Regan and Devon in 1988.

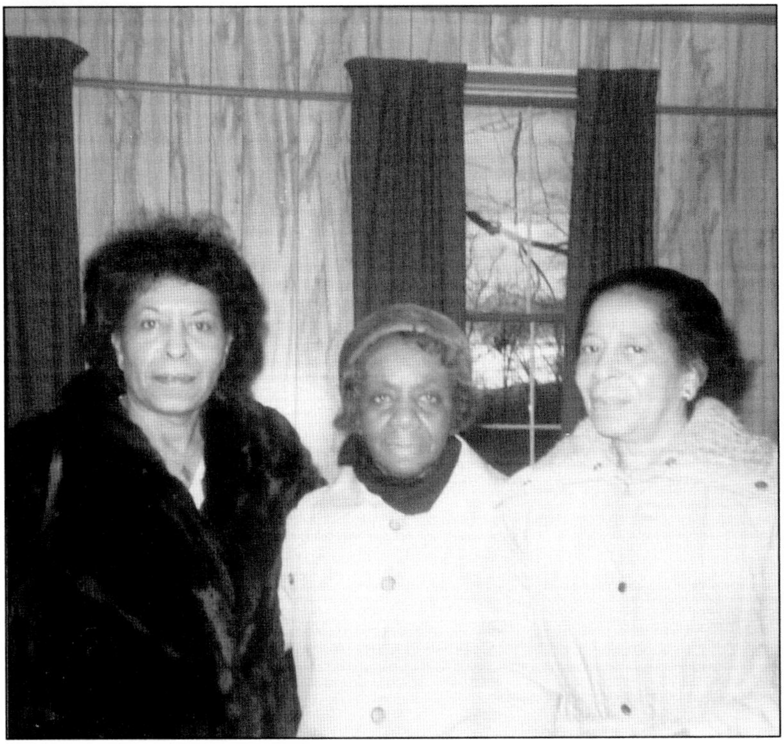

Pictured from left to right, Rena Barnett, Mable Jackson, and Florence Garrett are attending services at Love Chapel.

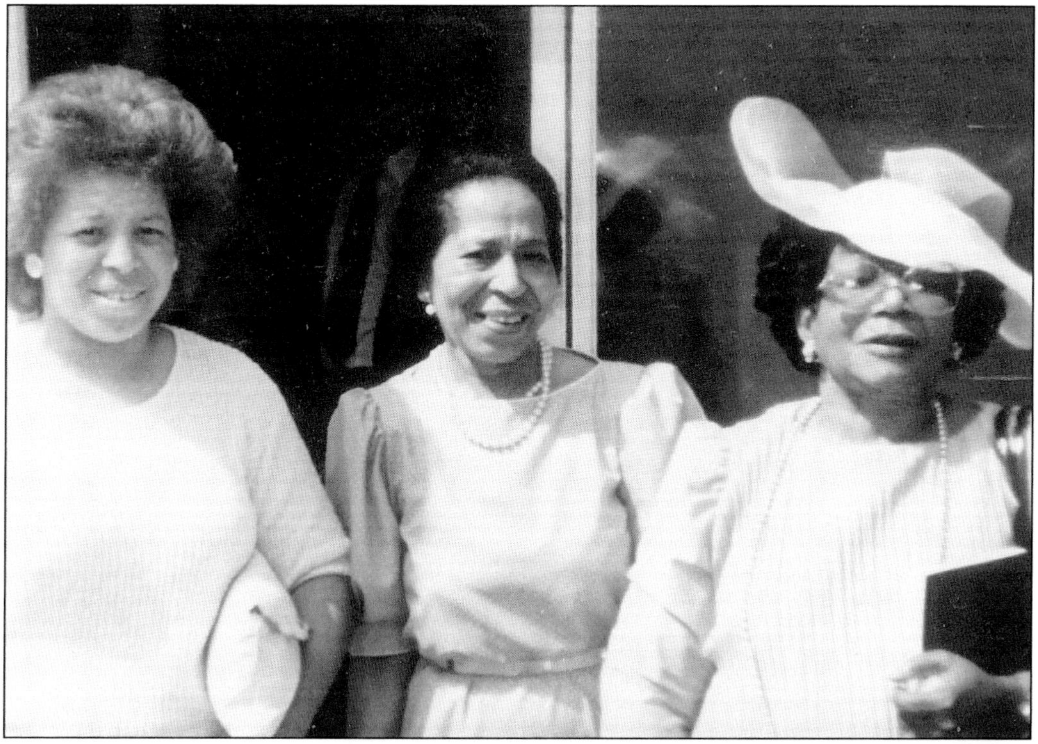

Joann Bussey, Florence Garrett, and Margaret Copney attend services at Love Chapel in 1990.

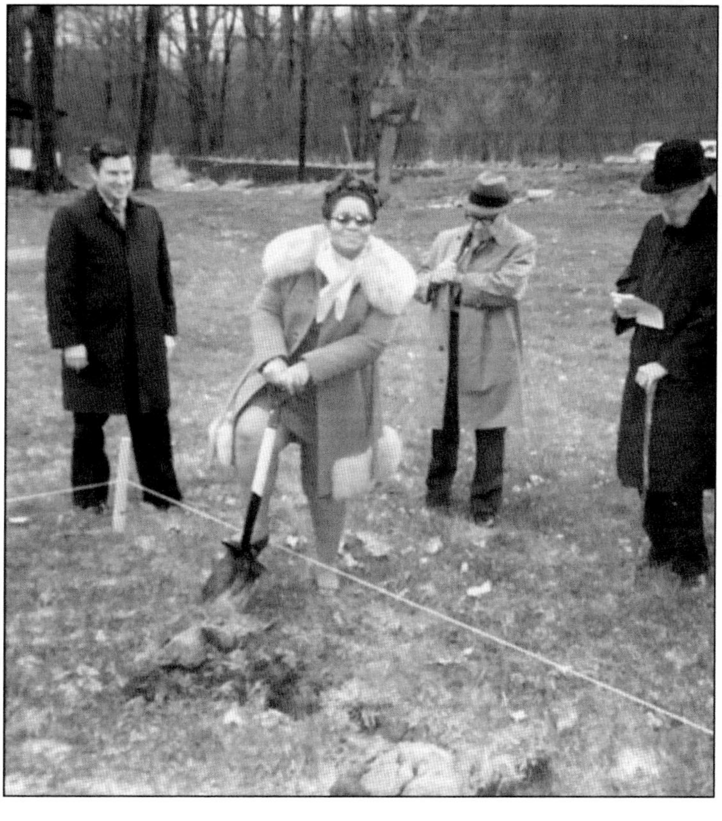

Nancy Jane Copney, the chairperson of the building improvement committee of the Love Chapel, helps in the groundbreaking ceremony for the fellowship hall in 1976. Also pictured are the Honorable Judge Robert C. Halbritter (left), the Honorable Mayor Al Unger, and Rev. C.P. Wilhelm of St. Michael's Episcopal Church.

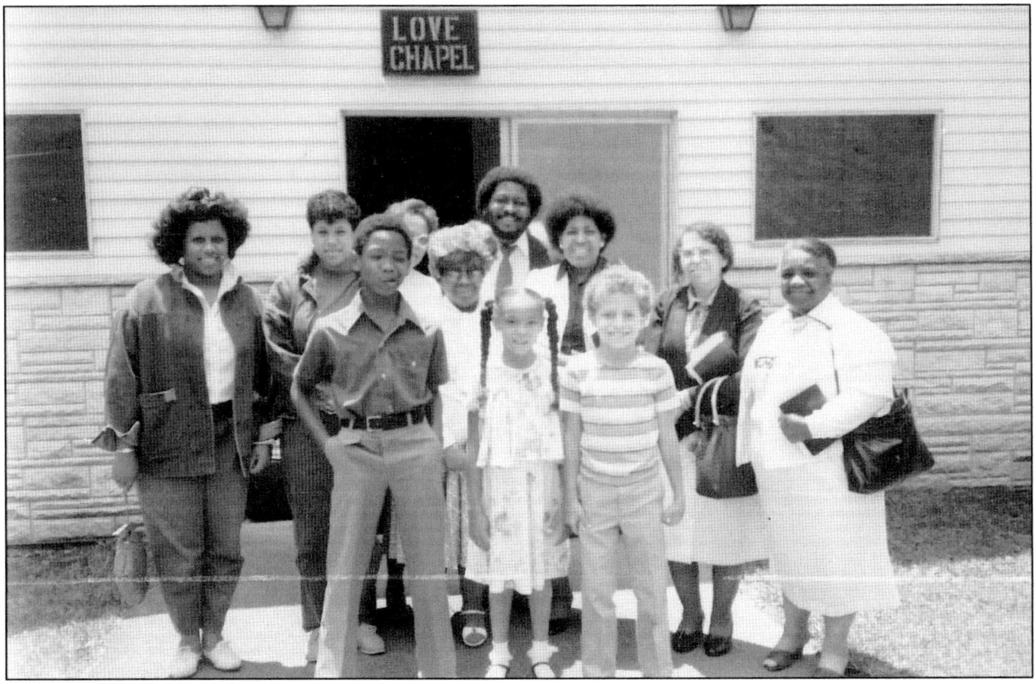

In front of the Love Chapel Church are, from left to right, (front row) Reverend Patterson's son, Grace McDonald, Devon Beckner, and Regan Jefferson; (back row) Kelly McDonald, Roxanne Smith, Helen McDonald, Reverend Patterson, Ruth Barnett, Viola Barnett, and Marietta Goines. Reverend Patterson was very instrumental in building a parsonage for ministers serving Love Chapel, Ottenbein, and Bethlehem Churches.

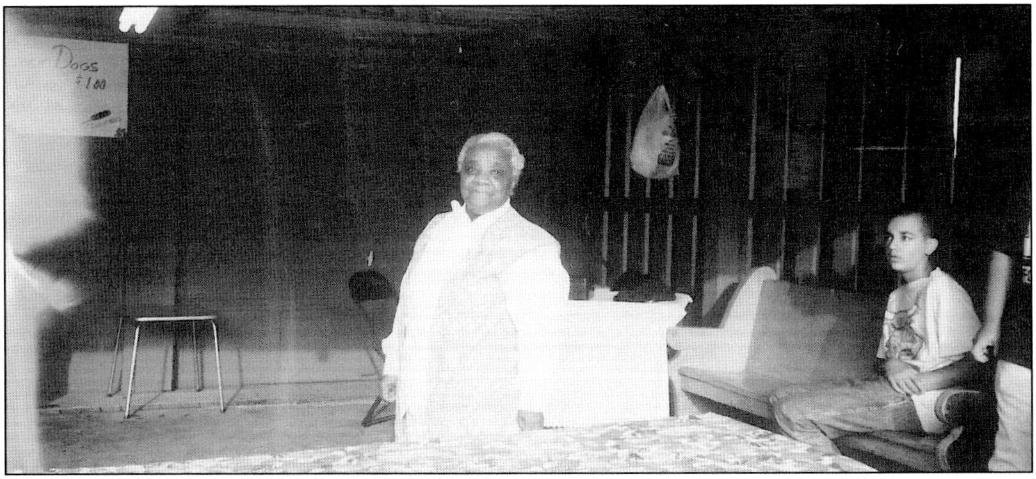

The Love Chapel Choir was invited to sing at a church in St. George, West Virginia, and while they were there, the choir members came upon a woman selling corndogs. The vendor shared her corndog recipe with the group. After returning home, Marietta Goines revised the original recipe, and she and her sister Grace began selling them on the street during the Buckwheat Festival as a means of raising money for the church's apportionment. This operation has grown over the years, and many volunteers from the community as well as church members, both current and former, help man the corn dog booth. This photo of Marietta Goines was taken in September 1998 as she celebrated 25 years of corn dogs.

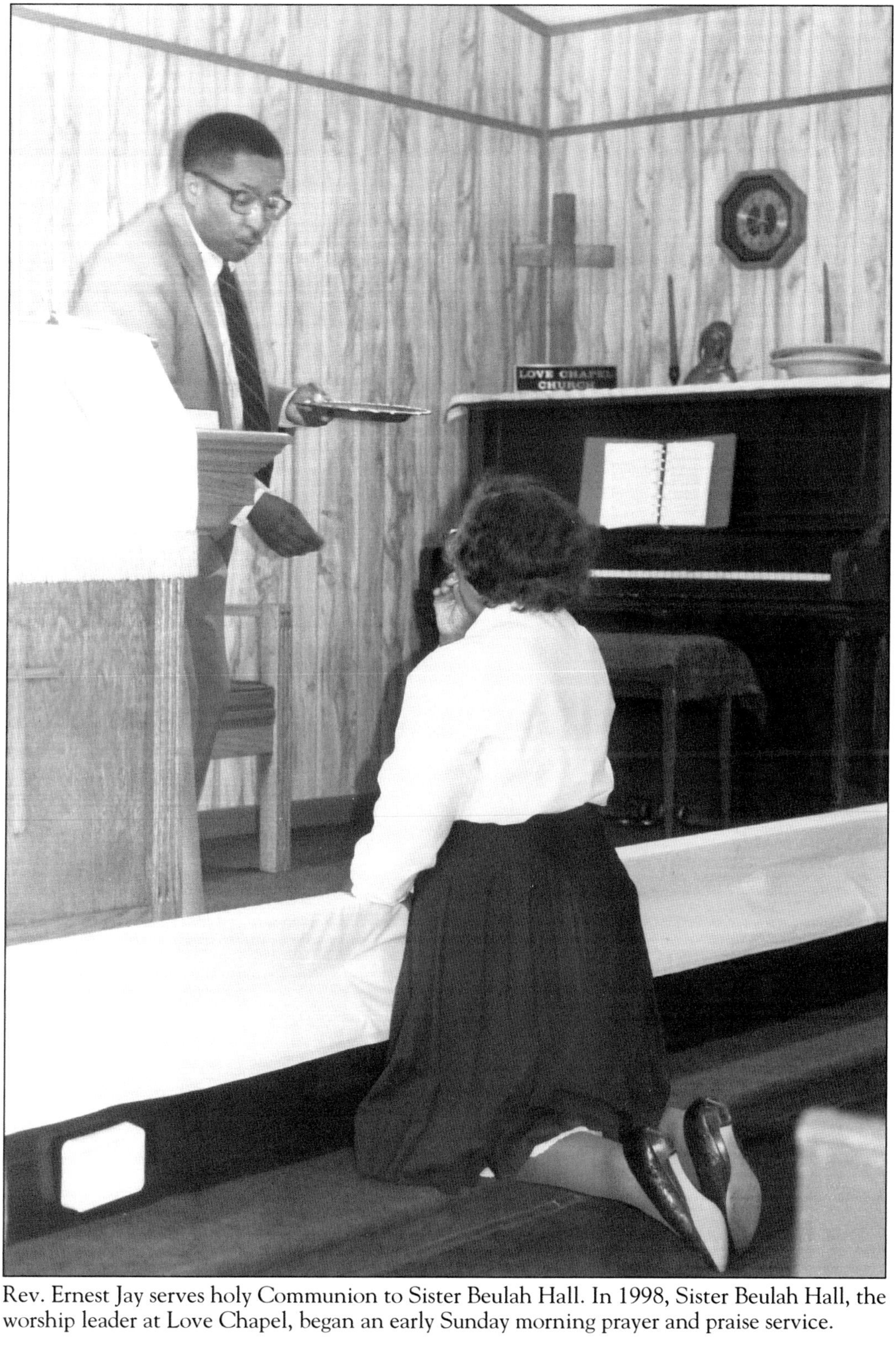

Rev. Ernest Jay serves holy Communion to Sister Beulah Hall. In 1998, Sister Beulah Hall, the worship leader at Love Chapel, began an early Sunday morning prayer and praise service.

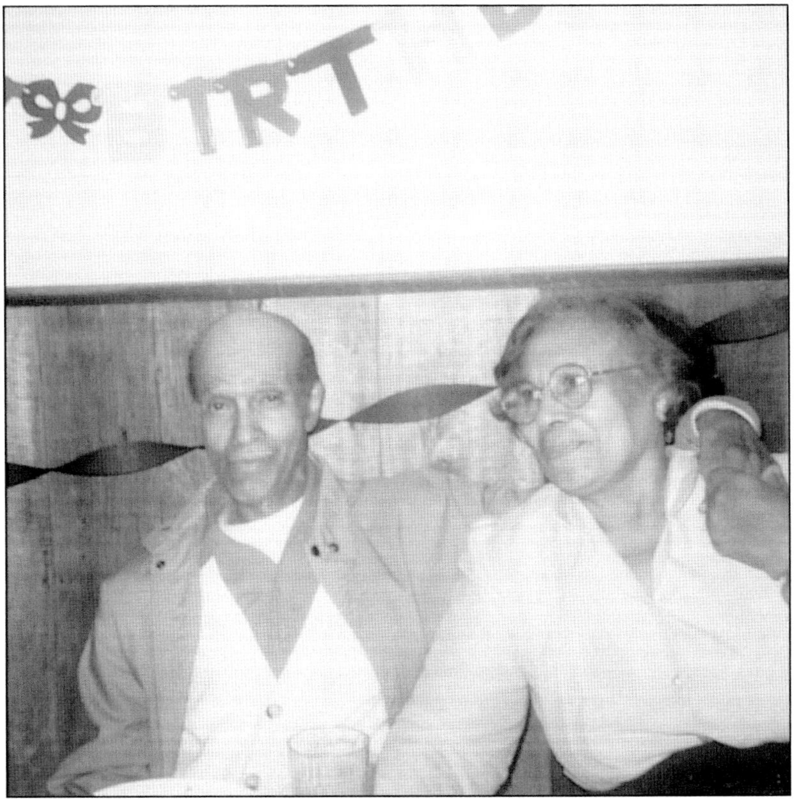

John and Beulah Hall are pictured here celebrating Beulah's birthday at the Kingwood Community Building in November 1991. She turned 68.

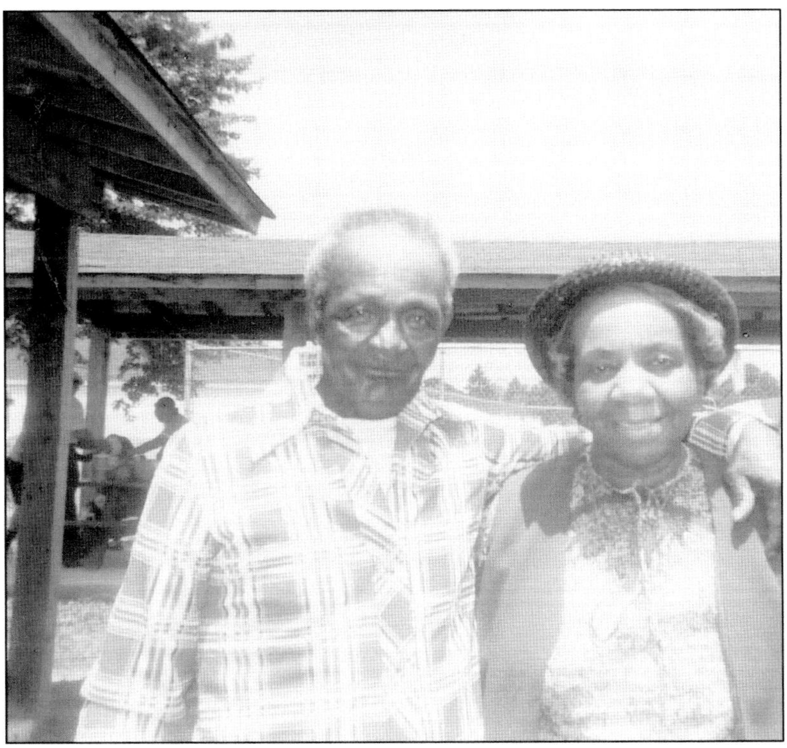

Siblings Norman Younger and Mable Jackson enjoy each other's company and the Younger family reunion where this picture was taken in July 1983.

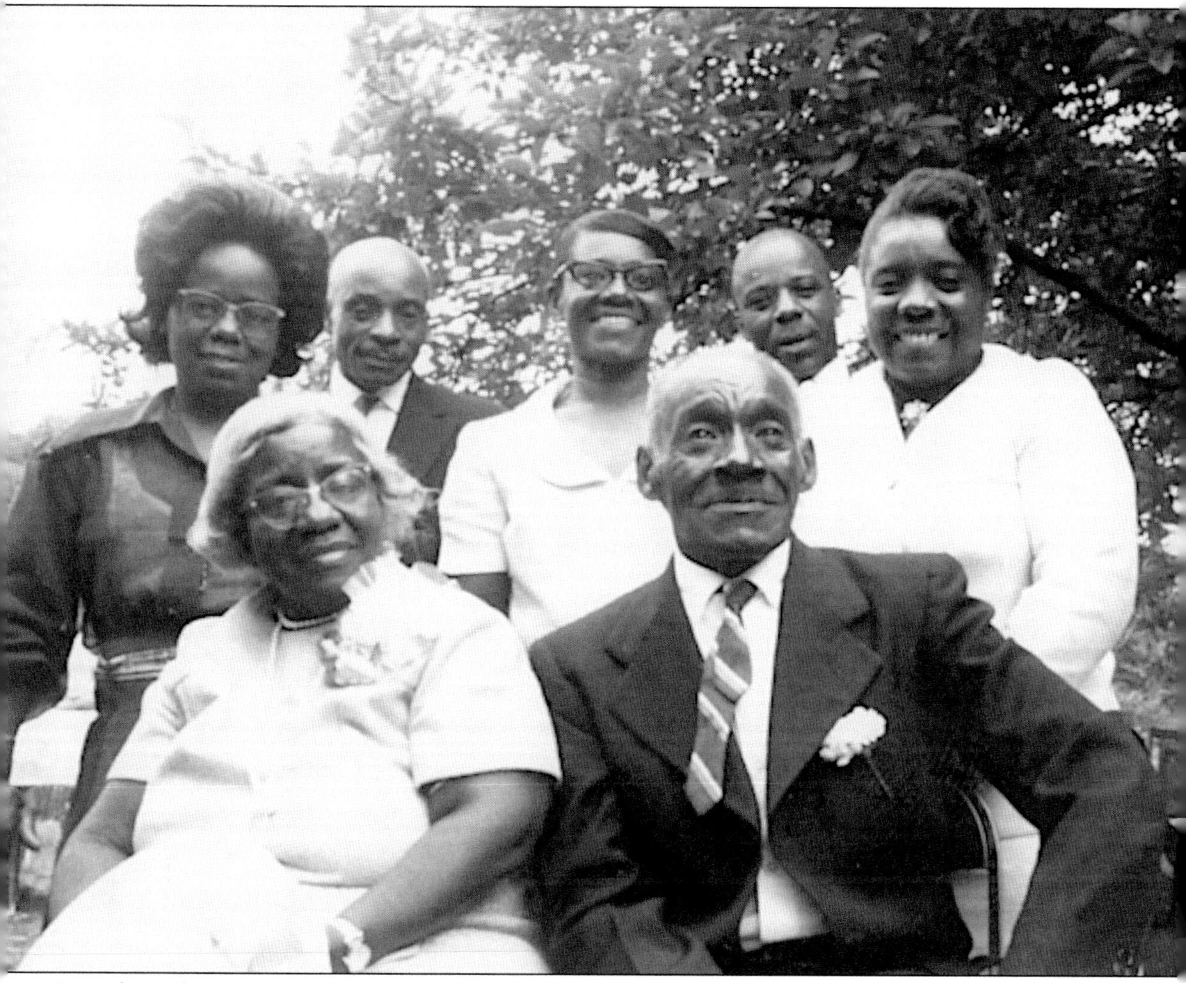

Seated in the front row, Mr. and Mrs. Jesse McDonald Sr. celebrate their 50th wedding anniversary with all of their children present, except son Calvin. This happy July 5, 1970 scene includes the couple's children, from left to right, Grace McDonald, Herbert McDonald Sr., Sarah McDonald Goines, Jesse McDonald, and Marietta McDonald Goines.

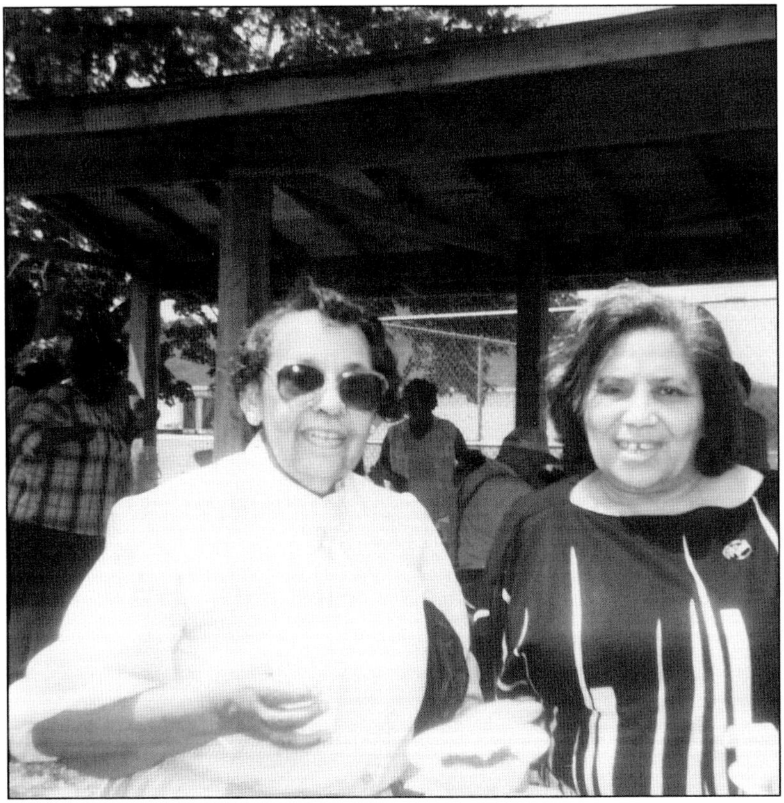

Virginia Younger (Mrs. Norman Younger) and her niece Mary Barnett Taylor take a moment from the reunion festivities to pose for this snapshot.

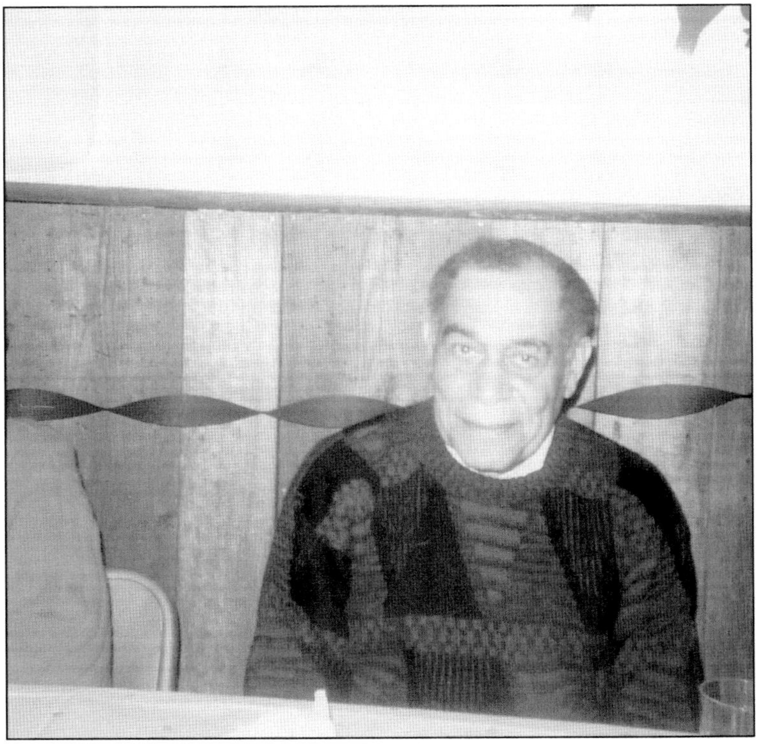

Earl C. Barnett, pictured here at a birthday celebration, owned Melva Coal Mine. This party was held in November 1991 for both Earl and his sister Beulah Hall. Earl was 73 years old.

Mary Barnett Taylor enjoys the same birthday party.

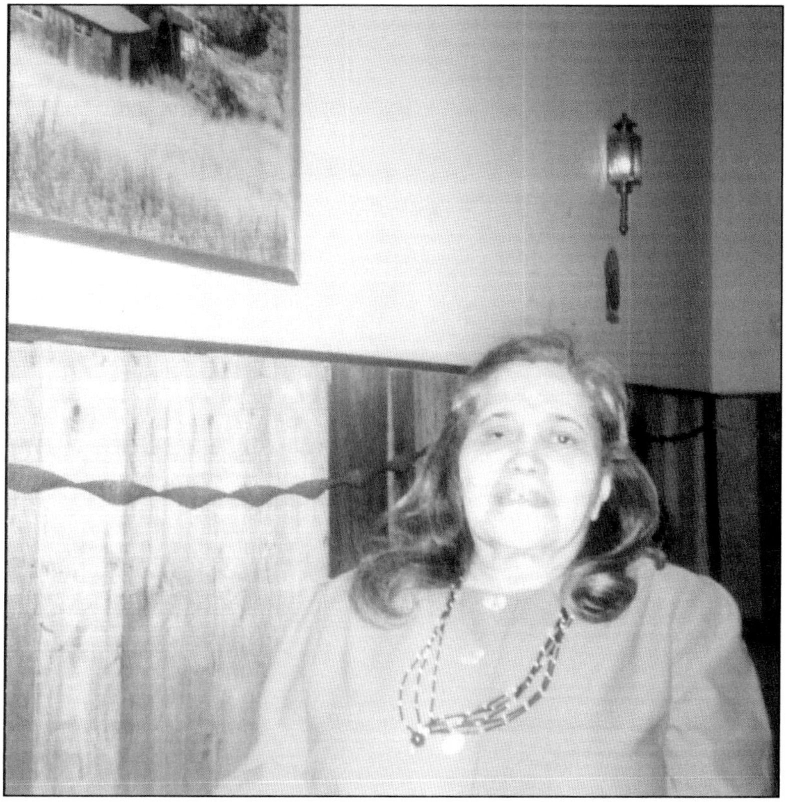

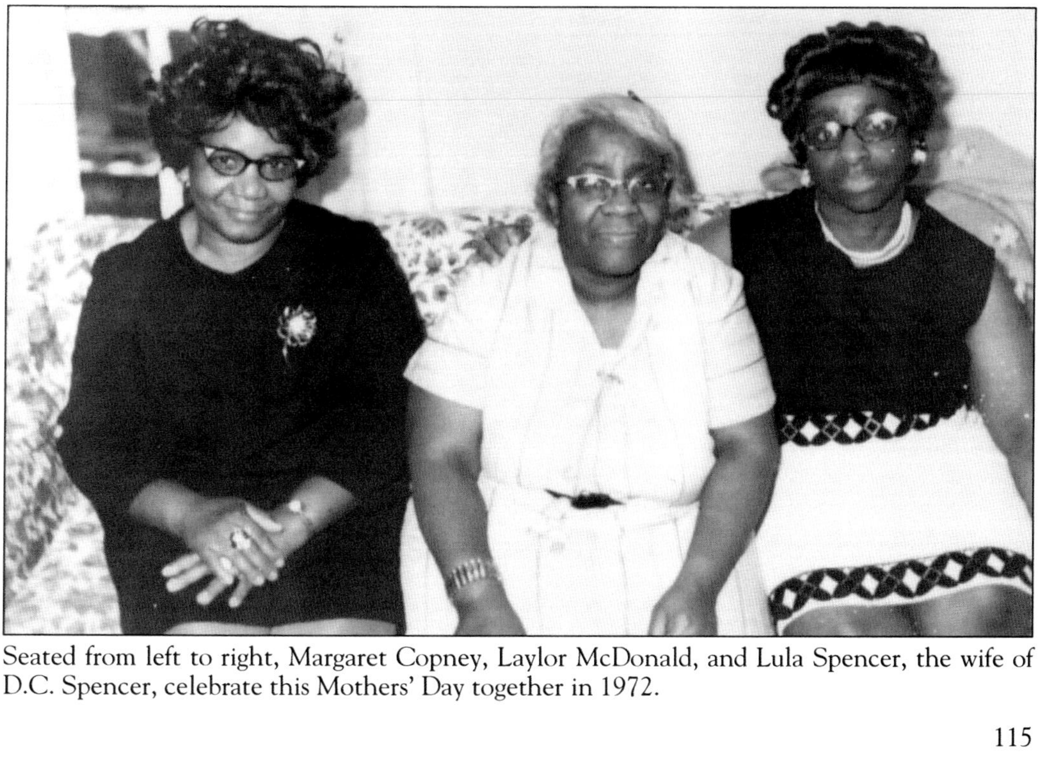

Seated from left to right, Margaret Copney, Laylor McDonald, and Lula Spencer, the wife of D.C. Spencer, celebrate this Mothers' Day together in 1972.

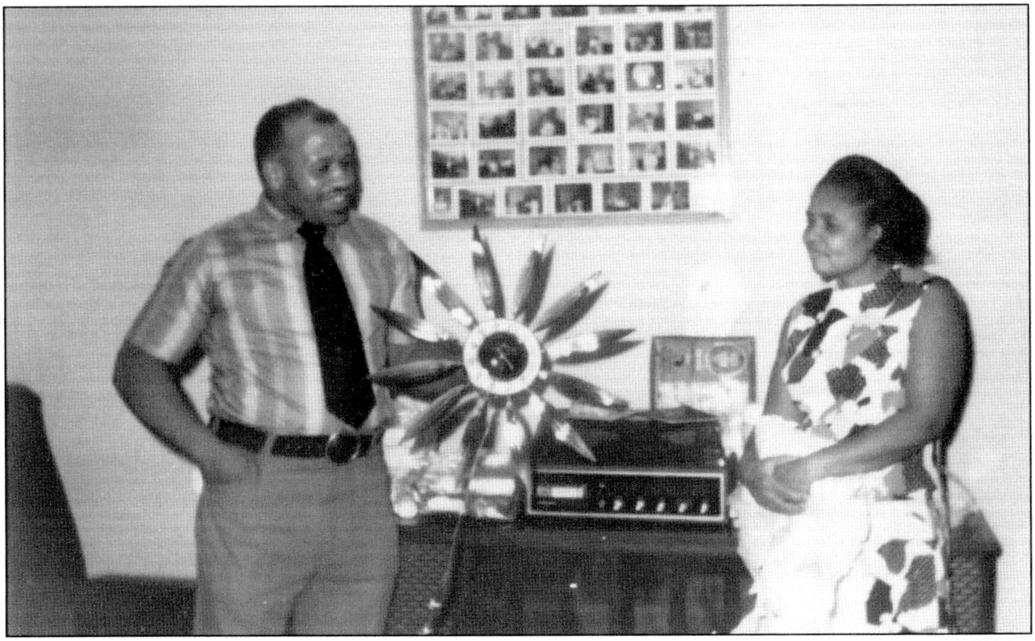

James "Eddie" and Elizabeth Smith are celebrating their 25th wedding anniversary in 1975. Eddie sponsored the Younger Family Reunion for several years. He was a faithful financial supporter of Love Chapel United Methodist Church. Eddie started a Little League in Kingwood. When other teams' managers wouldn't allow a team player to participate because they lived outside of Kingwood, he would personally drive to Howesville and other places to pick these players up. He also purchased equipment, clothes, and shoes for his players. Eddie really loved kids.

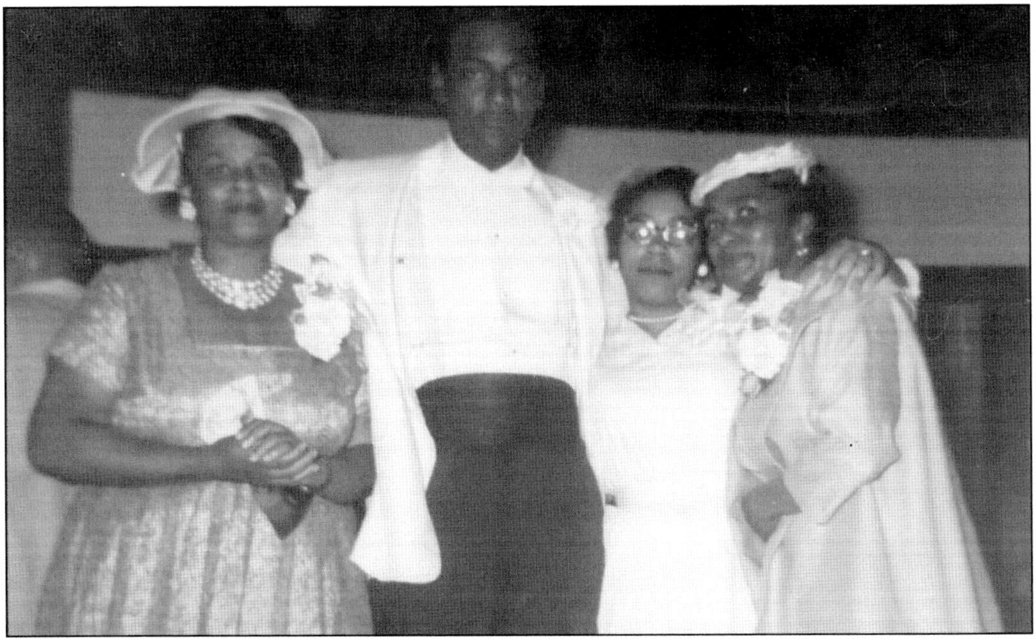

Mrs. Horton (mother of the groom), John Horton, Patsy Paige Horton, and Evelyn Paige (mother of the bride) are pictured here, from left to right, at the young couple's wedding.

The happy couple, Mr. and Mrs. John Horton, are pictured on their wedding day in May 1960.

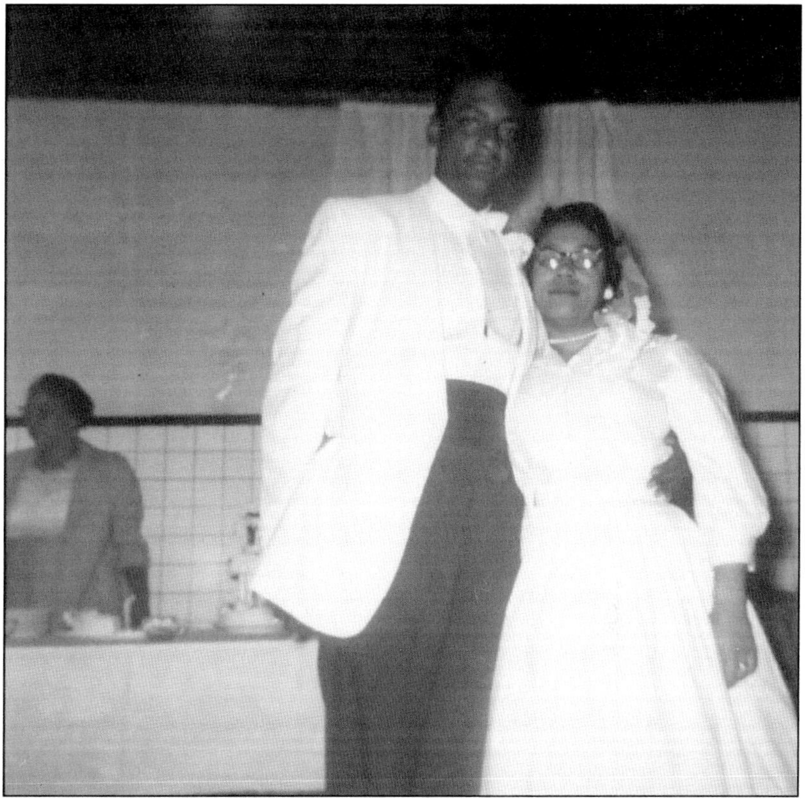

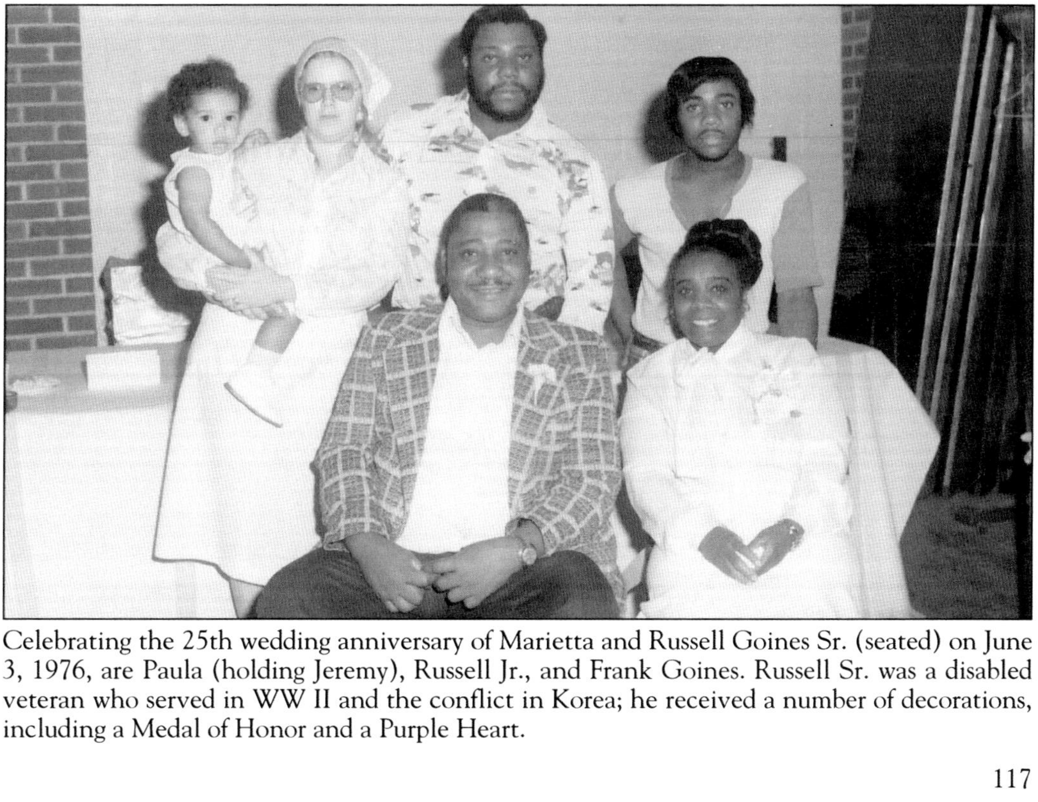

Celebrating the 25th wedding anniversary of Marietta and Russell Goines Sr. (seated) on June 3, 1976, are Paula (holding Jeremy), Russell Jr., and Frank Goines. Russell Sr. was a disabled veteran who served in WW II and the conflict in Korea; he received a number of decorations, including a Medal of Honor and a Purple Heart.

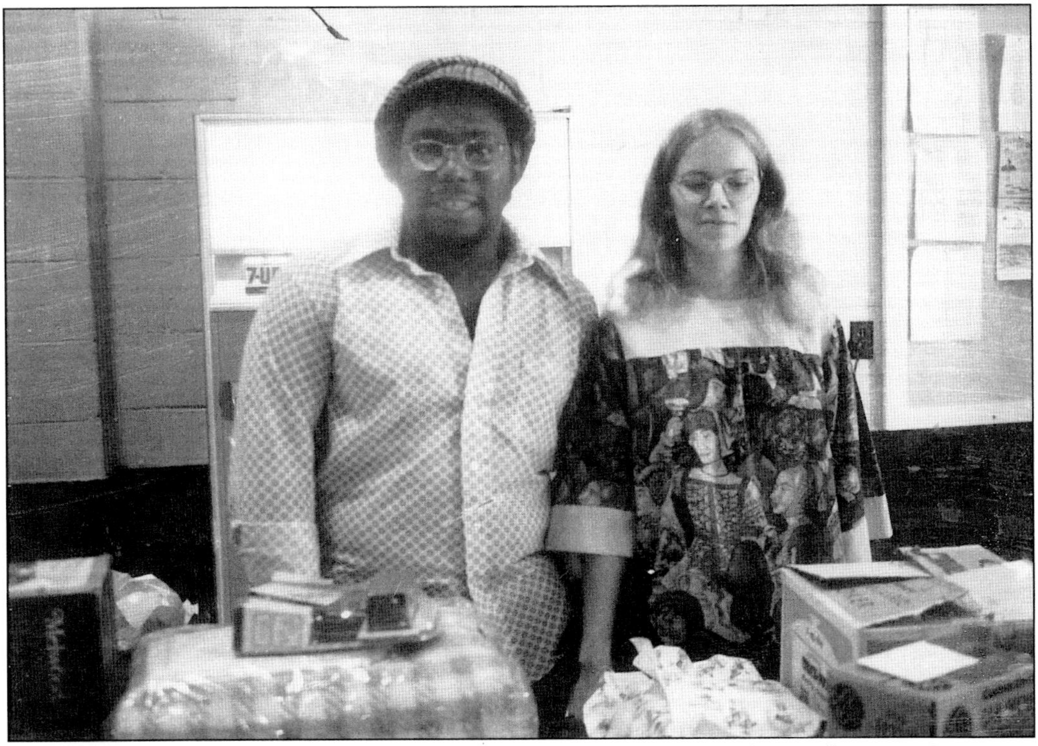

Paula Shrout and Russell Goines Jr. were married on July 6, 1975.

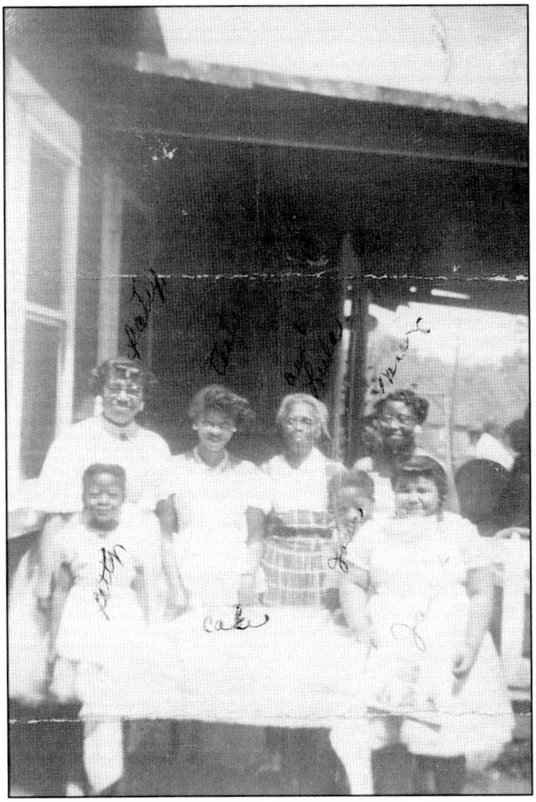

Celebrating Aunt Lula Whitley's birthday on this warm afternoon in the 1950s are, from left to right, (front row) Betty McDonald and Janet McDonald; (back row) Patsy Paige, Janie "Tootie" Hines, Lula Whitley, Joann McDonald, and Nancy Copney.

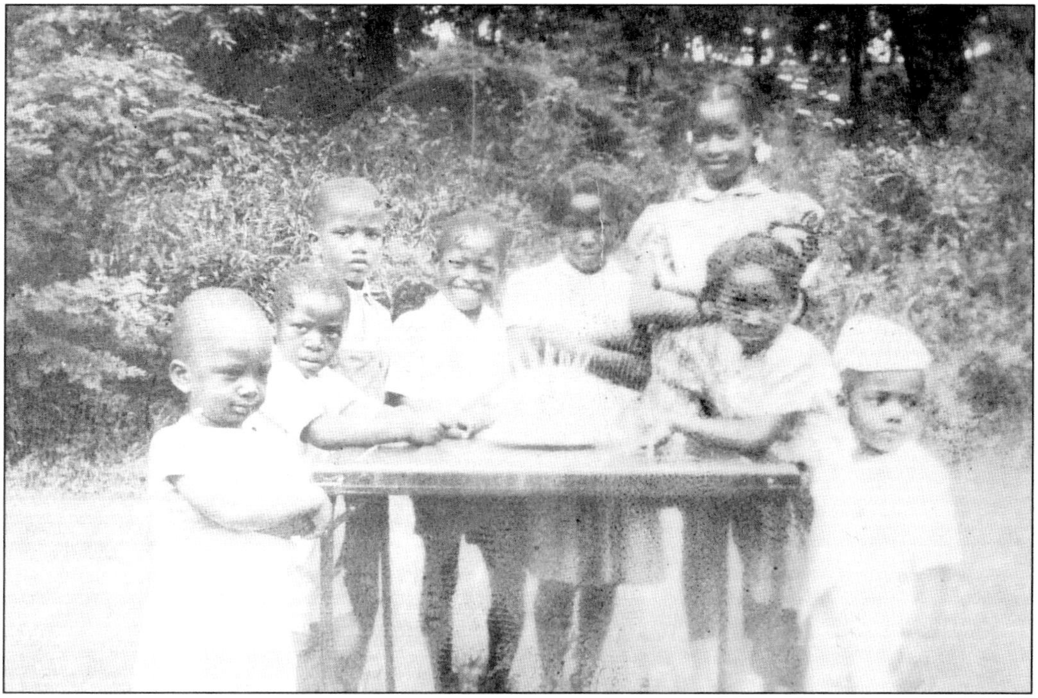

This double birthday celebration for Melvin Copney and Janie Hines in the 1940s was attended by, from left to right, John Jackson, Melvin Copney, George Jackson, Charles Copney, Nancy Copney, Shirley Grey, Janie Hines, and Leonard Smith.

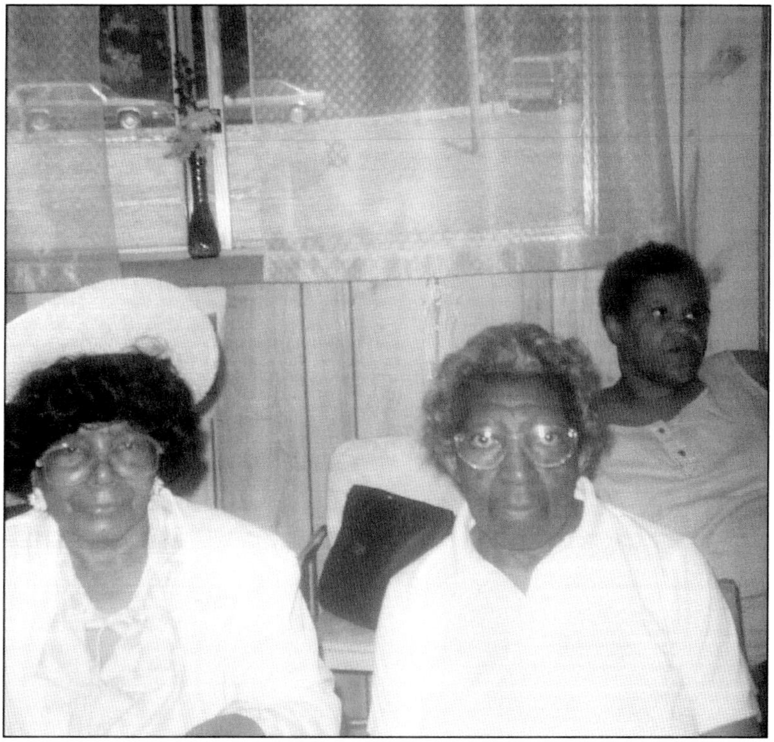

Margaret Younger Copney (in the hat) and her former schoolmate Catherine Davis Thomas are pictured together at the Edmond-McDonald reunion.

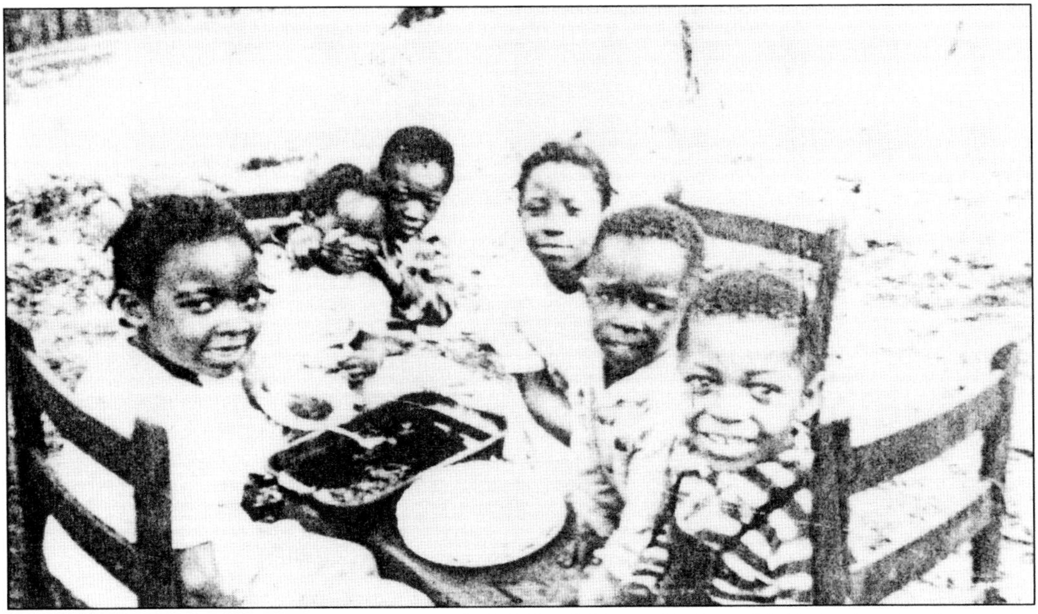

This early 1940s backyard party was given by Mildred Grace McDonald. Enjoying the festivities are, from left to right, Ruth Spencer, Laura Spencer, Charles Copney, Nancy Copney, Robert Spencer, and Melvin Copney.

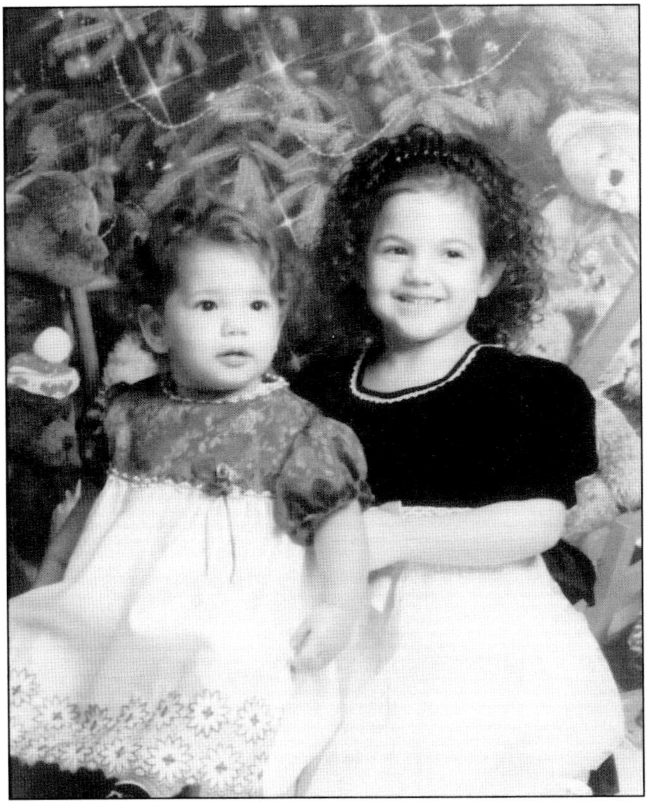

Alexis and Paige Goines are all dolled up for their 1998 Christmas portrait.

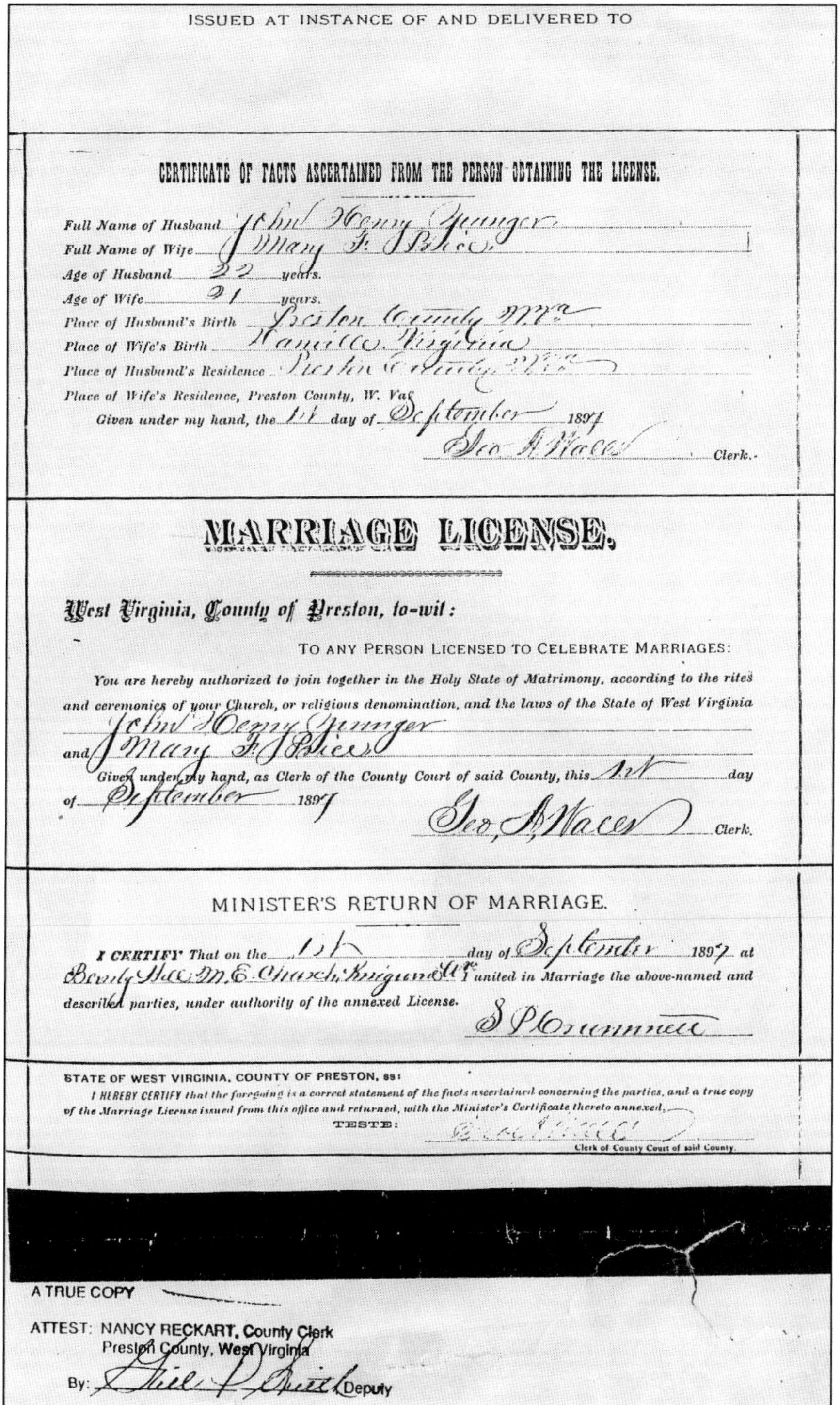
ISSUED AT INSTANCE OF AND DELIVERED TO

CERTIFICATE OF FACTS ASCERTAINED FROM THE PERSON OBTAINING THE LICENSE.

Full Name of Husband John Henry Younger
Full Name of Wife Mary F. Price
Age of Husband 22 years.
Age of Wife 21 years.
Place of Husband's Birth Preston County W.Va
Place of Wife's Birth [illegible] Virginia
Place of Husband's Residence Preston County W.Va
Place of Wife's Residence, Preston County, W. Va.
Given under my hand, the 1st day of September 1897
Geo. A. Wace, Clerk.

MARRIAGE LICENSE.

West Virginia, County of Preston, to-wit:

TO ANY PERSON LICENSED TO CELEBRATE MARRIAGES:

You are hereby authorized to join together in the Holy State of Matrimony, according to the rites and ceremonies of your Church, or religious denomination, and the laws of the State of West Virginia John Henry Younger and Mary F. Price

Given under my hand, as Clerk of the County Court of said County, this 1st day of September 1897
Geo. A. Wace, Clerk.

MINISTER'S RETURN OF MARRIAGE.

I CERTIFY That on the 1st day of September 1897 at Beverly Hill M.E. Church, Kingwood W.Va I united in Marriage the above-named and described parties, under authority of the annexed License.
S. P. Crummett

STATE OF WEST VIRGINIA, COUNTY OF PRESTON, ss:
I HEREBY CERTIFY that the foregoing is a correct statement of the facts ascertained concerning the parties, and a true copy of the Marriage License issued from this office and returned, with the Minister's Certificate thereto annexed.
TESTE: Clerk of County Court of said County.

A TRUE COPY
ATTEST: NANCY RECKART, County Clerk
Preston County, West Virginia
By: Deputy

This is a copy of the marriage license given to John Henry Younger and Mary F. Price. The couple was married by Reverend Crummett at the Beverly Hill M.E. Church in Kingwood on September 1, 1897.

THE WEST VA ARGUS.

Kingwood, September 2, 1897.

FOR BETTER OR WORSE.

Cupid Cutting Capers IN Colored Circles.

Another wedding was celebrated in town yesterday afternoon and colored circles are all agog over the event. It was the first marriage among the colored folks for a long time, and the affair was celebrated with becoming eclat. Invitations, both written and verbal were issued and preparations have been going on for some time. The contracting parties were Henry Younger and Miss Mary Price and the ceremony was performed at half past three yesterday evening, in the colored church on Beverly Hill, by Rev. B. P. Crummett, of the M. E. church, in the presence of a large crowd of invited guests, both white and colored. The latter came from all parts of the country and enjoyed the occasion immensely. Three o'clock was the hour set, but the wedding party did not arrive till half past. Miss Mabel Marsden presided at the organ and rendered Longehrins wedding march as the procession swept up the isle. The attendants were Samuel Younger and Miss Lizzie Workman. The house was handsomely decorated with flowers and evergreens and the bride looked very nice, attired in white satin and slippers to match. At five o'clock a reception was given at the home of the groom, to a large number of people and it was a very enjoyable affair. About the finest lot of cake ever served in the town, was a special feature and all in all the wedding was a great event and well celebrated. The bride received many handsome and valuable presents. Lots of good music both at the church and the house enlivened the occasion.

A *West VA Argus* newspaper clipping describes the happy event of the Younger-Price union the day before. It was "the first marriage among the colored folks for a long time."

Jeremy and Megan Goines are pictured on their wedding day in 1996.

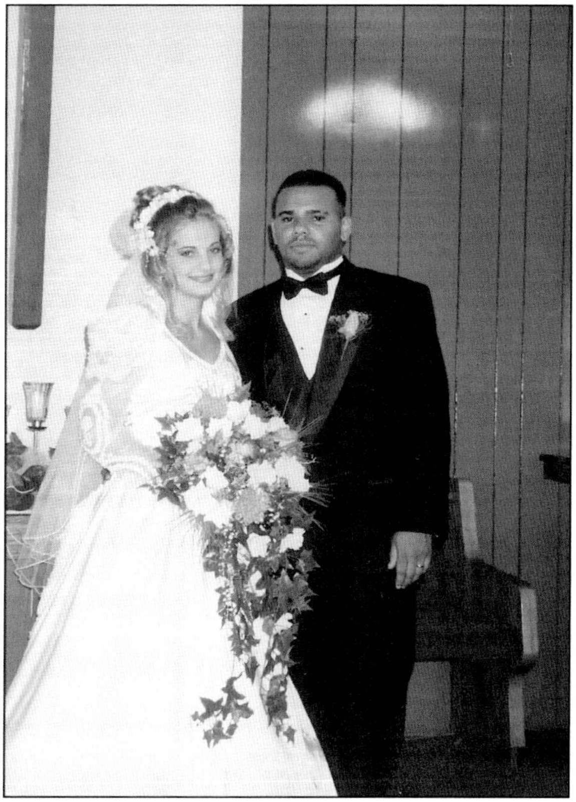

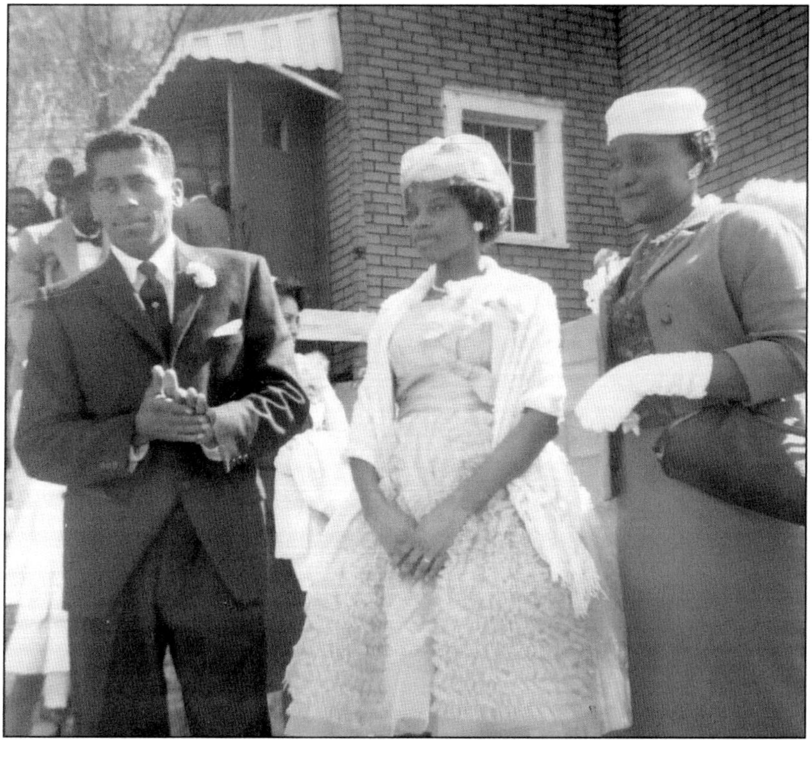

Donnie Barnett and Gloria Jean Jefferson are pictured here on their wedding day in the 1960s. The bride's mother, Mrs. Fannie Jefferson, stands on the right.

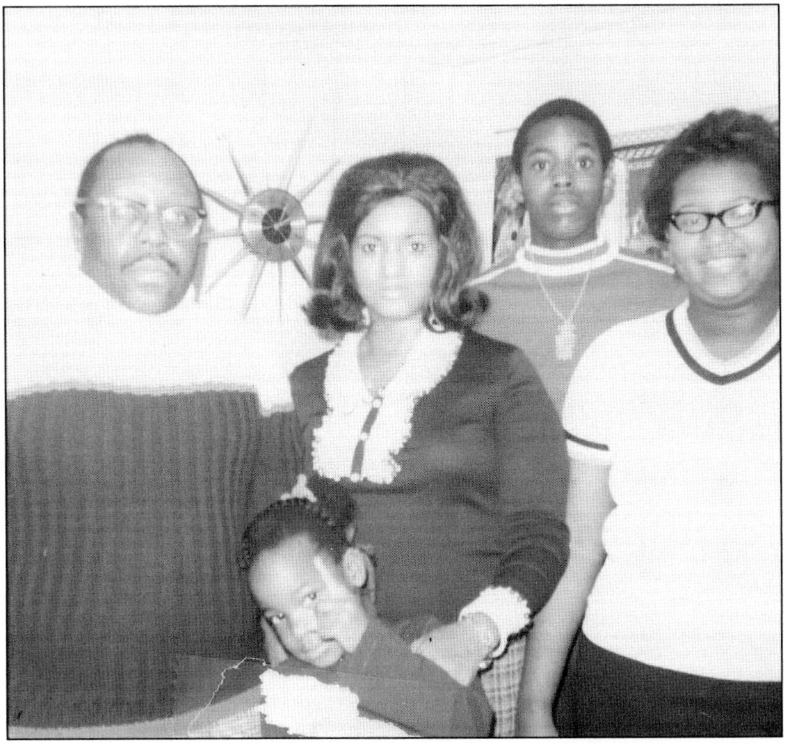

This Copney family Christmas celebration in 1973 includes, from left to right Ray, Ruth, Ray Alexander, JoAnn, and Joyce (standing in front). Little JoAnn was the first African-American train bearer for Queen Ceres in the history of the popular Buckwheat Festival.

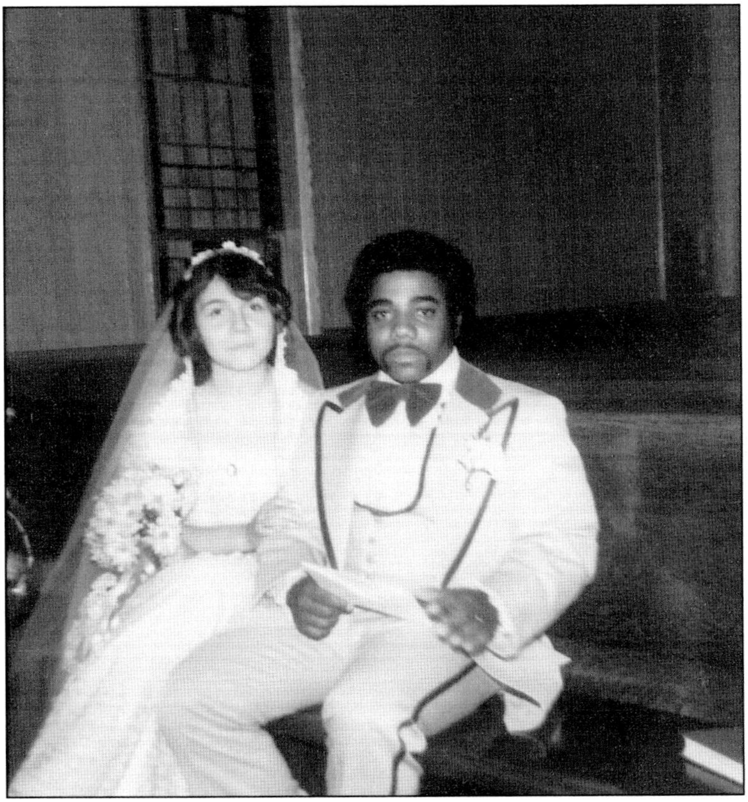

Frank and Melvonia Wilhelm Goines are pictured on their wedding day in December 1979.

Angela Barnett holds Katie Garrett and is joined by Florence Garrett and Eddie Barnett at Eagles Repass. After a funeral, the local churches usually served dinner to family and friends. The "Eagles" was the name of the place where this dinner was held. Brother Donnie Barnett had died.

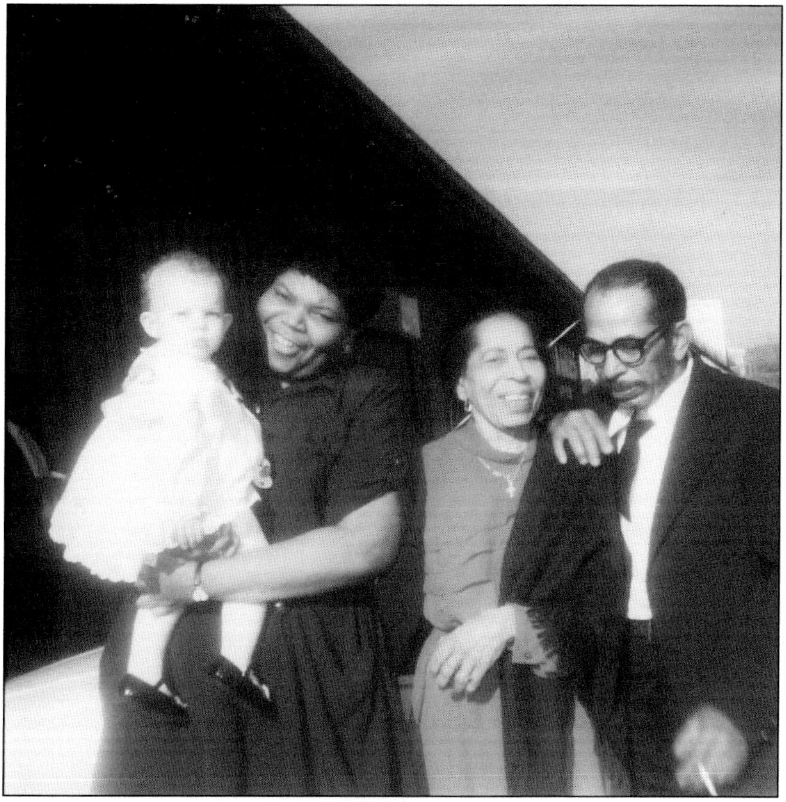

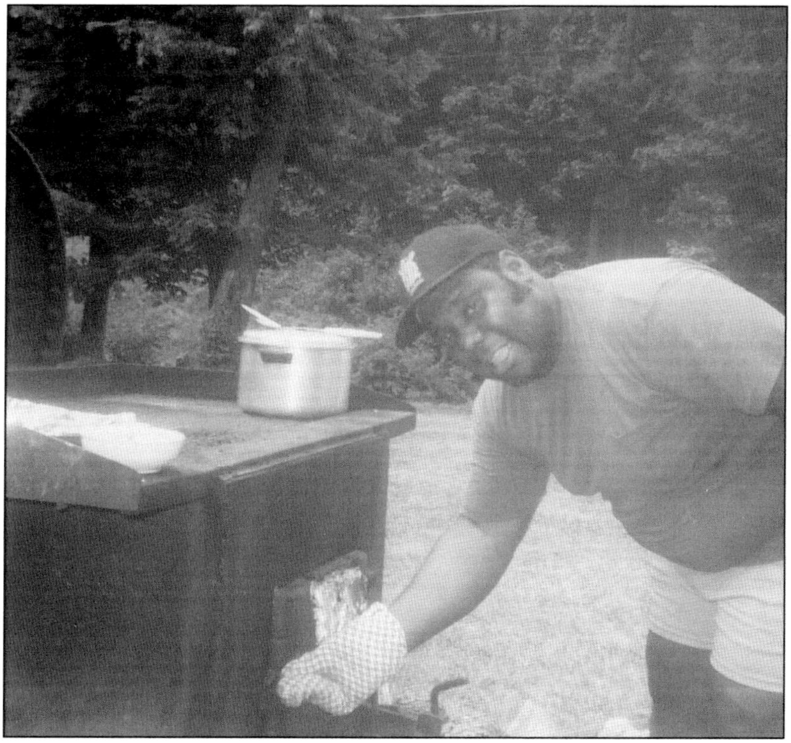

Russell Goines Jr. checks the fire in his homemade engine at the Edmonds-McDonald reunion in 1993.

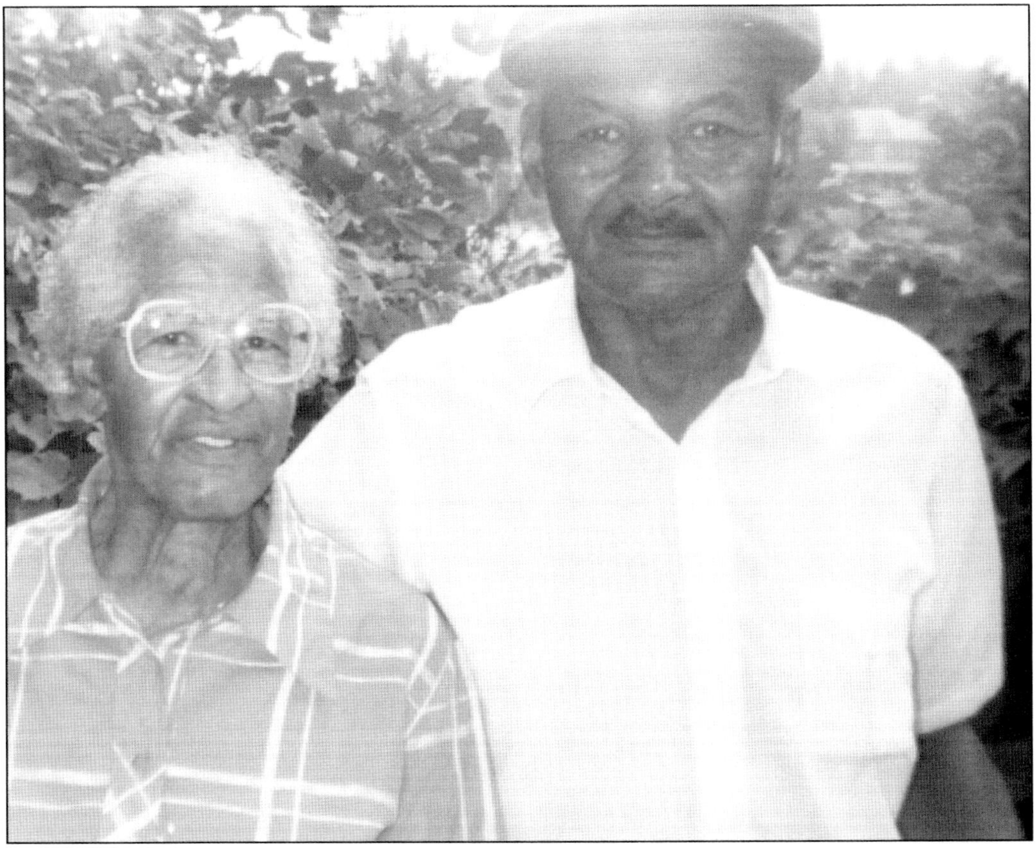

Pauline Gray and William Jones enjoy the Younger family reunion in Fireman's Park in 1983.

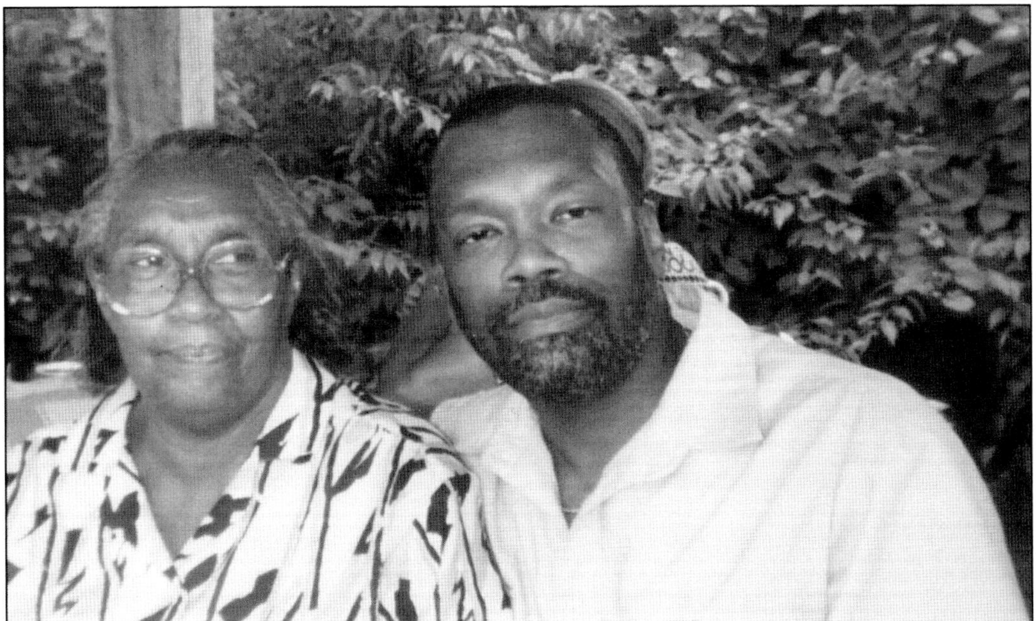

Inez McGee and her son Benjamin McGee also attended the Younger family reunion.

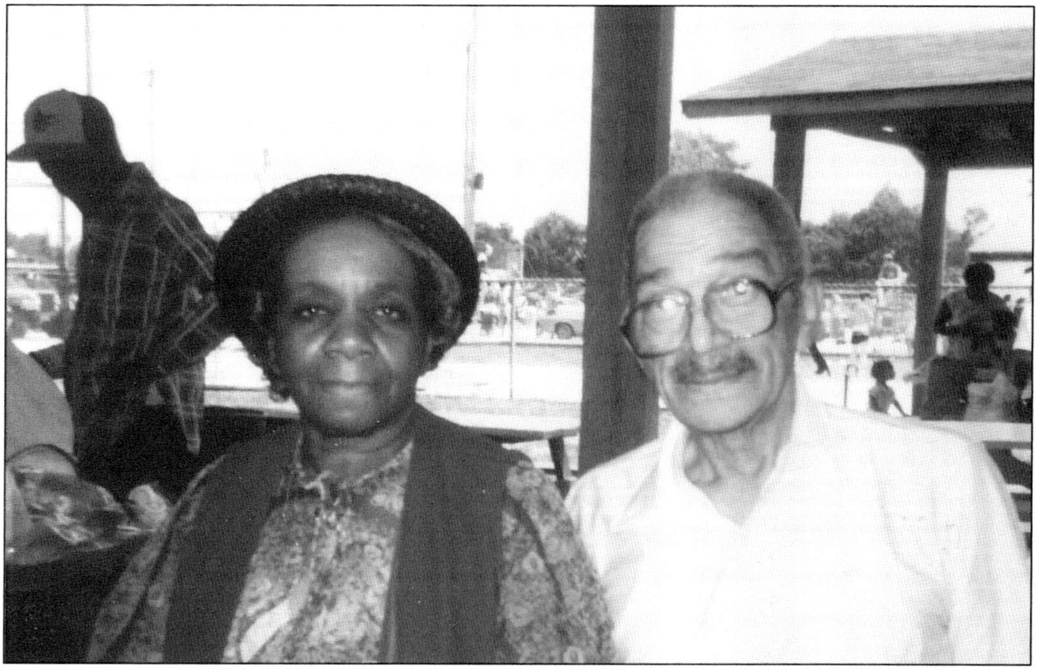

Mable and George Jackson participated in the 1983 Younger reunion.

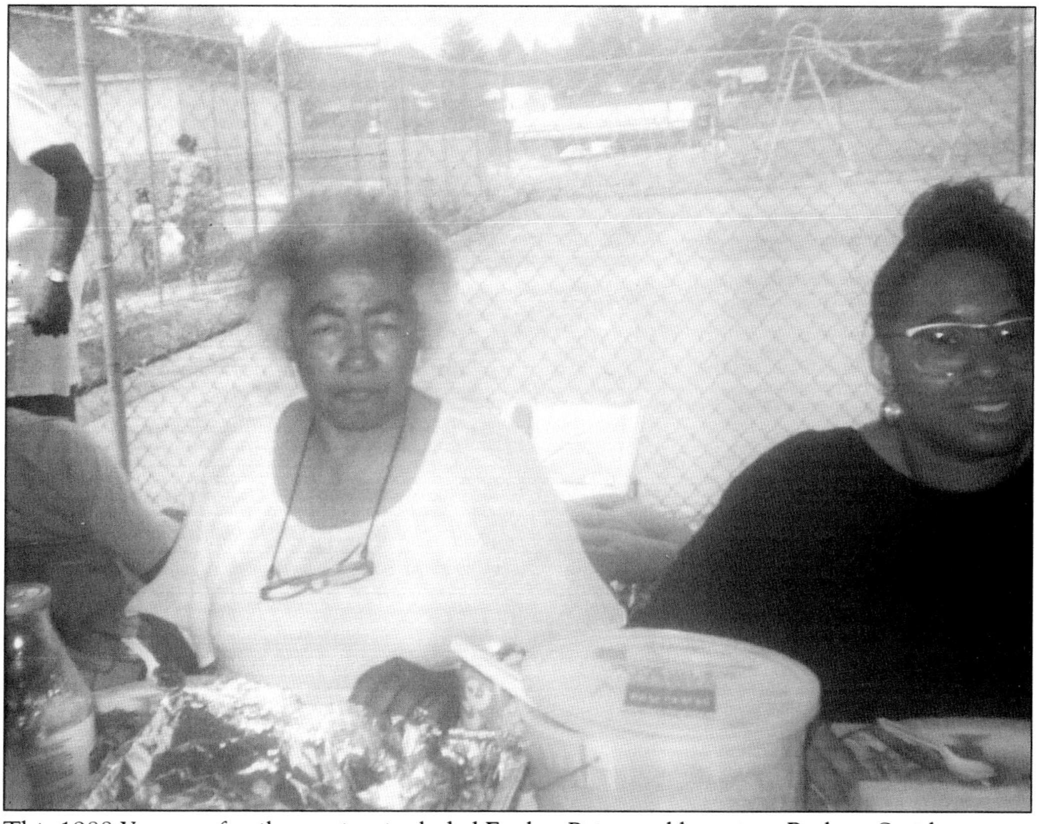

This 1988 Younger family reunion included Evelyn Paige and her niece Barbara Smith.

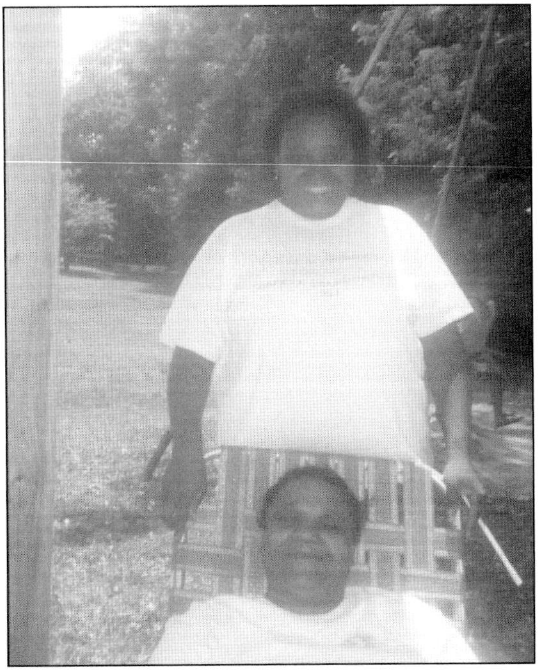

The smiling faces here are Ruby Lee Younger (seated) and her daughter Vera (standing).

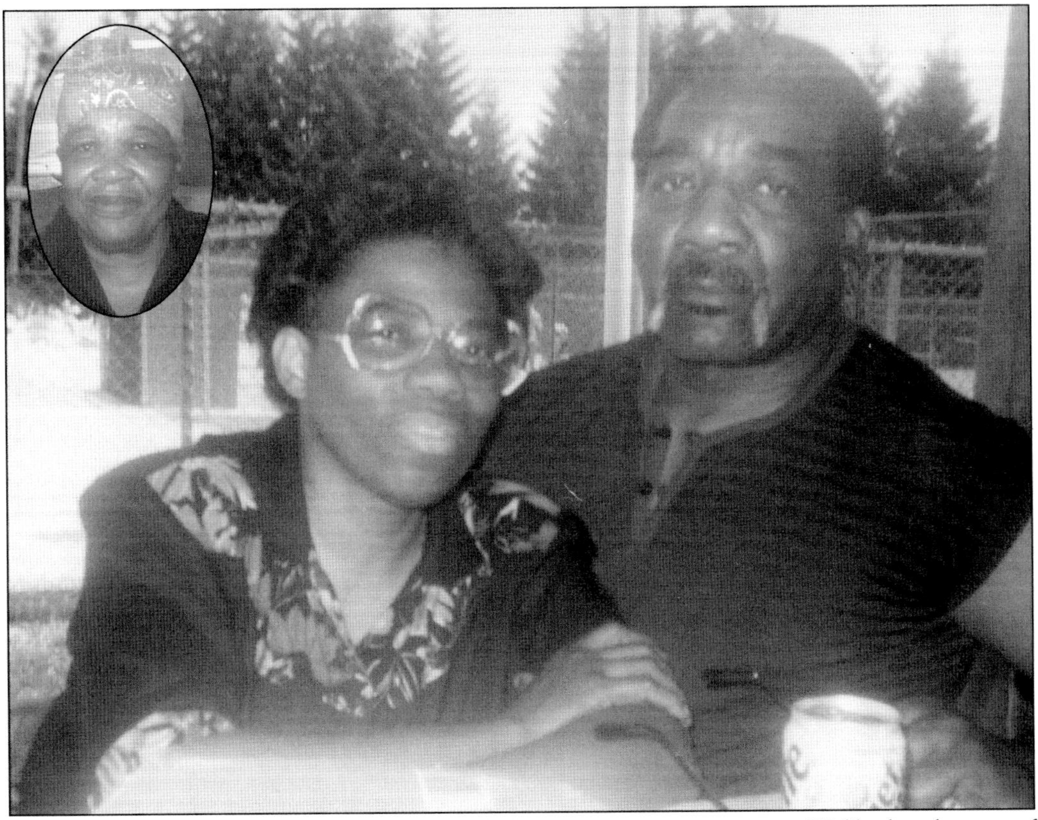

Mr. and Mrs. Wilford Younger also attended the 1988 Younger reunion. Wilford is the son of Lucille Younger Caldwell (inset).